RED ALC-CHINA
Red Académica de América Latina y el Caribe sobre China
UDUALC
FACULTAD DE ECONOMÍA
CENTRO DE ESTUDIOS CHINA-MÉXICO
UNIVERSIDAD NACIONAL AUTÓNOMA DE MÉXICO

LATIN AMERICAN EXPORTS TO China

LOCAL EXPERIENCES AND CHALLENGES

Edited by
Enrique Dussel Peters

RED ACADÉMICA DE AMÉRICA LATINA Y EL CARIBE SOBRE CHINA

Enrique Dussel Peters	*Coordinador General y Coordinador del eje temático Economía, comercio e inversión*
José Ignacio Martínez Cortés	*Coordinador del eje temático Relaciones políticas e internacionales*
Yolanda Trápaga Delfín	*Coordinadora del eje temático Recursos naturales y medio ambiente*
Liljana Arsovska	*Coordinadora del eje temático Historia, cultura y aprendizaje del chino*

http://www.redalc-china.org/

UNIÓN DE UNIVERSIDADES DE AMÉRICA LATINA Y EL CARIBE

Jorge Calzoni	*Presidente*
Roberto Escalante Semerena	*Secretario General*

http://www.udual.org

UNIVERSIDAD NACIONAL AUTÓNOMA DE MÉXICO

Leonardo Lomelí Vanegas	*Rector*
Patricia Dolores Dávila Aranda	*Secretaria General*
Tomás Humberto Rubio Pérez	*Secretario Administrativo*
Diana Tamara Martínez Ruiz	*Secretaria de Desarrollo Institucional*
Hugo Concha Cantú	*Abogado General*

http://www.unam.mx

FACULTAD DE ECONOMÍA

Lorena Rodríguez León	*Directora*
Adrián Escammilla Trejo	*Secretario General*
Juan Abelardo Mosqueda	*Secretario Administrativo*
Juan Puig Llano	*Coordinador de Publicaciones*

http://www.economia.unam.mx

CENTRO DE ESTUDIOS CHINA-MÉXICO

Enrique Dussel Peters	*Coordinador*
Silvia Jiménez Barba	*Responsable*

http://www.economia.unam.mx/cechimex

Latin American Exports to China. Local Experiences and Challenges

Enrique Dussel Peters	*Coordinador*
Yolanda Trápaga Barba	*Edición*
Socorro García	*Diseño y formación de interiores*

Primera edición: Mayo 2025
ISBN formato digital: 978-607-8937-22-6
ISBN formato impreso: 978-607-8937-21-9

Impreso y hecho en México/*Printed and made in Mexico*

Distributed by Lynne Rienner Publishers, Inc.
1800 30TH St., Boulder, CO 80301 USA
Tel +1(303) 444-6684, Fax: +1(303)444-0824 and email: questions@rienner.com

LATIN AMERICAN EXPORTS TO China

LOCAL EXPERIENCES AND CHALLENGES

Edited by
Enrique Dussel Peters

CONTENTS

Preface

Enrique Dussel Peters

The Academic Network for Latin America and the Caribbean on China (Red ALC-China) has been inviting its members, since its beginning in 2012, to improve the quality of research and to make efforts to engage in new analysis relevant for understanding the socioeconomic relationship between Latin America and the Caribbean (LAC) and China. As a result, Red ALC-China has been publishing contributions on Chinese outward foreign direct investments in LAC since 2013, the impact of the LAC-China foreign trade in LAC's regional trade integration process, the relevance of Chinese infrastructure projects in LAC, China's impact in LAC's employment generation, and LAC's outward foreign direct investment in China, among others. After more than a decade these contributions have become important pillars to understand the complexity, depth, and extension of the socioeconomic LAC-China relationship and have allowed for improving this initial analysis for new countries, sectors, and territories within countries in LAC.

Based on the already existing research on the trade relationship between LAC and China, both at Red ALC-China and in multiple other institutions, the goal of this book is to examine the territorial impact of LAC's exports to China in specific global value chains (GVC), i.e. this book acknowledges the massive literature on

LAC-China trade and contributes in examining the local impacts in LAC as a result of exports to China. While there are important case studies on the topic, so far, and surprisingly, today a systematic approach and publication on this topic does not exist.

The seven chapters of the book are based on two foundations. On the one hand, a common understanding of the methodological approach of GVC. On the other, such a methodological understanding of GVC requires the authors to understand the details –processes and products of the segments of specific GVC – in order to empirically present the impact of exports to China in specific territories. Beyond this common basis all authors were free to discuss on the territorial impacts in terms of employment, suppliers, technologies used, potential territorial tensions, learning processes within the region and by Chinese firms, as well as how these topics have changed over time. In several of the cases the authors depend on the publicly available information on the GVC and interviews, considering that firm-level information is very difficult to obtain. In several cases, firms were unwilling to grant interviews, even after being assured of the confidentiality of the information provided. The confrontation between the United States and China is deeply affecting LAC-countries, and LAC and Chinese firms engaged on trade with China could easily be confronted in public based on the provided information through interviews.

The results of the seven chapters could be systematized in at least eight important topics.

First, in practically all cases the contemporary confrontation between the United States and China plays an important territorial role. The chapter of Dussel Peters and Pérez Santillán invites us to consider the concepts of security-shoring since 2022, particularly since the wave of executive orders issued during the second Trump presidency beginning on January 20, 2025, as well the concept of "new triangular relationships", which is of particular relevance for LAC as a region and its countries. Carlos Eduardo Piña elaborates on how Venezuela has been entangled in this new triangular relationship at least since 1999 with the presidency of Hugo Chávez, as well as in the cases of Argentina, and Ecuador. Brazil's dialogue and cooperation directly with China and through the G20 and BRICS (Brazil, Russia, India, China, and South Africa) since 2003 (chapter 4 by Pedro Henrique Batista Barbosa) presents another form of profound integration with China. Free Trade Agreements with China by Chile (2005), Peru (2009), and Ecuador (2023) reflect additional forms of engaging socioeconomically with China.

Second. The first chapter of the book offers an aggregated perspective of LAC's value-added in its exports, based on input-output matrixes. Relevant for the aforementioned confrontation between the US and China, the results are relevant for the rest of the chapters: Chinese value-added in LAC's exports to the US have increased significantly during 1995-2020 –from 0.-8 % of its foreign value-added to 20.4 % in 2020– with important differences between countries: Mexico with the highest value (21.2 %) in 2020 and Costa Rica with the lowest (10 %); Argentina, Brazil, Chile, Colombia and Peru with coefficients in between. The falling value-added of the United States in LAC exports to the US for the period and the increasing presence of China is an important basis for the rest of the chapters. In addition, the chapter explains the recent extreme dynamics of LAC trade (exports and imports) to China, which is discussed in all chapters in detail.

Third. The analysis on LAC exports to China reflect enormously different GVC which are critical for understanding the increasingly complex and mature relationship between LAC and China in the 21st century. Commodities such as oil (discussed in chapters 2 and 3 for Venezuela and Brazil) and copper (chapter 6 for Peru) present substantially different characteristics in their production, transportation and distribution in China when compared to soybeans in Argentina, shrimps in Ecuador and cherries in Chile. The latter, as examined by Dorotea López, Andrés Bórquez, and Juan E. Serrano-Moreno in Chapter 3, are characterized by their delicacy and high perishability, which are crucial for ensuring quality. Additionally, their seasonality and strict sanitary and phytosanitary regulations are essential considerations for harvesting and transportation. The analyses in chapters 2-7 are extremely rich in capturing the specific conditions and implications of these GVC and their territorial impacts.

Fourth. The relevance of the selected GVC is very different for the respective countries in their exports to China, as well as for Chinese imports. From a LAC perspective, oil from Brazil, as well as Argentina's soybeans, play a minor role in their exports to China, while Peru's copper, Chile's cherry's and Ecuardor's shimps are much more important in their contribution to their national exports to China. In the case of Argentina's soybean exports to China (examined by Eduardo Daniel Oviedo in chapter 5), Argentina has implemented different policies to industrialize and upgrade its production and exports (92.6 % of soybean complex exports are in industrialized products such as meals and pellets, oil (crude and refined) and biodiesel, among others. As a result, Argentina's soybean exports to China are highly concentrated in raw materials (90.3 % in 2023), but account for only 9 % of its exports of the soybean GVC in 2023. The case of Peru's copper exports (examined by Kehan Wang and Marco Curi in chapter 6) is on the other extreme: copper concentrated 67 % of Peru's exports to China in 2023; Venezuela's oil exports to China even accounted for 68 % of its total exports to China. From a Chinese perspective, Chile's cherries and Peru's copper are major players in their respective GVC; oil imports from Brazil and Venezuela, as well as shrimps from Ecuador and soybeans from Argentina compete with other countries in China's imports and play a secondary role considering other respective major imports. Clearly, these initial results will require future detailed analysis in China's import demand and respective markets.

Fifth. LAC's exports, based on the analysis of specific GVC exported to China in chapters 2-7, reflect that in several cases (such as Ecuador's shrimps and Chile's cherries) exports are pursued by national and local firms, without an explicit Chinese presence. For the cases of Brazil and Venezuela, as well as copper in Peru and soybeans in Argentina, there is an important presence of Chinese firms at the national and local level. In the case of Brazil, firms such as Sinopec, CNPC, CNOOC, and Sinochem (which are discussed in detail) have invested massively since the first decade of the 21st century in exploration and production projects, especially those in the pre-salt area. Similarly, chapter 2 examines how Chinese loans by China Development Bank (CDB) and foreign direct investments by CNPC directly affected crude oil production in Venezuela to be exported to China. The topic is fundamental for discussions on exports to China and their territorial impacts, as well as policy proposals (see below).

Sixth. The territorial analysis of LAC exports to China within specific GVCs also provides a valuable contribution to understanding the upgrading processes within the respective territorial GVCs, as well as those transferred by Chinese firms. Surprisingly the most important upgrading processes have taken place in those territories in which Chinese firms were not present (i.e. in Chile and Ecuador, see 5.). The case of Chile is particularly relevant in developing new technologies and processes locally and nationally through private investments, including innovations in transport, harvesting techniques, selection technologies, and packaging, all aimed at exporting fresh cherries to China. Brazil is another extreme, where firms such as CNOOC, CNOOC, and others benefitted from already existing pre-salt (i.e. Petrobras´ expertise in ultra-deepwater drilling). The other case studies do not reveal significant technological upgrading processes or transfer of technologies by Chinese firms at the local or national level.

Seventh. Chapters 2-7 are substantial for understanding the deep territorial impacts through their exports in specific GVC to China, without exception. In all cases exports have generated important direct and indirect new employment. Considering that in several cases territorial exports to China are minor (such as in the Argentinian Pampas and Brazil's oil), in other cases the new employment generation is substantial: 3,933 shrimp firms account for 195,000 jobs in Ecuador, particularly in the Guayas and Oro provinces, and only the Las Bambas copper project in Peru operated by China's MMG generated over 8,000 direct and indirect jobs in the Apurímac region. Other positive results of these exports to China refer to technological upgrading processes discussed above.

These exports have also generated important local challenges, most of them regarding the environment and social unrest. While Brazil's oil exports in the Río region have not generated any particular new environmental and social confrontations, the territorial experiences in Peru's, Ecuador's Guayas province and the Pampa's soybean complex in Argentina have all been significant from this perspective. In the case of Perú, for example, copper mining has resulted in lead contamination and waste accumulation, as well as water grabbing and conflicts on land usage; 60 % of all social unrests in Peru are related to mining. The criminalization of conflicts has also increased violence. In the case of Chinese firms in Peru, Chinese firms have engaged in an important learning process on environmental and social challenges in the last decades. Nevertheless, even in the cases of cherries in Chile and shrimps in Ecuador, with no presence of Chinese firms, generalized water scarcity is a common challenge that has intensified rapidly due to the growing demand from China. The case of shrimps in Ecuador, analyzed by Carolina Viola-Reyes and Giuliana Vera-Díaz (chapter 7), presents a particularly drastic case of environmental devastation of its mangroves, added to high levels of poverty, lack of basic services, and high levels of homicides associated with the main regions exporting shrimps.

Eight. All chapters of this book present a variety of research and policy proposals. It is clear that the book points into a topic that has huge potential, considering massive territorial experiences of LAC exports to China in specific GVC; seven case studies are clearly not sufficient. Nevertheless, the book clarifies the complexity and maturity of the socioeconomic relationship between LAC and China at the territorial level. In most of the cases the national governments in LAC are responsible for improving learning processes and offering and implementing regulations, technological upgrading options, and the transfer of technology; the effective implementation of labor and environmental laws is also the responsibility of federal, provincial, and local governments. In other specific cases, particularly regarding public Chinese firms, they should and could also commit to improving efforts to overcome techno-logical, labor, and environmental challenges. All these cases should be significant for institutions such as the CELAC (Community of Latin American and Caribbean States)-China Forum, which was established in 2015 and explicitly integrates these themes in the working programs since 2015.

1. Chinese Value-Added in Latin American and Caribbean Exports: Conditions and Challenges

Enrique Dussel Peters and Lesbia Pérez-Santillán

There is a long-standing conceptual and empirical tradition of measuring the value-added of foreign trade, particularly exports, for countries using input-output tables (Hummels *et al.* 2001; Johnson and Noguera (2012); Koopman, Wang, and Wei 2008; Rasmussen 1963), also in Latin America and the Caribbean (LAC) (Durán Lima and Banacloche 2021; Rodil Marzábal 2017). Surprisingly, given the increasing confrontation between the United States and China since the "great power competition" in 2017 and security-shoring since 2022, research in LAC has been limited on this topic, with some exceptions.[1]

The goal of this chapter is to examine the main foreign trade trends in the 21st century from a Latin American and Caribbean (LAC) perspective, particularly in light of the U.S.-China confrontation. Particularly important will be the discussion, empirical results and main structures that have evolved for LAC's exports –total and to the U.S.– regarding its value-added structure and concentrating on China's value-added. In the U.S.-China confrontation this discussion is at the center of the U.S.-LAC trade debate. Surprisingly, think tanks have contributed little to this discussion.

1 For a full discussion see: Pérez-Santillán (2022, 2024).

This chapter will focus on LAC's foreign trade and its value-added by major countries, particularly the contributions of China and the U.S., in order to understand current policy discussions since the Biden and second Trump presidencies *vis a vis* LAC. The chapter will be divided into three sections. The first will introduce two concepts –new triangular relationships and security-shoring– to understand the depth of the contemporary U.S.-China confrontation. In addition, it will include some general trade structures of LAC *vis a vis* the U.S. and China. The second section will highlight LAC's value-added structure in its (total and to the US) exports and the increasing presence of Chinese value-added. Input-Output Matrixes (IOM) will be useful for examining the main trade structure for a group of LAC countries and the region as a whole, and a group of LAC countries, during 1995-2020. The last section will conclude with the main issues of the analysis and a group of policy recommendations.

1. Implications of US-China Confrontation for LAC and Main Foreign Trade Structures in the 21st Century

This section will begin by introducing two concepts relevant for understanding the depth of the U.S.-China confrontation, with important implications for the contemporary and future socioeconomic relationship of LAC with the U.S. and China. The second part will highlight a group of LAC foreign trade structures. Both issues will be relevant for the subsequent analysis.

1.1 New Triangular Relationships and Security-Shoring[2]

The concept of new triangular relationships is particularly useful in the context of the profound confrontation between the U.S. and

2 For a full historical and conceptual analysis see: Dussel Peters (2025).

China since 2017.[3] The concept is valuable in situating bilateral relations today and also in the near future given the great power competition and profoundly diverging political and economic perspectives between the United States and China. Third countries and regions such as LAC will have to examine their relationship with the United States and China in depth on specific issues that have important socioeconomic repercussions. Among these are: using 5G, acquiring weapons systems, building ports and airports, financing, trade and FDI, but also setting up Confucius Institutes and special economic zones, among many others.

What is the historical context of the U.S.-China confrontation, and how has it shaped new triangular relationships in regions such as LAC? In December of 2017, for the first time, the United States acknowledged China as an equal –initially framing it as a global challenge to American power (NSS 2017:2). In the 2017 National Security Strategy, China was most often mentioned in association with Russia, highlighting the "return of great power competition. China and Russia began to reassert their influence regionally and globally" (NSS 2017:27). A few years later a strategy based on 'principled realism' was proposed by the White House (WH 2020:7) explicitly *vis a vis* China. The basis of the analysis is that "America possesses unmatched political, economic, military, and technological advantages" (NSS 2017:3) compared to the rest of the world and China; explicitly referring to China and its relationship to the Western Hemisphere, including LAC, since "China seeks to pull the region into its orbit through state-led investments and loans" (NSS 2017:51). The most coherent arguments regarding the United States' new policy toward China under Trump were delivered by Vice President Pence in 2018. In his analysis of China (which did not include Russia), he once again emphasized the concept of 'great power competition' in U.S.-China relations (Pence 2018:1). The analysis, from this perspective, is striking: the United

3 The concept has been discussed and used for at least a decade (Dussel Peters, Hearn and Shaiken 2013) and a growing body of literature has emerged around it.

States supported China historically, particularly since the Second World War, "but soon after it took power in 1949, the Chinese Communist Party began to pursue authoritarian expansionism" (Pence 2018:2), and 'after the fall of the Soviet Union, we assumed that a free China was inevitable... America agreed to give Beijing open access to our economy, and bring China into the World Trade Organization. Previous administrations made this choice in the hope that freedom in China would expand in all forms, not only economically, but also politically, with a newfound respect for classical liberal principles, private property, religious freedom, and the entire family of human rights... but that hope has gone unfulfilled... Over the past 17 years [2000 to 2017], China's GDP has grown 9-fold; it has become the second-largest economy in the world. Much of this success was driven by American investment in China' (Pence 2018:2). China, from this perspective, is ungrateful towards the United States and will not change politically and economically while it is led by the CPC which uses "an arsenal of policies inconsistent with free and fair trade, including tariffs, quotas, currency manipulation, forced technology transfer, technology theft, and industrial subsidies doled out like candy... has set its sights on controlling 90 % of the world's most advanced industries, including robotics, biotechnology, and artificial intelligence" (Pence 2018:3).

In light of this "great power competition," since 2017 the United States and China have participated in a dramatic deterioration in their bilateral relationship, with different arguments, intensities, suggestions, laws, and, in some cases, negotiations. These negotiations range from the trade war –which has received the widest attention– to a wide range of topics that have received much less attention until the end of 2023, including the closing of massive numbers of Confucius Institutes in U.S. universities, scaling down of visiting students, scholarships and joint research, as well as an overall review of Chinese researchers in particular facilities, extending even to the threat of drastically reducing and banning passenger airlines, the persecution of respective firms under "entity lists", the scaling back of journalists on both sides, up to the constant escalation on economic and financial issues.

On the one hand, the Biden administration –under the headings of 'invest, align, compete' and 'managing competition' (Blinken 2022; Sullivan 2024)– has continued the same policies initiated by President Trump, butno important policy regarding China has been cancelled or substantially changed since. In addition to the recognition of 'great power competition,' however, the Biden Administration enabled economic policies to counter China's increasing competition. Assuming that "companies in economies disciplined by the market cannot effectively compete with both Chinese companies and the Chinese state" (USTR 2022:4), the U.S. is making massive investments in its productive sector to catch up in high-tech industries, counter China's competition, and maintain its absolute advantage, alongside its allies U.S.. As a result, in 2022 the Biden Administration was able to pass three major laws –the Inflation Reduction Act, the ° and Science Act, and the Infrastructure Law (McNeece 2023)– whose combined costs accounted for almost 15 % of the U.S. GDP. All three initiatives make specific reference to China and require a resilient process against it. This is particularly true in infrastructure, and also in innovation and technology, as well as in advanced manufacturing and semiconductor tools (Sullivan 2024). As we shall see below, the implications extend to third countries. On the second element of the new strategy, 'align' –i.e., to "shape the strategic environment around Beijing to advance our vision" (Blinken 2022)–, the U.S. has integrated other countries and groups of countries into its policies vis-à-vis China, referring to this as a 'network of alliances and partnerships' (Blinken 2022). Finally, investments and alignment would ensure, from a U.S. perspective, a fair competition process based on reciprocity and protecting 'against efforts to siphon off our ingenuity or imperil our security' (Blinken 2022). They would also generate an 'allied techno-industrial base' (WH 2021:33) with the goal of 'extending absolute advantage,' according to the National Security Council (Wang 2022:2).

What are the implications for other countries of Biden's strategy towards China?

The Biden administration's strategy *vis a vis* other countries, including LAC (see below), has been much more subtle –under the under the headings of 'invest, align, compete', as discussed earlier, and against Trump's unilateral decisions against China.

Increasingly since 2022-2023, however, the Biden Administration has made clear in its strategy against China that national security (Blinken 2022) will be the guiding principle, i.e. socio-economic and international relations with China and third countries will be subordinated to the national security of the U.S., that is (free) trade, investment, culture, educational exchange, as well as other bilateral relations will have to be reviewed from a national security perspective (and thus security-shoring) (Yellen 2023). From this perspective, and in contrast to the recent trend of multiple shorings –including nearshoring, offshoring, onshoring, ally-shoring, and friend-shoring, which are generally understood as the relocation of segments of global value chains but fail to acknowledge that such relocations have occurred globally since the 1950s (Dussel Peters 2000; Piore and Sabel 1984)– the concept of security-shoring introduces several contributions. First, it defines a relatively recent process, initiated in 2022–2023 by the Biden Administration, which prioritizes national security interests over nearly all other aspects of its international relations. Second, security-shoring is a strategy against China that increasingly invites third countries –under the heading of "align"– to participate in this strategy. Third, there is an enormous potential that this strategy will continue beyond the US-election in November of 2024, also given the incremental addition of policies against China since 2018 under both the Trump and Biden administrations. The impacts of security-shoring –and responses by China– will be significant in the U.S. (for example in terms of the costs of such policies in 2022, as discussed earlier), particularly internationally. Under security-shoring, third countries –and in the confrontation of the United States versus China– will have to decide to benefit from US-incentives against China or to be left aside. The founder of the current global trading, investment, and financial system, established since the Bretton Woods Agreement in the 1940s, is now advocating for its own national interests (against China) and opposing the policies that the U.S. has followed for decades under multilateralism and reciprocity U.S. . With this background, third countries could easily begin taking unilateral policies in these and other socioeconomic fields and quickly result in chaotic pre-World War II conditions.

Under the second presidency of Donald Trump, since January 20, 2025 security-shoring has again escalated to new military levels, i.e. immigration and organized crime have resulted in an "invasion" (Trump 2025), which justifies the use of new instruments for preserving the US' national security (and thus security-shoring). They are also the basis to justify new tariffs against U.S. imports from Canada, China, and Mexico since February 1, 2025.[4] Robert Lighthizer has been one of the few authors close to the new Trump administration who has been able to propose a medium-term strategy explicitly linking U.S. national security with a new global trade regime. This strategy envisions a group of countries operating "based on long-term trade balance, and the new system should enforce an equilibrium … Indeed, John Maynard Keynes proposed a similar structure at the Bretton Woods conference that established the post–World War II trade order"[5]

4 In the case of China The Executive order to justify 10 % additional tariffs beginning on February 1, 2025 refers to synthetic opioid supply (WH 2025/a), while the Executive order for 25 % tariffs on Mexican imports refers to unlawful migration, illicit opioids, and Mexican drug trafficking organizations (WH 2025/b).

5 Lighthizer (2025) also asserts that the U.S. 'have become victims either because they believe in the myth of free trade or because they are not good at defending themselves against these aggressive strategies … In the last 20 years, we have transferred some $ 20 trillion of our wealth … to the governments and citizens of the exploiting countries … We are not competitive in important products like personal computers, semiconductor manufacturing, solar panels, shipbuilding and much more.' He explicitly refers to "real villains" such as Canada, Germany, Mexico, and Vietnam, but particularly to China.

1.2 LAC's Foreign Trade by Main Countries[6]

The LAC-China trade relationship has been examined in detail in the last years (Damares Lopes *et al.* 2021; Dussel Peters 2024, 2025). In order to set the overall foreign trade basis of LAC for the next chapter, two topics are significant.

First. China has become LAC's second main trading partner since 2009, only after the U.S. (Figure 1); in a rather short period China increased its share over LAC's total foreign trade to 17.11 % (in 2023). Intraregional trade suffered significantly, falling from 21.45 % in 2008 to 14.60 % in 2023, the lowest level in the 21st century. The main loser in LAC's trade has been the US, accounting for 54.21 % of LAC' s trade in 2000 with levels below 38 % since 2020.

Figure 1. LAC Main Trading Partners (2000-2003) (percentage over total trade)

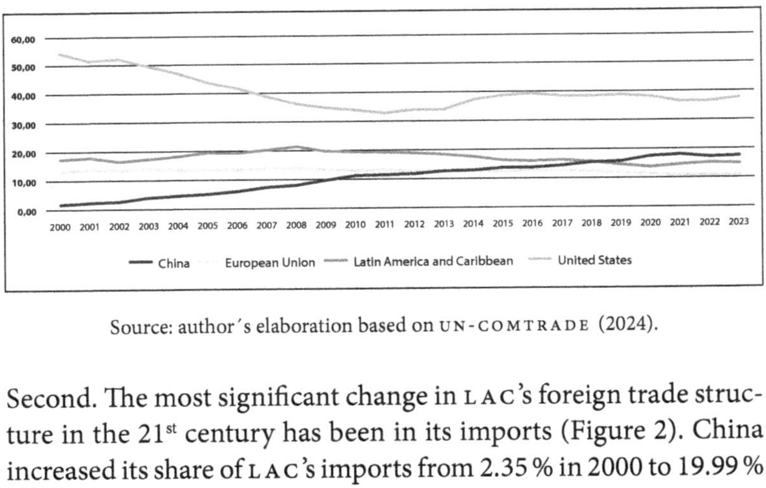

Source: author's elaboration based on UN-COMTRADE (2024).

Second. The most significant change in LAC's foreign trade structure in the 21st century has been in its imports (Figure 2). China increased its share of LAC's imports from 2.35 % in 2000 to 19.99 % in 2023, while the U.S.'s share fell sharply from 49.62 % in 2000 to 30.70 % in 2023. Both LAC and the European Union maintained rather low shares for the period (Figure 2).

6 For a full historical and conceptual analysis see: Dussel Peters (2025).

Figure 2. LAC: Main Importing Countries (2000-2023)
(percentage over total trade)

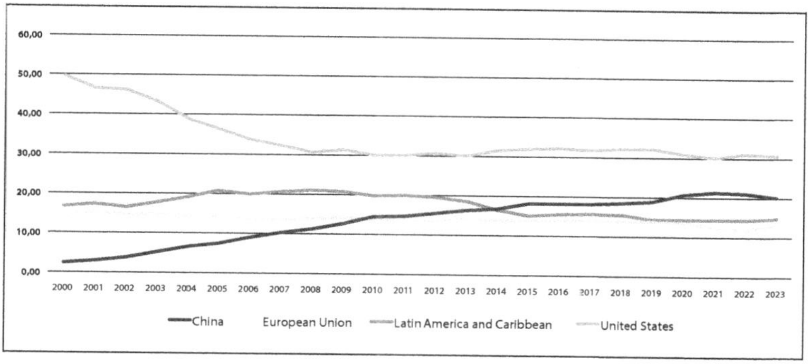

Source: Author´s elaboraion based on UN-COMTRADE (2024).

Other analyses have highlighted additional characteristics of LAC-China foreign trade, including LAC's exports, details on specific global value chains, intra-industry trade, trade concentration, transportation costs, and trade deficits, among others. These trade structures, however, are sufficient for understanding the important contribution of the next chapter, in light of the discussion and accusation by the U.S. that LAC, and particularly Mexico, are exporting Chinese goods and services to the U.S. The argument has been particularly strong and important –given the new triangular relationship and debates on security-shoring vis-à-vis China– explicitly against Mexico. While the U.S. has confronted China with direct tariffs since 2018, Mexico has increasingly become a 'back door' for Chinese imports entering the U.S. (USTR 2024:25).

2. LAC's Value-Added in its Total Exports and to the U.S. (1995-2020)

In order to examine China's value added in LAC's foreign trade we will use the Organisation for Economic Co-operation and Development's (OECD) Inter-Country Input-Output Tables (ICIO). These input-output matrixes include information for 78 countries and the rest of the world; disaggregated in 45 sectors; they allow to distinguish inputs according to the domestic or foreign origin between 1995-2020. Latin America and the Caribbean includes 7 countries: Argentina, Brazil, Colombia, Costa Rica, Chile, Peru, and Mexico.

ICIO allows to calculate: a. the GDP or value-added by country, b. the decomposition of gross exports in: i. domestic content, ii. foreign content, which can be disaggregated by country.[7] This type of analysis is particularly fruitful as it allows for estimates of the foreign content in a country's gross exports by source country (for example, the U.S. and China) U.S. . Results will focus on the discussions posed in the first section of this chapter.

Four types of results are relevant for our discussions.

First. China's presence in LAC's economy calculated by China's GDP absorbed in the economy in LAC (or in final goods completed in China and consumed in LAC). Figure 3 reflects that LAC's

Figure 3. Chinese Value-Added Absorbed by LAC's Economies (1995-2020) (percentage of respective GDP)

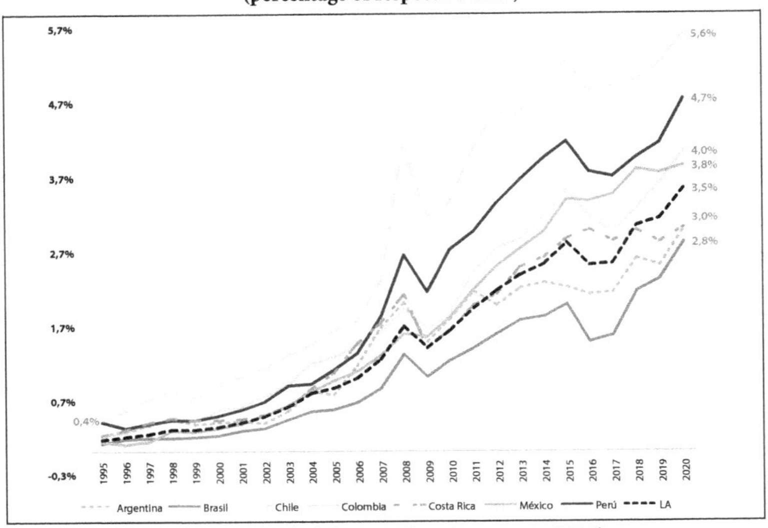

Source: Author's elaboration based on OECD (2023).

7 For a full discussion see Borin and Mancini (2019) and Pérez-Santillán (2024).

absorption of Chinese GDP has increased significantly during 1995-2020, from 0.2% of LAC´s GDP in 1995 to 3.5% in 2020. This process has deepened for all considered countries of LAC, and particularly for Chile (5.6% of its GDP), Peru (4.7%), Colombia (4.0%), and Mexico (3.8%).

Second. Decomposition of gross exports to the United States. As discussed above, gross exports are disaggregated by domestic and foreign content. Table 1 reflects for an important fall of LAC's domestic content in its gross exports to the US, from 73.3% in

Table 1. LAC´s Exports to the US: Domestic Value-Added (1995-2020) (percentage over gross exports to the US)

	Argentina	Brazil	Chile	Colombia	Costa Rica	Mexico	Peru	LAC
1995	89.8	87.9	84.7	88.5	79.1	67.1	90.6	73.3
1996	89.6	88	84.1	88.4	78.5	65.6	90.5	71.5
1997	89	86.9	83.9	88.6	78.6	64.7	90.4	70.6
1998	89.6	86.9	82.6	89.1	78.3	62	90.4	68.1
1999	90.2	85	83.3	92	78.8	61.6	90.5	67.7
2000	90.7	84.6	81.5	87.7	78.5	61.6	89.8	66.8
2001	91.2	82.9	79.6	86.7	79	61.8	89.4	66.8
2002	89.9	83.6	79.5	86.7	79.3	52.3	88.6	67.2
2003	89.3	84.2	78.2	87	79.1	51.5	88.2	66.9
2004	87.1	84	79.1	87.5	78.2	52.7	87.2	68.1
2005	87.2	85	77.3	88.4	76.9	53.5	84.6	68.9
2006	87	85.5	79	88.6	75.2	53.5	82.9	68.9
2007	86.1	86	78.5	88.6	76.1	63.4	80.7	68.6
2008	85.3	85.4	75.5	88.2	74.6	64.8	79.3	69.9
2009	87.4	87	79.3	90.7	79.1	63.9	83.9	69.8
2010	87.3	86.4	80	91.3	79.6	63.3	82.3	69.2
2011	86.9	85.6	77.7	90.9	79	65	81.5	70.9
2012	87.1	84.8	78.5	91.1	79.3	64.5	82.2	70.3
2013	87	83.7	78.3	91.2	80.6	64	83.1	69.4
2014	88.7	84.3	79.8	88.1	81	64.1	83.9	69.1
2015	88.8	83	82	87.3	83.2	62.4	86.1	67.3
2016	87.2	84.3	83.6	86.8	83.6	61.5	86.9	66.9
2017	87.1	84.4	83.2	87.5	82.3	61.6	86.1	66.9
2018	86.5	82.4	81.6	87.1	81.1	61.9	85.5	66.6
2019	86.5	82.1	81.7	86.7	82.2	63.3	86.7	67.7
2020	88.4	82.3	82.2	88.1	81.8	64.3	88.5	68.7

Source: Authors´s elaboration based on OECD (2023).

1995 to 68.7 % in 2020, i.e. the foreign content accounts for 31.3 % in 2020. Differences among countries are most significant: Mexico is by far the country with the lowest domestic content in gross exports to the US, of 64.3 % in 2020, in contrast to Peru, Argentina and Costa Rica, with 88.5 %, 88.4 % and 81.8 %.

Third. Tables 2 and 3 reflect the profound changes in LAC's trade (as discussed in section 1.2) and specifically regarding the value-added of its exports to the U.S. as a percentage of its foreign value-added. Table 2 accounts for the increasing relevance of

Table 2. LAC Exports to the US: Chinese Value-Added in LAC´s Foreign Value-Added (1995-2020) (percentage)

	Argentina	Brazil	Chile	Colombia	Costa Rica	Mexico	Peru	LAC
1995	1.6	0.9	1.4	1	0.6	0.7	1.8	0.8
1996	2	1.4	1.9	1.5	0.7	0.5	1.7	0.6
1997	2.4	1.5	2.4	2.1	1	0.7	1.8	0.8
1998	3	1.6	2.7	2.7	1.2	1.4	2.2	1.5
1999	2.7	1.5	3.2	3	1.1	1.4	2.2	1.5
2000	2.5	1.4	2.3	2.8	1.2	1.5	2.2	1.5
2001	2.7	1.7	2.5	3.1	1.3	2.3	2.6	2.3
2002	2.9	2.4	2.8	3.8	1.4	3.4	3.1	3.3
2003	3.3	3.2	2.8	4.2	1.7	5	3.8	4.8
2004	3.9	3.3	3.2	5.8	2.3	6	3.8	5.7
2005	3.7	3.3	3.1	5.5	2.7	6.8	4.4	6.4
2006	4.8	3.6	3.7	5.6	3.8	7.6	4.7	7.2
2007	6.7	4.5	4.4	6.3	4.1	9	5.1	8.5
2008	8.3	5.7	6.4	7.2	4.8	10.6	6	9.9
2009	7.2	5.2	5.9	7.3	4.6	11.8	7.7	11.1
2010	7.7	6	6	7.7	5.2	12.8	7.1	12.1
2011	9.1	6.1	6.2	9.3	5.4	13.4	6.8	12.5
2012	9.2	6.4	7.3	10	5.6	14.6	7.7	13.6
2013	9.9	7.3	7.9	10	6.7	15.1	7.9	14.2
2014	11	8.1	10	9.4	7.1	16.2	10.2	15.3
2015	11.7	10.3	11.8	11	8.5	17.2	13	16.5
2016	11.2	8.5	11.4	9.8	8.9	16.6	12.8	15.9
2017	10.8	8.6	11.4	9.5	8.6	16.8	11.5	16.1
2018	11.5	11.7	11.1	10	8.7	17.6	11.4	16.9
2019	13.4	11.3	12	10.2	8.7	18.3	14	17.5
2020	15.7	13	14.8	13.3	10	21.2	18.7	20.4

Source: Author´s elaboration based on OECD (2023).

Table 3. LAC´s Exports to the US: US Value-Added (1995-2020) (percentage over gross exports to the US)

	Argentina	Brazil	Chile	Colombia	Costa Rica	Mexico	Peru	LA
1995	20	22.3	21.4	34.4	42.9	64.7	24.7	59.1
1996	19.8	20.9	21	33.1	41.6	71.9	22.5	66.2
1997	21.3	22.9	21.1	34.9	44.1	71.7	22.1	66.3
1998	20	24.5	18.6	31.8	45.4	65.8	22.6	61.8
1999	20.7	24.1	18.7	34.9	42.7	65.9	21.1	62
2000	21.8	23.1	17.7	32.8	41.2	64.9	19	61
2001	23.5	22.7	16.5	30.6	40.7	58.7	18.4	55
2002	22.6	20.3	15.5	30.4	42.4	55.2	16.6	51.6
2003	22.1	18.7	13.9	28.7	43.5	53.7	16.7	50
2004	20.6	17.4	14.6	27.2	39.8	48.8	16.3	45.1
2005	19.7	17	14.5	25.8	37.9	45.5	14.4	41.9
2006	19	16	15	26.5	40.2	44	13.8	40.7
2007	17.3	16.1	16	26.1	38.1	41.4	13.5	38.5
2008	15.9	16.3	17.6	25.9	37.8	40.5	15.6	37.4
2009	19.6	18.4	16.9	29	36.6	41.4	19.4	38.9
2010	18	18.9	16.2	26.5	42.5	40.3	17	38
2011	17.6	19.2	18.7	26.9	40.1	39.6	16.4	37
2012	18.8	19	20.5	26.5	42.6	40.1	16.4	37.7
2013	18.9	20	21.9	31	42.1	41.2	19.5	39
2014	19.5	19.6	21	35.9	41.2	41.5	21.6	39.5
2015	20.1	21	21.9	33.4	40.7	41.6	25.6	39.8
2016	20.1	23.4	22.5	30	40.6	40.8	27.8	39.3
2017	19.8	23.1	22.1	28.4	39.5	39	25.1	37.6
2018	19.3	22.3	23.3	32.8	39.3	38.7	24.7	37.3
2019	19.4	23.3	24.1	30.2	37.9	39	29	37.6
2020	15.9	22.3	22.4	30.9	35.9	37.2	27.1	35.8

Source: Author´s elaboration based on OECD (2023).

China's value added in LAC's exports to the U.S., from less than 1% until 1997 to 20.4% of foreign value-added. Mexico stands out for the highest Chinese value-added in 2020 (21.2%), while Costa Rica (10%), Brazil (13%), and Colombia (13.3) reflect a much lower Chinese value-added in their exports to the U.S. Table 3 accounts for the U.S.' value added in LAC's foreign content. The U.S. is still the most important source of LAC's foreign value-added, but fell drastically from 59.1% in 1995 to 35.8% in 2020, i.e. the U.S.' share over LAC's trade has not only fallen significantly (as discussed in Section 1.2.), but in addition its value-added in LAC's exports to the U.S. This is particularly the case for Mexico (from 64.7 % in 1995 to 37.2 % in 2020), but also for Brazil, Chile, and Peru (Table 3). There are other countries in LAC's trade, in addition to China and the U.S, that are important in terms of their foreign value-added to LAC's gross exports, such as other Asian countries, the European Union, and LAC countries.

Fourth. Additional calculations, such as those for Mexico. The ICIO calculations allow for additional estimations for sectors and countries, in addition to China and the U.S. for 1995-2000. Based on the discussion in the first section, three results are of interest.

A. Figure 4 deepens profound structural changes in Mexico's foreign trade and exports. During 1995-2020 Mexican exports to the US have drastically increased Chinese valued-added, now as a percentage of Mexico's value-added in gross exports (from 0.24 % in 1995 to 7.5 % in 2020) in comparison to the U.S. (from 21.09 % to 13.13 %). Thus, while the U.S. is still the major source of Mexican foreign value-added by country, it has fallen significantly, particularly in comparison to China. Equally relevant, however, is

Figure 4. Mexico: Exports to the United States and Value-Added from China and the US (percentage over value-added in gross exports) (1995-2020)

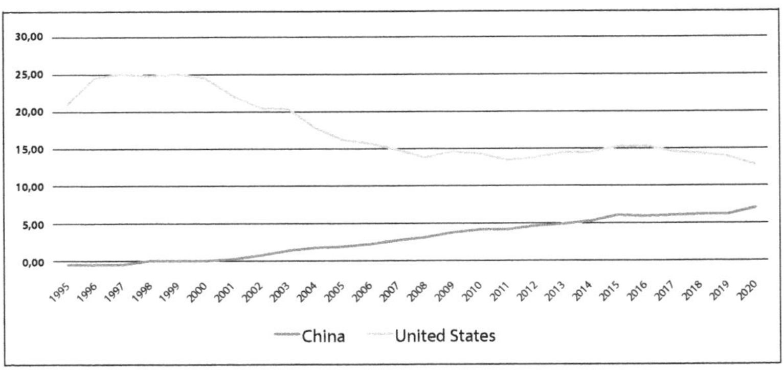

Source: Author´s elaboration based on OECD (2023).

that foreign companies –particularly those from the U.S.– account for 70 % of Mexico's imports, including those from China (Tolama and López 2024).

B. The United States' domestic value-added in its exports is much higher than for any other LAC country (see Table 1), including the US exports to Mexico: its domestic value-added over gross exports have remained relatively stable at around 87 % during 1995-2020. Nevertheless, China's value-added share in its total value-added to exports to Mexico increased from 0.4 % in 1995 to 1.8 % in 2020. Canada's value-added in exports to Mexico also increased from 0.3 % in 1995 to 3.0 % in 2020 (Figure 5).

Figure 5. United States and Canada: Chinese Value-Added to Exports to Mexico (1995-2020) (over respective gross exports to Mexico)

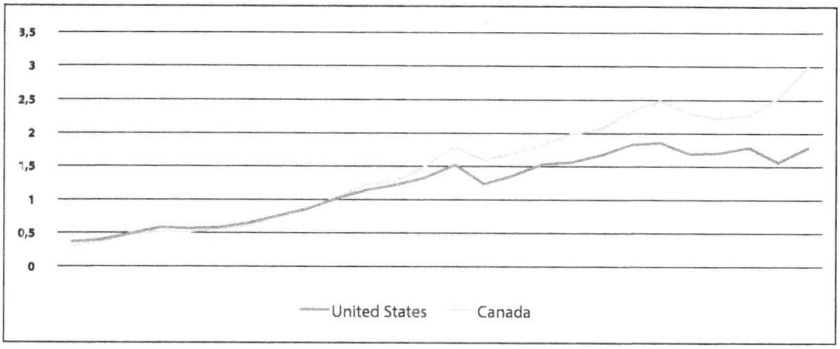

Source: Author´s own ellaboration based on OECD (2023).

3. Conclusions and Discussions

The analysis has highlighted the importance of the U.S.- China confrontation, particularly in its first section in terms of the concepts of new triangular relationships and security-shoring. The profound U.S.- China confrontation goes far beyond trade, high-tech commodities and electric vehicles, and it includes tourism, education, and academics, as discussed. Third regions and countries will have to specify concrete steps regarding an agenda *vis a vis* the U.S. and China. The security-shoring agenda of the

U.S. since 2022 poses enormous challenges for LAC and other regions and countries, particularly since 2025 and the aggressive strategy of the second Trump presidency.

The analysis contributes to understanding the increasing presence of China in LAC's foreign trade in the 21st century, particularly in comparison to the U.S., LAC, and the European Union. As discussed in Section 1, LAC's foreign trade has significantly substituted for the U.S., specifically regarding its imports, and affecting LAC's intraregional trade during the 21st century.

A key contribution of the analysis is its examination of LAC's value-added in gross exports by country, along with the growing share of Chinese value-added. The substantial increase in Chinese value-added, compared to the U.S.'s –still the most significant, though with a notable decline in the 21st century– is one of the chapter's most important findings.

The Mexican analysis invites to a more profound analysis for the rest of the region and each of its countries. The Mexican case is substantial considering its low domestic value-added content, and, in addition, the substantial growth of Chinese value-added to its exports to the U.S., of 7.5 % in 2020. Even in the Mexican case, however, the concept of new triangular relationships is fundamental: yes, Mexican export increase its Chinese value-added, but the imports of Chinese parts and components are pursued by foreign firms, particularly from the US. In addition, Chinese value-added has also increased importantly in the US' and Canada's exports to Mexico, although with lower levels than Mexico (Figure 5). These trade structures –excluding other specific analyses such as foreign direct investment flows and structures– have not been sufficiently understood and have been overlooked by U.S. policymakers in recent years, particularly in the context of security-shoring.

The results also set the basis for detailed analysis of specific global value chains in LAC, mainlyfor those exported to China.

References

Blinken, Antony J. 2022. *The Administration´s Approach to the People´s Republic of China*. The George Washington University: Washington, D.C.

Damares Lopes, Afonso, Quinet de Andrade Bastos, Suzana, and Salgueiro Perobelli, Fernando. 2021. "América Latina y China: ¿beneficio mutuo o dependencia?". *Revista de la* CEPAL 135, pp. 159-176.

Durán Lima, José E. and Banacloche, Santacruz. 2021. *Análisis económicos a partir de matrices de insumo-producto. Definiciones, indicadores y aplicaciones para América Latina*. CEPAL: Santiago de Chile.

Dussel Peters, Enrique. 2000. *Polarizing Mexico. The Impact of Liberalization Strategy*. Lynne Rienner: Boulder.

Dussel Peters, Enrique. 2024. "Tendencias de los costos de transporte en el comercio internacional : análisis de las importaciones de los Estados Unidos procedentes de América Latina y el Caribe y otras regiones o países". *FAL Boletín* (CEPAL) 402, pp. 1-21.

Dussel Peters, Enrique. 2025. *Latin America, China, and Great Power Competition. New Triangular Relationships*. Lynne Rienner Publishers: Boulder, Colorado.

Dussel Peters, Enrique, Hearn, Adrian H. and Shaiken, Harley (edits.). 2013. *China and the New Triangular Relationships in the Americas. China and the Future of* US*-Mexican Relations*. University of Miami/CLAS, University of California-Berkeley/CLAS and UNAM/CECHIMEX: Mexico.

Gereffi, Gary, Humphrey, John and Sturgeon, Timothy. 2005. "The Governance of Global Value Chains". *Journal of International Economics* 48(1), pp. 78-104.

Hummels, David, Ishii, Jun, and Yi, Kei-Mu. 2001. "The Nature and Growth of Vertical Specialization in World Trade". *Journal of International Economics* 54, pp. 75-96.

Johnson, Robert and Noguera, Guillermo. 2012. Accounting for intermediates: Production sharing and trade in value added. *Journal of International Economics, 86(2), 224–236.*

Koopman, Robert, Wang, Zhi, and Wei, Shang-Jin. 2008. "How Much of Chinese Exports is Really Made in China? Assessing Domestic Value Added When Processing Trade is Pervasive." NBER *Working Paper* 14109, pp. 1-51.

McKibbin, Warwick J. 2025. *Trump´s threatened tariffs projected to damage economies of* US, *Canada, Mexico, and China.* PIIE (Peterson Institute for International Economics): Washington, D.C.

McNeece, John. 2023. "President Biden´s Industrial Policy and Prospects for North American Regionalization". *North American Competitiveness Working Group*, pp. 1-29.

NSS (National Security Strategy). 2017. *National Security Strategy of the United States.* The President of the United States: Washington, D.C.

NSS. 2022. *National Security Strategy.* The President of the United States: Washington, D.C.

OECD (Organisation for Economic Co-operation and Development). 2013. *Interconnected Economies. Benefiting from global value chains.* OECD: Paris.

OECD. 2023. *Inter-Country Input Output Tables.* OECD: Paris.

Pence, Michael. 2018. *Remarks by Vice President Pence on the Administration´s Policy Toward China.* The Hudson Institute: Washington, D.C.

Pérez-Santillán, Lesbia. 2022. "Relación económica y comercial de China con América Latina: los casos de Brasil y México, 2000-2020". *Cuadernos de Trabajo del Cechimex* 6, pp. 1-21.

Pérez-Santillán, Lesbia. 2024. "Cambios recientes en la producción internacional de bienes, valor agregado e insumos importados en las manufacturas en México y China". In, Dussel Peters, Enrique (coord.). *América Latina y el Caribe y China. Economía, comercio e inversión 2024.* Red ALC-China, UNAM and Cechimex: Mexico, pp. 223-248.

Piore, Michael J. and Sabel, Charles F. 1984. *The Second Industrial Divide. Possibilities for Prosperity*. Basic Books: New York.

Rasmussen, P. Norregaard. 1963. *Relaciones intersectoriales*. Aguilar: Madrid.

Rodil Marzábal, Óscar. 2017. "Las relaciones intersectoriales de América Latina con China en el marco de las cadenas globales de valor". In, Dussel Peters, Enrique (coord.). *América Latina y el Caribe y China. Economía, comercio e inversión 2017*. Red ALC-China, UNAM y Cechimex: Mexico, pp. 337-358.

SteelOrbis. 2024. "US warns of possible reinstallation of Section 232 tariffs on Mexican steel and aluminum". *SteelOrbis*, February 20.

Sullivan, Jake. 2024. *Remarks and Q&A by National Security Advisor Jake Sullivan on the Future of U.S.-China Relations*. Council on Foreign Relations: Washington, D.C.

Tolama, Jimena and López, Italia. 2024. "México tiene que estar abierto a la inversion china: subsecretario de Comercio Exterior". *Bloomberg Línea*, November 13.

Trump, Donald. 2025. "The Inaugural Address". The White House: Washington, D.C. January 20.

USTR (United States Trade Representative). 2022. *2021 Report to Congress on China´s WTO Compliance*. USTR: Washington, D.C.

USTR. 2024. *Report to Congress on the Operation of the United States-Mexico-Canada Agreement with Respect to Trade in Automotive Goods*. USTR: Washington, D.C.

WH (White House). 2020. *United States Strategic Approach to the People´s Republic of China*. Washington, D.C.: WH.

WH. 2021. *Building Resilient Supply Chains, Revitalizing American Manufacturing, and Fostering Broad-Based Growth*. WH: Washington, D.C.

WH. 2025/a. *Executive Order – Imposing Duties to Address the Synthetic Opioid Supply Chain in the People´s Republic of China*. WH: Washington, D.C.

WH. 2025/b. *Executive Order – Imposing Duties to Address the Situation at Our Southern Border*. WH: Washington, D.C.

Yellen, Janet. 2023. *Remarks by Secretary of the Treasury Janet L. Yellen on the* U.S.*- China Economic Relationship at Johns Hopkins School of Advanced International Studies.* John Hopkins School of Advanced International Studies: Washington, D.C.

2.
The Local Impact of Venezuela's Oil Exports to China: An Analysis Based on the New Oil-Based Global Value Chain (2000-2023)

Carlos Eduardo Piña

Introduction

The main objective of this analysis is to analyze the local impacts in the main economic levels of analysis (macro, medium, micro and territorial) generated by Venezuelan oil exports to China during the 21st century. For this purpose, two main sources will be considered, such as: 1) the cumulative knowledge of the methodology on GVC developed by the Academic Network of Latin America and the Caribbean on China (Red ALC-China), especially the approach that assumes the integration of micro, medium and macroeconomics as a methodological tool to understand the economic engagement between China and Latin America and the Caribbean (LAC) (Dussel Peters 2019); and 2) the publicly available information related to Venezuelan oil exports to China during the first twenty-three years of the new century. It is crucial to note that oil is the most important natural resource produced in Venezuela and the country's main exportable product; moreover, this product has been the main driving force in consolidating bilateral relations between China and Venezuela and promoting their current "All-weather strategic partnership".

In terms of economic impact, the decision to research this topic is part of the academic effort to identify and understand

Latin America's economic engagement with China in recent years. For many countries, including Venezuela, China has become an important trading partner, but also an important investor in infrastructure projects and/or a source of foreign direct investment, in the form of greenfield projects and/or mergers and acquisitions. This economic engagement has generated new jobs, technology transfers, new and valuable upgrading activities and, in general, economic growth in the host countries. Furthermore, this chapter attempts to integrate new knowledge, understanding and information on how the new oil-based GVC with China has brought economic advantages or disadvantages, depending on the case, to Venezuela.

In order to achieve this goal, the following pages will explain some topics related to Sino-Venezuelan trade relations and, especially, the creation, consolidation and stagnation of the new oil-based GVC between these countries. In this regard, the structure of this chapter is made up of a summary of the diplomatic relations between China and Venezuela, which commemorated its fiftieth anniversary in 2024; for this purpose, this half-century period will be explained in two different stages: 1974-199 and 1999-2024. The following part explains the main characteristics and figures of the Sino-Venezuelan trade relations during the fifty years of their bilateral relations, emphasizing the period 2000-2023, which is the most dynamic and relevant in commercial terms. After this explanation, the next part of this chapter will focus on the local impact at four economic levels (macro, medium, micro and territorial) of Venezuelan oil exports to China. Finally, the chapter closes with the main conclusions of this study and a set of policy recommendations.

1. China and Venezuela: Fifty Years of Diplomatic Relations (1974-2024)

Venezuela and the People's Republic of China (PRC or China) officially established diplomatic relations in 1974, during the administration of President Carlos Andrés Pérez (1969-1974) (Brandt and Piña, 2019). Since then, both countries have already commemorated their fifty years of diplomatic relations (MINCYT, 2024); according to the literature and studies on this bilateral relationship, it is possible to divide it, with the aim of better understanding its historical process, in two different periods such as 1974-1999, a stage that can be described as the "beginning of the relationship", and 1999-2024, a period considered the "consolidation of the relationship".

The First Stage of Sino-Venezuelan Relations (1974-199)

Regarding the beginning of the relationship, it is important to mention that the bilateral diplomatic recognition between China and Venezuela came at a time when other Latin American countries such as Chile, Mexico, Peru, Jamaica, Guyana, Brazil, Trinidad and Tobago, and Argentina had also begun to shift their diplomatic stance from Taiwan to China as the legitimate representative of the Chinese state (Connelly and Cornejo 1992).

It is important to note that most of these new diplomatic positions were influenced by the meeting between the two presidents Richard Nixon and Mao Zedong in Beijing in 1972, an event that marked a turning point in China's diplomatic relations with the Western world (Department of State 2024). At that time, most Latin American countries were politically, militarily and economically influenced by the United States (US). Thus, the approach that this North American country chose for managing its relations with the PRC marked a path for other countries in the region to follow.

A few years after the diplomatic recognition between China and Venezuela, the Asian country started a huge transformation of its economic system, based on the improvement of its industrial sector. The main objective of this strategy was to create the conditions for a more effective integration into the world economy. However, due to the complexity of this work, China could not integrate its economy with the world as much as it wanted to, at least during the decades of the 1970s and 1980s (Anguiano Roch 1997).

This did not prevent the country to advance in the signature of different types of bilateral agreements to strengthen its diplomatic relations with the countries that began to recognize the PRC in those years. In this context, Venezuela and China, during 1974 and 1990, signed eight diplomatic agreements related to scientific cooperation, cultural exchanges, commercial issues, elimination of visas for their diplomats and other public officials, and technical cooperation in areas such as mining, oil-related research, including petrochemical issues (MRE 2010).

At the diplomatic level, Venezuelan President Luis Herrera Campins visited Beijing in November 1981, the first official visit to China by a Venezuelan president. This meeting was preceded by the visit of his Foreign Minister, Alberto Zambrano Velasco, to the Chinese capital on February 25, 1981. After this visit, three different Chinese delegations arrived in Caracas: the first, which arrived in March, was a group of representatives of the National People's Assembly; the second was led by the Deputy Foreign Minister, Zhang Wen Jing, in April 1981; finally, in August of that year, China´s Minister of Foreign Affairs, Huang Hua, visited Caracas to prepare the official trip of President Campins (Molina 2018).

Norbert Molina, a professor at Venezuela's Universidad de Los Andes, explains that the next high-level visit by a Venezuelan diplomat took place in 1991, when Venezuela's foreign minister, Armando Durán, arrived in Beijing on a five-day trip in October of that year. Two other high-level visits were made by Venezuelan officials in the 1990s; in 1997, Foreign Minister Pedro María Burelli was in Beijing in February. Later, in 1999, the Chief of Staff of the Ministry of Foreign Affairs, Carlos Bivero, visited the Chinese capital at the head of a special delegation (Molina 2018).

On the other hand, there are records of some Chinese delegations coming to Venezuela in the 1980s and 1990s. The main objective of these trips was to establish political and economic ties with Venezuela. In this context, during the decade of the 1990s, both Chinese and Venezuelan officials were interested in signing agreements to buy/sell "Orimulsion", a product made from bitumen oils and used to generate electricity in power plants. According to the Venezuelan Ministry of Foreign Affairs, both parties explored the possibility of building a power plant to produce Orimulsion, signing three letters of intent (LOIs) and two feasibility studies on the idea (Ministerio del Poder Popular para las Relaciones Exteriores de la República Bolivariana de Venezuela 2010). Finally, the construction of this plant became a reality in 2001, when, according to official sources, 350 million USD were invested in its construction (Romero 2000).

At the same time, it is important to note that Venezuela received the first Chinese investment in its oil sector when the state-owned China National Petroleum Corporation (CNPC) acquired the rights to explore and produce oil in two fields called "Caracoles" and "Intercampo". This investment represented a milestone in the region, as the Intercampo and Caracoles projects were the second of this type signed by CNPC in the region, after the agreement reached with the Peruvian authorities to explore the "Talara" oil field (CNPC 2013).

The Second Stage of Sino-Venezuelan Relations (1999-2024)

The second stage of the China-Venezuela relations started in 1999 when Hugo Chávez came to power in the South American country. The arrival of Chávez marked a turning point in bilateral relations, setting the stage for increased economic engagement between the two countries, but also for the establishment of a new type of diplomatic relationship. During his time as head of state (1999-2013), Chávez made four visits to China in 2001, 2004, 2006, and 2009 (CVECH 2018). The strengthening and integration of his country with the "rising powers" such as China was one of the main foreign policy goals of Chávez; the former Venezuelan president was always able to promote a "multipolar" world that undermines American influence in the international arena (González Urrutia 2006).

At the time when the Venezuelan president outlined this "multipolar" approach, China was implementing a strategy aimed at integrating its economy with the rest of the world (People's Daily News 2001). This strategy, also known as the "going global" policy, was crowned by the acceptance of this Asian country as a member of the World Trade Organization (WTO) and, a few years later, by the decisive role that it played in the recovery of the global economy during the 2008 financial crisis (Jingjing 2019).

Authors such as Enrique Dussel Peters have pointed out that behind the going global agenda was a clear intention to adapt the country and its economy to the global dynamics characterized by globalization, but with its own approach; Dussel Peters called this process a globalization with Chinese characteristics. Some years earlier, Joseph Stiglitz noted a similar analysis, saying that the Chinese strategy for facing globalization combined: a) a strong presence of the state in defining its economic policies, b) a controlled liberalization of its economy, and c) ensuring the technology transfer process from the companies that invested or established their operations in China (Stiglitz 2016).

For many political and ideological reasons, the Chinese approach to globalization was of interest to President Hugo Chávez, who always saw in the Chinese development model an alternative to the US-led model of liberal democracy (Diez 2006). For this reason, it is appropriate to consider the coincidence of goals and interests of both China and Venezuela, especially in issues related to cooperation among developing countries, promotion of a multipolar world, and economic development.

Once both the Chinese and Venezuelan authorities understood that they agreed in most of their foreign policy principles and objectives, the next step to engage their relationship was to create an institutional common ground in various areas of cooperation.

In this sense, in 2001, these countries agreed the creation of the China-Venezuela High-Level Joint Commission (CMAN, in Spanish), with which both countries would discuss and agree on all issues related to their bilateral relations (Chinese Embassy in Venezuela, 2006). The first CMAN meeting brought the signing of several agreements to strengthen the bilateral cooperation in areas such as technology, agriculture, transportation, and eventually energy. Because of this new stage, that year China and Venezuela decided to elevate their bilateral relations to the "Strategic Partnership for Shared Development" (Piña 2024).

In the following years, both countries were able to increase their bilateral economic exchange, but the internal situation in Venezuela did not allow it. From 2002 to 2004, the Chávez administration faced a major challenge in securing the country's governance from opposition movements and political parties. This situation led to an attempted coup d'état against Chávez in April 2002 and a two-month blockade of the Venezuelan National Petroleum Company (PDVSA). After these events, the political parties decided to resolve their differences by holding a referendum to decide whether Chávez should remain in power. Ultimately, the Venezuelan president won the election, and the political crisis was over; however, the economic cost to the country and to the advancement of bilateral relations with China was significant (Todo Chavez 2004).

The period 2004-2007 was very dynamic for both countries in terms of advancing their bilateral relations. During these years, China and Venezuela signed 131 different agreements, increased their technical cooperation in many fields, secured new Chinese direct investments in Venezuela and, last but not least, made progress in negotiating a new framework for the disbursement of loans from China to Venezuela in exchange for oil. These important results shown by both countries in those years were possible after two new official visits made by President Hugo Chávez to Beijing in 2004 and 2006, when both countries celebrated two meetings of the High-Level Joint Commission (MRE 2010).

In 2007, the consolidation of this relationship reached a new level with the creation of the China-Venezuela Joint Fund (CVJF), a loans-for-oil scheme negotiated by both sides in previous years. This program brought nearly 62 billion USD to the Venezuelan economy over the period 2007-2015 (Piña 2019a). The benefits for both countries were significant; for China, a new Global Value Chain (GVC) focused on the oil trade was created with the aim of supplying part of its current (at the time) and future oil consumption; for Venezuela, the opening of the Chinese market was not only an opportunity to diversify its oil exports to a country other than the United States, but also a way to increase its revenues from the sale of this commodity.

As will be shown in the next pages of this chapter, the amount of money that came from the Sino-Venezuelan joint funds was invested in various projects and factories, as well as in the purchase of many products such as cars, televisions, air conditioners, washing machines, etc., produced in China. At the same time, these purchases stimulated Chinese companies to make direct investments in Venezuela in sectors such as telecommunications, the automotive industry, and the oil industry, in which CNPC established four joint ventures with PDVSA (Petróleos de Venezuela, S.A. 2016).

In the years that followed, bilateral relations continued to improve. Meanwhile, the death of Hugo Chávez did not stop the two countries from the path they had embarked on in 2001. In fact, a year after the new Venezuelan president, Nicolás Maduro, took office, China decided to upgrade the bilateral relationship to a "strategic comprehensive partnership" (Embassy of the People's Republic of China in Nepal 2014). This new attitude brought new investments and loans to the Venezuelan economy in 2015 and 2016. In the oil sector, CNPC made new investments in these two years to maintain oil production in the fields where they have joint ventures with PDVSA (Petróleos de Venezuela, S.A. 2016).

Despite the importance of this new stage in Sino-Venezuelan relations, the economic situation in Venezuela and the direct confrontation that this country had with the United States caused a stagnation in all economic indicators between China and Venezuela. However, this situation did not prevent both countries from continuing their cooperation process; for example, in 2016 and 2018, China allowed Venezuela to renegotiate the terms of the bilateral debt service (Reuters 2016). Later, the Asian country supported Venezuela during the period when the American president, Donald Trump, imposed some economic sanctions against the Venezuelan government, and Beijing provided health assistance to Caracas for facing the covid pandemic (Brandt Siem 2020). For its part, Venezuela has kept intact its diplomatic support to China in all the difficult issues that this country faces at the international level, such as: the Hong Kong security law, the claim for sovereignty in the South China Sea, the Taiwan dispute and the denunciations related to the treatment that Beijing applies in the Xinjiang region (Piña 2024)

All this political support shown by the two countries in the first quarter of the twenty-first century motivated them to reach a new level in their bilateral relations, such as the "All-Water Strategic Partnership" (Reuters 2023). This new diplomatic consideration was reached during the last visit of President Nicolás Maduro to China in September 2023.It marked the consolidation of a bilateral relationship that looks like a mature partnership not only in the economic field, but also in the political and foreign policy aspects. It is important to note that the main driver of the Sino-Venezuelan model has been the oil trade, and the energy agreements related to this industry, by far the most important in the Venezuelan economic system.

2. An Historical Review of the China-Venezuela Trade Relations (1974- 2023)

Sino-Venezuelan trade relations have gone through at least two different stages during the 50 years of bilateral relations. The period 1974-1999 showed a slow engagement between these countries due to the economic reform process experimented in China in the

1970s and 1980s, but also because of the economic integration between Venezuela and other countries/regions such as the US and/or Europe. Taking this into consideration, the Chinese Embassy in Venezuela noted that the commercial exchanges of this Asian country with Venezuela during the period 1974-1999 accumulated around 400 million dollars; of this amount, most was transacted during the decade of 1990, especially after 1996, when these countries singed two sale-purchase agreements (SPA) related to Orimulsion; the trade balance rose from about 388 million USD (Ríos 2009). In addition, it is important to note that in 1974 both countries had an exchange of 1.4 million USD. So, in this first stage, growth was considerable, but not at the same level as experimented in the second stage of this relationship.

The second period (2000-2024) was more dynamic than the first. According to the World Bank's World Integrated Trade Solution (WITS), economic exchanges between China and Venezuela grew from 351 million USD in 2000 to 4.1 billion USD in 2023. However, these figures do not show the complexity of these commercial relations, especially because of the consolidation of a new GVC based on oil and its derivative products, both countries registered a peak in their commercial exchanges in 2012, when they transacted products for a joint value of 23.8 billion USD, as it can be seen in figure 1 (WITS 2024).

During the first six years of the new century, China and Venezuela maintained their existing bitumen supply agreements; bitumen was the main raw material used in the production of Orimulsion. However, starting in 2003, Venezuela began to increase its oil exports (crude oil and its derivatives) to China, a situation that quickly led to an increase in the trade balance between the two countries in the following years. In addition, China was interested in buying non-agglomerated iron ore preparations and iron and steel products. To get an idea of the importance of these four commodities in the Venezuelan export matrix to China in the first five years of the new century, it must be said that they represented about 81 % (2.3 billion USD) of the total exports (2.9 billion USD) to this Asian country (WITS 2024).

Figure 1. Venezuela: Trade with China (2000-2023) ($US million)

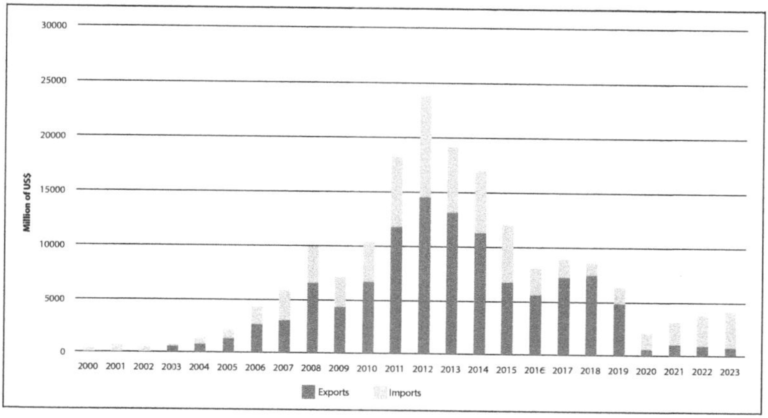

Source: Own elaboration based on WITS (2024).

In particular, from 2005 to 2006, the trade relations between both countries doubled, starting a growth path that will continue until 2012, with the only exception being the year 2009, when the world economy was affected by the consequences of the global economic and financial crisis. This increase can be explained taking into account two events. The first one, the signing of several bilateral trade agreements between 2004 and 2006, brought a new dynamic in the relationship; the second one was the signing in 2007 of the Chinese Venezuelan Joint Funds (CVJF), which was a loans-for-oil scheme that allowed these countries to increase their bilateral trade based on oil shipments (PDVSA 2016).

The CVJF, which consisted of two different mechanisms, the Heavy Fund and the Long-Term Fund, brought about 50.3 billion USD to the Venezuelan economy during the period 2007-2015. The main characteristic of these funds was that they had to be paid with Venezuelan crude oil or also with crude oil derivatives (Piña, 2019a). As already mentioned, these oil payments were made after the advance payment of loans in different tranches; moreover, this new scheme secured a new market for Venezuela to collocate its oil production. The results were impressive for this South American country, considering the figures presented by PDVSA in its 2016 annual report, which confirms the export of 1.34 billion barrels of oil to China between 2008 and 2016 (PDVSA 2016).

According to the data downloaded from WITS, the amount of money transacted by both countries in crude oil, bitumen and the other oil derivatives such as fuel oil, coke and asphalt between 2000 and 2023 was about 100.1 billion dollars. This amount represents about 89.5 % of the total Venezuelan exports to China in this whole period. Of these oil exports, 93.6 billion USD were transacted after the signing of the CVJF, which reveals the link between this loans-for-oil scheme, which since then has been the main foundation of the new oil-based GVC between both countries.

Table 1 shows the disaggregated exports from Venezuela to China between 2000 and 2023, taking into account the first twenty subheadings. Apart from petroleum products (crude oil, bitumen and petroleum derivatives), it is possible to see several raw materials, especially minerals such as non-agglomerated iron ores, ferrous products, aluminum, ferro-nickel, etc. In addition, in this table it is possible to observe only one type of food product (frozen shrimps and prawns), as well as only one subheading code related to a manufactured product, as in the case of bovine and equine leather products. In general, it is relevant to note the high concentration of Venezuelan exports to China in twenty products during this period, which reinforces the mono-producer pattern shown by Venezuela in the last one hundred and fifty years.

On the other hand, Table 2 shows the disaggregated information on Venezuelan imports from China during the first twenty-three years of the century. As can be seen, most of the purchases that Venezuela made during this period were related to high-value products such as telephones, air conditioners and/or computers. Moreover, during the 2007-2015 period, the Venezuelan government bought several vehicles, buses and motorcycles made for Chinese companies, a path that favored the later establishment of both a bus and a vehicle Chinese assembly factory in Venezuelan soil. Finally, it is possible to notice the purchase of some products related to the oil industry, especially drilling machinery and

Table 1. Venezuela: Exports to China Based on Sub-Heading Codes (2000-2023)

Position	Sub-heading code	Description (Sub-heading code)	Amount (US$ Million)	Share (%) of total
1	270900	Crude oil	76,347	68.20%
2	271000	Crude oil derivatives	22,522	20.10%
3	260111	Non-agglomerated iron ores and concentrates	6,636	5.90%
4	720310	Ferrous products obtained by direct reduction	2,041	1.80%
5	290511	Methanol (methyl alcohol)	812	0.72%
6	271311	Petroleum coke, not calcined	803	0.71%
7	740400	Waste and scrap, copper or copper alloy	486	0.43%
8	271490	Bitumen and asphalt; natural asphaltites	465	0.41%
9	281820	Aluminium oxide, other than artificial corundum	273	0.24%
10	260112	Agglomerated iron ores and concentrates	174	0.15%
11	550200	Artificial filament tow	153	0.13%
12	760120	Aluminium unwrought, alloyed	118	0.10%
13	720260	Ferro-nickel	102	0.09%
14	30613	Frozen shrimps and prawns	91	0.08%
15	250310	Crude or unrefined sulphur	86	0.07%
16	760200	Waste and scrap, aluminium	82	0.07%
17	410429	Other bovine and equine leather, tanned	71	0.06%
18	261900	Slag, dross, etc, from the manufacture of iron	61	0.05%
19	740321	Copper-zinc base alloys, unwrought	59	0.05%
20	720712	Semi-fin prod,iron or n-al steel,rect/ sq cross	41	0.04%
1- 20	Top twenty sub-headings (subtotal)		111,423	99.6%
All	Total exports		111,861	100%

Source: Own elaboration based on WITS (2024).

carbon steel pipes, both important products to be used in upstream activities (oil exploration and production).

Contrary to the pattern shown in Table 1, the information on the twenty first subheadings imported by Venezuela from China during the period 2000-2023 shows a more diversified basket of products than the one offered by Venezuela to China. For example, the mentioned twenty subheadings represented only 30.1 % (20.1 billion USD) of the total Venezuelan imports from China (67 billion USD). In this respect, the trade pattern of both countries

Table 2. Venezuela: Imports from China Based on Sub-Heading Codes (2000-2023)

Position	Sub-heading code	Description (Sub-heading code)	Amount (US$ Million)	Share (%) of total
1	852520	Transmission apparatus incorporating reception	3,122	4.60 %
2	841510	Air conditioners	1,662	2.48 %
3	847120	Digital computers with cpu and input/ output units	1,611	2.40 %
4	871120	Motorcycles	1,587	2.37 %
5	843041	Drilling or sinking machinery	1,405	2.09 %
6	730420	Carbon steel pipes	1,234	1.84 %
7	852810	Televisions and/or television receivers	1,175	1.75 %
8	640299	Footwear with rubber soles and uppers	1,110	1.65 %
9	870323	Automobiles with reciprocating piston engine	860	1.30 %
10	401120	New pneumatic tyres	850	1.30 %
11	851730	Telephonic or telegraphic switching apparatus	730	1.08 %
12	843049	Boring or sinking machinery nes, not self-prope	725	1.08 %
13	870210	Diesel powered buses with a seating capacity of	621	0.92 %
14	730890	Structures and parts of structures, of iron or steel	573	0.85 %
15	950390	Toys	551	0.82 %
16	848180	Taps, cocks, valves and similar appliances, ne	502	0.75 %
17	890510	Dredgers	490	0.73 %
18	851740	Apparatus, for carrier-current line systems, ne	474	0.70 %
19	71333	Dried kidney beans, incl. white pea beans, shel	460	0.68 %
20	851782	Telegraphic apparatus, nes	454	0.68 %
1- 20	Top twenty sub-headings (subtotal)		20,199	30.13 %
All	Total imports		67,026	100 %

Source: Own elaboration based on WITS (2024).

reveals the traditional central-peripheral relationship, in which a country concentrates its exports on a few raw materials in exchange for a series of products with high added value. Over the years, this pattern has strengthened due to the progress of the Chinese economy and its impressive advances in technological processes, but also because of the Venezuelan process of reprimarization.

At this point of the trade explanation, it is important to add a brief clarification about the 2019-2023 period, which, as can be seen in Figure 1, showed a significant decline in bilateral trade between China and Venezuela, but also a change in the pattern that both countries had during the century. This was possible due to the imposition of US-led sanctions against the Venezuelan government in 2019, specifically a ban on countries buying crude oil produced in Venezuela. As a result, Venezuela, which exported nearly 5 billion USD in crude oil in 2019, saw China reduce its oil purchases. The significance of this new reality lies in how externalization, such as sanctions and the oil embargo, affected oil-based GVCs between the two countries. Instead, China focused its purchases from Venezuela on methanol, ferrous products, iron ore concentrates, and non-calcined petroleum coke, all of which were not subject to embargoes or purchase bans (WITS 2024).

In general, China's integration as one of the main customers of Venezuelan oil exports, but also the adaptation of the CVJF and the sale and purchase agreements (SPA) between both countries, as part of these loans-for-oil programs, allowed it to be Venezuela's second trading partner during the period 2008-2017, but also to become the main trading partner in 2019, 2021 and 2022, according to the data published in WITS. Finally, it is important to mention that during the period 2019-2023, the trade balance has been favorable for the Asian country, because of the aforementioned sanctions, but also because China is trying to couple its wholesale sector to the Venezuelan economy, diversifying its exports to this Latin American country.

3. The Economic Effects of the New Oil-Based Global Value Chain (GVC) Conformed by China and Venezuela in the TwentyFirst Century

Given the explanation of the historical development of Sino-Venezuelan trade relations, the analysis of the oil-based GVC will focus on the twenty-first century. In this respect, the subchapter will be divided into two parts; the first one is related to the conformation of the new oil-based GVC between China and Venezuela during the first twenty-three years of the new century; the second one, in turn, is related to the local impacts stemming from Venezuelan oil exports to China during the same period. Finally, this subchapter concludes with an explanation of the local impact of the aforementioned GVC taking into account its territorial impact.

3.1 The New Oil-Based GVC Between China and Venezuela (2000-2023).

Since the beginning of his first presidential term, Hugo Chávez was able to change the main foundations of Venezuela's foreign policy, including economic issues. In his first government development plan for the period 2000-2007, the then-president clearly defined his intention to move towards a multipolar world by connecting with new "centers of power" other than the United States and Western Europe. Among these countries, Chávez considered India, Iran, Russia, and, last but not least, the People's Republic of China (MPP 2001).

Motivated by this goal, Chávez traveled to Beijing as soon as he took office in 1999. Since his first trip, this politician has offered Venezuela's oil potential to deepen bilateral relations with China. These efforts became a reality in 2001, when the two countries not only established the CMAN, but also signed a "Ten-Year Energy Cooperation Agreement (2001-2011). This document was the basis for how China and Venezuela defined their intentions regarding their relationship around Venezuelan oil production (MRE 2001).

This step was taken at the same time as both countries signed new supply agreements to sell bitumen to China. As part of this effort, they agreed to new purchases of bitumen from Venezuela to China but also decided to invest in a new Orimulsion plant in Venezuela. This plant was to be built at an estimated cost of 350 million USD and its main objective was to create an Orimulsion-based GVC that would supply the industrial sector in China (Piña 2019a). It is important to note that bitumen production was located in the Orinoco Oil Belt (OOB), and, in 2006, the Venezuelan government and the state-owned oil company, PDVSA, considered bitumen an extra-heavy oil and reduced exports of this commodity to China (PDVSA 2010). As a result, the sales of bitumen remain relevant until 2005, when both parts decided to focus their SPA energy on crude oil and its derivatives (Prensa PDVSA 2006).

The ban on bitumen exports was part of Hugo Chávez's strategy to increase Venezuelan oil exports to China in the new century. Previously, the former Venezuelan president had visited Beijing in 2001, 2004 and 2006 to intensify his efforts. In those moments, Chávez tried to secure the opening of the Chinese market to Venezuelan oil, offering a wide range of options to integrate both countries through this raw material; the proposal included: 1) promoting Chinese direct investment in Venezuelan oil fields; 2) selling new fuel oil shipments; 3) maintaining the trade between both countries; 4) investments in both the petrochemical and gas industries and; 5) selling asphalt. The intentions of said leader were recorded in a speech given in 2004 after a meeting with President Hu Jintao, in which he said: "Venezuela has all the oil China needs to ensure its development and economic growth" (Todo Chávez 2004).

The agreements reached by Presidents Chávez and Hu Jintao after their meeting in Beijing in 2004 led to a rapid increase in oil trade between China and Venezuela. Since then, Venezuelan oil sales to China have increased tenfold, from $75 million to about $700 million in the first six years of the new century. These revenues, although important, were not comparable to the revenues that PDVSA received from its sales to the United States during the same period. Nevertheless, it is important to say that these new revenues were invested in social programs, especially in 2004, when Chávez put his leadership to the test by proposing a referendum to decide on his continuation in power (D'Elia and Cabezas 2008). At that moment, the former Venezuelan president understood that his political project needed huge economic resources to survive in the long run. The rapprochement with China was also part of this political calculation.

To complete this strategy of integrating both economies through Venezuela's oil industry, the Chávez government developed a plan called "Siembra Petrolera" (Oil Seed), which envisioned the possibility of increasing Venezuela's oil exports to China to more than two million barrels per day (IESA 2014). This plan was to be implemented by PDVSA, the national oil company, in order to integrate the different stages of business with the Chinese oil companies. Since 2006, both countries–especially Venezuela–have been in talks to propose building two refineries in China to process Venezuelan crude arriving in the country. The intention of this proposal was to secure and integrate a new value chain based on Venezuelan oil supplies (OPCh 2009).

Along with this proposal, the Venezuelan president sought ways to generate more revenue from oil shipments to China. To achieve this, Chávez and his government, after signing several agreements that strengthened bilateral cooperation in the oil industry, developed a strategy to link oil shipments with the financial sector.: the creation of the China-Venezuela Joint Fund (CVJF), a loans-for-oil mechanism that implied the advance disbursement of loans to Venezuela in exchange for oil shipments to China. This proposal was made by Chávez during a visit to Beijing in August 2006 and was approved by China in 2007 (Todo Chávez 2007). Its approval marked the final consolidation of the new oil-based GVC between the two countries and provided Chávez with the necessary funds to build several infrastructure projects throughout the country.

While Chávez was negotiating the creation of the CVJF with China, the ruling party in Venezuela was able to reform the

Organic Law of Hydrocarbons, a legal instrument that transformed the oil business in the country and reserved a large share of the oil business for the Venezuelan state (Brewer-Carías 2008). As a result, a new entity was created to carry out oil projects: the Joint Ventures, which had to be formed by the National Oil Company, PDVSA, and any other foreign company that wanted to be part of the oil business.

This measure, which amounted to the nationalization of upstream activities in the Venezuelan oil industry, was not without controversy. Some American companies, such as ExxonMobil and ConocoPhillips, rejected it and filed a lawsuit against PDVSA at the World Bank's International Center for Settlement of Investment Disputes (ICSID) (Reuters 2014). As a result, the EMBI country risk index rose and Venezuela's access to the international credit market became more difficult and expensive. In this adverse situation, President Hugo Chávez decided to decisively advance his country's financial integration with China by pushing for the creation of the CVJF (Piña 2019a).

At the same time, it is important to mention that PDVSA and its counterpart in the CVJF agreements, CNPC, consolidated the oil-based GVC with China through the creation of four new joint ventures, viz: Sinovensa (2007), Petrolera Sinovenezolana (2006), Petrozumano (2008), and Petrourica (2010) (PDVSA 2016). All of these joint ventures operated in Venezuela and were established as part of a strategy aimed at securing oil production for China to meet Venezuela's debt commitments. Also, the Venezuelan legislation assures the property over the oil reserves to the foreign oil companies that decide to conform JVs along with PDVSA. This disposition gave both economic and legal protection to CNPC, a company that secured a collateral in case the Venezuelan part, represented by PDVSA, refused or was not able to pay the debt services (PODE, 2016). Then, the oil-based GVC created by these two countries involved different stages of the business and provided China with enough security to invest in a country considered risky in the international credit market.

In addition, in 2012, the former China International Trust Investment Corporation (CITIC) (now CITIC Group) received the 10% of a JV that PDVSA operated together with the American Chevron in the Orinoco Oil Belt (OOB) (Vyas, 2012). A similar transaction was made by CNPC in 2018, when PDVSA negotiated the transfer of 9.9 % of Sinovensa, the aforementioned JV between China and Venezuela operating in the OOB (Banca y Negocios 2019).

Along with this information, it is possible to refer to another related to oil supply contracts signed by China and Venezuela between 2008 and 2009. According to Giacalone and Ruiz, PDVSA signed at least four supply contracts in 2008 and 2009 with subsidiaries such as China Zen Hua Oil company, UNIPEC, and PetroChina (Giacalone and Briceño Ruiz 2013). These contracts were very specific in terms of how much oil Venezuela had to import to China, but they contributed to the increase of national oil exports to China.

In Figure 2, it is possible to observe the evolution of revenues from oil exports to China, noting an exact coincidence between the signing of the energy agreements (including the CVJF) and the increase of oil exports from Venezuela to China. In addition, the existence of at least four subheadings related to oil exports to the Asian country can be seen, such as crude oil, oil derivatives (fuel oil, kerosene, etc.), bitumen (especially during 2000-2005) and non-calcined coke (especially during 2019-2023). Among them, crude oil and oil derivatives were the most relevant products, generating revenues of more than 10 billion USD every year between 2011 and 2014. It is also important to remember that China's national statistics did not include purchases of crude oil or oil derivatives from Venezuela during 2020 and 2023, due to the US-led economic sanctions against the South American country.

At this point, it is also worth noting that most of the oil exports from Venezuela to China are usually directed to Guangdong Province, a place where Venezuelan crude oil is usually processed to provide part of the energy production for residential and industrial purposes. On this basis, China planned long-term oil supply contracts with Venezuela, as was the case with the CVJF. These contracts, for example, maintained the supply of oil from Venezuela during 2019, the time in which the US government measured an oil embargo against the Venezuelan oil; at that moment, China claimed that its government needed to collect its debts from Venezuela as the main reason to maintain the oil supplies for one year (SWI Swissinfo.ch 2019). In this sense, it can be seen how the energetic interdependence between both countries was able to ensure the maintenance of the Venezuelan oil shipments to this Asian country during an unfavorable context for this South American country.

Figure 2. Venezuela: Oil Exports to China (Sub-heading codes) (million USD) (2000-2023)

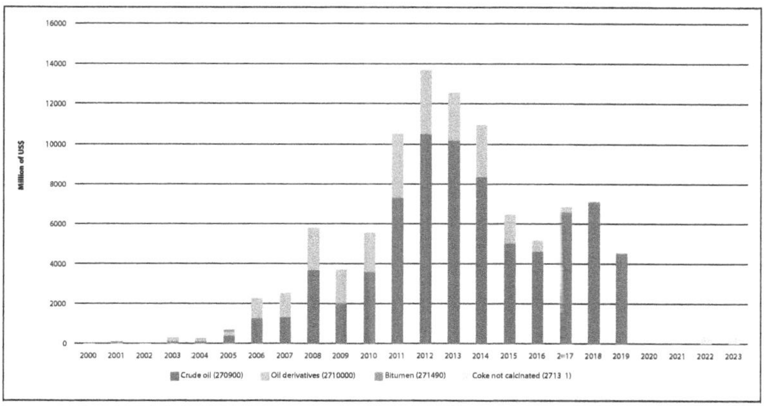

Source: Own elaboration based on WITS (2024)

In addition, it is important to mention another financial system, beyond the CVJF, that was created by these countries to secure investments in the fourth JVs between CNPC and PDVSA. Specifically, between 2013 and 2016, both CNPC and the CDB disbursed approximately 6.6 billion USD to finance oil production in these JVs (Brandt and Piña, 2018). This money was used to finance an oil upgrader, a new terminal port in the city of Anzoátegui, and, more generally, the maintenance of drilling and transportation equipment in the oil fields. It is important to note that these loans were also approved under the Loans for Oil program (Dussel Peters, 2024). In 2016, the CDB, the Social, Economic, and Development Bank of Venezuela (BANDES), and PDVSA renegotiated the terms of Venezuela's debt service with China. This measure allowed Venezuela to avoid for two years the payment of principal and interest related to the CVJF funds and the loans directed to the oil sector; moreover, this scheme served the South American country to manage the pressure that its currency, the bolívar, had suffered so it would be devalued (Reuters, 2016).

In general, according to WITS data, the mix of Venezuelan oil exports has changed over the period 2000-2023. For example, at the beginning of the century, in 2000, Venezuelan oil exports to the United States accounted for more than 79 % of the total, leaving China with only 3.4 %. By 2018, the year before the oil embargo, China's share had grown to 25 % of the total, reducing the U.S. share to 38 %, with India (33 %) and others (5 %) dividing up the rest of the destination (WITS, 2024). In 2022, these figures changed, showing new partners such as Spain, a country that received about 88 % of the total oil exports, and Italy, a country that received the remaining 12 %. In 2023, the United States regained its position as main destination to the Venezuelan oil due to the approval of a license that benefited the oil company Chevron to import oil from Venezuela, making a partial exception to the embargo. However, this exception only benefited Chevron (USA), Repsol (Spain) and ENI (Italy); in any case, the US allowed China to import oil from Venezuela (Reuters 2022).

The final picture shown until 2018 revealed the success Hugo Chávez and Nicolás Maduro's strategy, which aimed to replace the dominant position of the United States in Venezuela's oil export mix. As already mentioned, this objective was influenced by a political approach, but also with the clear intention of diversifying the oil markets in which Venezuela could finally place its oil production. At this point, it is not only relevant to note how Caracas achieved its goals after a long period of trying to diversify its markets, but it is also interesting to note how the Venezuelan administration integrated Chinese capital and companies at different stages of the business of its national oil industry. However, after 2019, the dominant position of the United States in the world economy has contributed to the virtual disappearance of Venezuelan oil exports to China between 2020 and 2023, at least officially, because some reports suggest that Caracas sent this raw material to China through third countries such as Malaysia (Aizhu *et al.* 2021). Despite this information, at the time of writing, there is no official information that could prove these allegations.

3.2. Impact of the China-Venezuela Crude Oil-Based GVC on the Venezuelan Economy (2000-2023)

The establishment of the new Sino-Venezuelan oil-based GVC in the twenty-first century has generated different types of effects at the macroeconomic, meso-economic, and microeconomic levels in Venezuela. Also, the governments headed by both Hugo Chávez (1999-2013) and Nicolás Maduro (2013-2024) have integrated some discussions and debates about the territorial impact of crude oil and its derivatives exports to China. Then, in the following pages, it will contribute with these discussions referring to the existing knowledge made by the Academic Network of Latin America and the Caribbean on China with new sources of information found during the preparation of this chapter. It is important to remember that this analysis will focus on the period 2000-2023, which has been the most important in the consolidation of oil-based GVC.

A) Macroeconomic Level

The main driver of the bilateral economic relationship between China and Venezuela during much of the 21st century was the loans-for-oil mechanism. This scheme, which materialized in the CVJF, allowed the integration of a new oil-based global value chain, increasing Venezuelan oil exports to (and imports from) China, but also other activities such as the outflow of foreign direct investment (OFDI) from this Asian country to Venezuela. In this sense, it can be seen how the oil-based GVC between both countries has affected different types of macroeconomic variables.

Regarding the loans-for-oil schemes, as mentioned in the previous pages, Venezuela considered borrowing from China at a time when, despite the high revenues accumulated from its oil exports, confidence in its economic indicators had been diluted over time, especially at the international level, because of the nationalization policy of private companies. Even in this context, in 2007/2008, China decided to lend Venezuela its first 4 billion dollars to develop a series of infrastructure projects in the South American country (Piña 2019c). This situation was clearer in 2009, a year after the world financial crisis that affected global economic growth, China, through its China Development Bank (CDB), disbursed a new 4 billion loan for oil to Venezuela. After this approval, a new 20 billion loan of this type was approved in 2010, followed by two more 4 billion loans in 2011 and 2012, respectively. In total, the Chinese CDB disbursed about 36 billion USD in loans-for-oil to Venezuela during 2007-2012 (Brandt and Piña 2018)

Later, in the period that comes from 2013-2015, Venezuela, now under the government of Nicolás Maduro, began to face the first steps of an economic crisis, strongly related to the fall of the Venezuelan oil industry, but also because of the fall of international oil prices (Stocker *et al.* 2018). Even if the panorama was not the most hopeful for the Venezuelan economy, China, now under the government of Xi Jinping, approved three new tranches of loans-for-oil in a two-year period (Piña 2024). These new loans brought nearly 14 billion USD more to Venezuela and allowed the Maduro government to keep some of its most important social programs functioning. Figure 3 graphs the evolution of the CVJF loans-for-oil and incorporates a description related to the loans disbursed to grow the oil production (PDVSA 2016).

Various studies have analyzed the consequences for Venezuela of contracting this debt from China. One of them, made by Carlos Piña, pointed out that the financial relations between China and Venezuela based on the loans-for-oil schemes brought

Figure 3. Venezuela: Loans Disbursed by Chinese Financial Institutions (2007-2015)

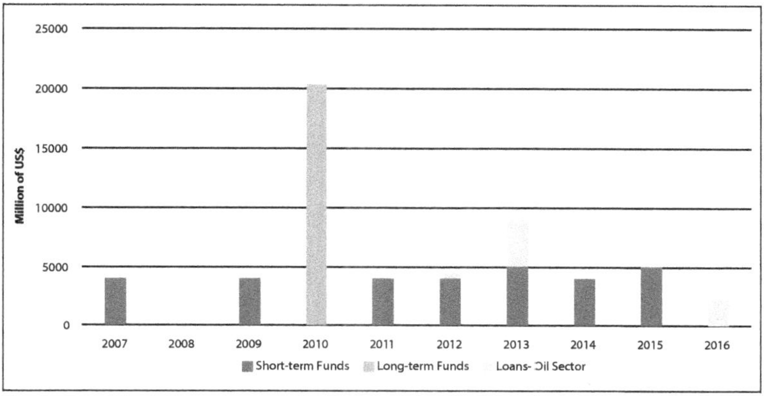

Source: Own elaboration with information from PDVSA's 2016 annual report and Venezuela's Ministry of Planning.

contradictory results to the country. According to this author, on the one hand, Venezuela could obtain resources in the midst of a difficult situation at the international level, taking on debt at better conditions than the market offered in those years. On the other hand, Piña states that the contracting of these loans did not bring a significant level of improvement in the country's economic capacities, especially because, as will be shown in the following pages, the investments made by the Venezuelan government in several infrastructure projects with money from the CVJF were not only not completed, but they also did not invest in modernization activities (Piña 2019b).

Also, Micolta and Piña studied the evolution of eighty-two projects financed with money from the CVJF between 2000 and 2022. The results of this work concluded that this financial mechanism did not benefit the economic development to Venezuela, mainly because of the management of economic resources by the Venezuelan government, which in most of the projects did not have enough governance processes to ensure their completion. This situation led to many irregularities and possible cases of corruption, but also to several criticisms related to the lack of controls and a long-term vision on how to use the important revenues generated by the oil sales to China. As a conclusion, these authors considered that this loans-for-oil mechanism favored China more than Venezuela, because the former could secure future oil supplies and used some of its national companies in several projects in Venezuela. In contrast, the latter did not take advantage of the huge amount of money received from the CVJF and committed an important future oil production that must be sent to China to pay the debt obligations (Micolta and Piña 2023).

For its part, the NGO Venezuelan Transparency analyzed the impact of the contracted debt from the CVJF on Venezuela's external debt variables. In this sense, the main conclusion of this research indicated that the oil collateral agreed as part of the CVJF forced Venezuela to prioritize the payment of these debt obligations over others, such as a sovereign debt and/or bonds issued by PDVSA in the international credit market. As a result, the pressure on the sovereign debt and other private instruments grew at the time the government focused its attention on the payment of an instrument that still represented more than the 15 % of the country's total external debt (Paredes 2022).

In addition, Sino-Venezuelan economic integration through the oil-based GVC encouraged new Chinese FDI in Venezuela. This phenomenon was the result of a calculated policy by President Hugo Chávez, who sought to create incentives to attract Chinese investment and used the money his government received from the CVFJ to achieve this goal. Specifically, Chávez developed a strategy that consisted of buying a series of specific products from some Chinese companies but securing from them a commitment from the Chinese side to build a factory on Venezuelan soil, which had to be a joint venture in association with a Venezuelan state-owned company (Piña 2019). The results of this plan can be seen in Table 2, where it is also possible to identify the evolution of the Chinese OFDI stock in Venezuela during the period 2000-2021 (there are only data available until 2021); usually the trend was upward, but in the years 2016, 2019, 2020 and 2021 negative OFDI inflows were registered, which led to a reduction in OFDI stocks (MOFCOM 2020; Dussel Peters 2024a).

Regarding this indicator, it is accurate to mention that the importance of Chinese OFDI in Venezuela has increased over the years. For example, according to the data published by the United Nations Trade and Development (UNCTAD), in 2005, the total amount of OFDI Stocks in Venezuela was 44.5 billion USD, of which 13 million USD came from China (about the 0.04%). However, in 2018, the total amount of OFDI Stocks in Venezuela was 22.9 billion USD; in that year, the same indicator from China was around 3.2 billion USD, which represented around the 14% of the total. Two different conclusions can be drawn from these indicators, such as: 1) the importance of Chinese OFDI in Venezuela has grown over the years until it became the second most important in 2018, and 2) the more the Venezuelan economy has declined, the more China has become relevant for this South American country. The latter explanation is related to the fact that Chinese capitals have represented over the years a more significant portion of the Venezuelan economy, a situation that has increased even at the time the US has been reducing its participation in it (UNCTAD 2024).

Figure 4. Venezuela: Chinese OFDI Stocks (2000-2021) (million USD)

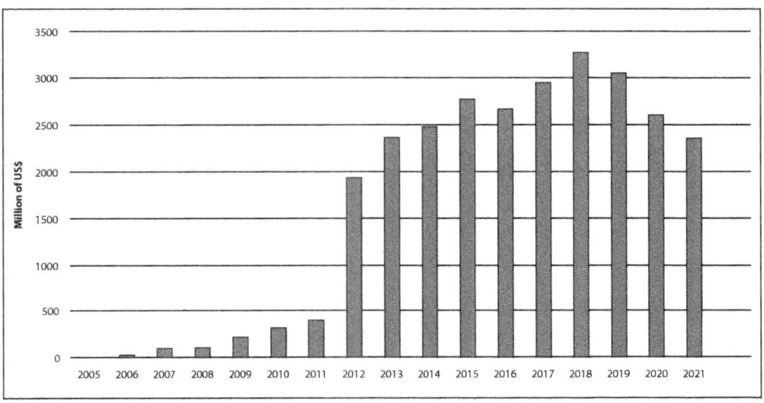

Source: Own elaboration with data from MOFCOM and the RED-ALC's Chinese OFDI Monitor (2024).

As mentioned above, most of the Chinese OFDI transactions were carried out by companies linked to a Venezuelan partner. This was the case for companies such as ZTE, Huawei, Inspur, Haier Group Company, or Yutong, which partnered with Venezuelan public companies to develop joint ventures in telecommunications, home appliances, buses, and crude oil. Some of these Chinese companies landed in Venezuela after the governments of Hugo Chávez and Nicolás Maduro bought millions of products and used their power to ensure that all of them were sold to the local population under favorable conditions. Carlos Piña documented that the Venezuelan government used a capital control to establish an exchange rate that favored the purchase of Chinese products at the expense of other foreign products. This allowed the Chinese companies to compete in an advantageous position over other foreign companies, but also to gain an important market share in their specific sector. Once a better market position was achieved, some of these Chinese companies were open to establishing operations in Venezuela (Piña 2019a).

Finally, it is important to refer to the CVJF apports to the social programs financed by both the Hugo Chávez and Nicolás Maduro governments. Despite the intersection of different sources, the 2016 annual report published by PDVSA shows a cumulative amount of 38.1 billion USD (PDVSA 2016). This figure includes investments in public infrastructure, purchases of products such as electronics, telephones, vehicles and buses, as well as the payment of scholarships, hospital and school donations, among others. Social spending was an important part of Hugo Chávez's political project to maintain his popularity among the Venezuelan people.

B) Mesoeconomic Level

China-Venezuela relations have been governed by a state-to-state approach. This means that most issues related to the political and economic engagement between the two countries are discussed, planned and decided by the high-level authorities of each country in the bilateral context, as mentioned above, the main institution where both countries sign their agreements and/or discuss the relationship is the High-Level Joint Commission (CMAN, in Spanish). The meetings of the CMAN are usually composed of high-level officials of each country; from these meetings come the decisions on the diplomatic positions of both sides, but also the plans related to their bilateral economic engagement, as is the case of the new GVC based on crude oil.

From the Venezuelan side, the main institution that participates in the CMAN meetings is usually the Ministry of Planning and Development, while from the Chinese side it is usually the National Development and Reform Commission (NDRC). In addition, officials who are heads of some ministries or secretaries of state have participated in these meetings, depending on the topic that both governments have previously decided to discuss and negotiate. It is also important to highlight the participation of state-owned companies like PDVSA and CNPC in the CMAN meetings (CVECH 2019).

Given this explanation, it is important to note that during the years 2000 and 2023, all these public institutions and their representatives participated in the consolidation of the oil-based GVC between China and Venezuela. Moreover, during the subperiod 2000-2012, the former Minister of Planning of Venezuela, Jorge Giordani, was one of the masterminds behind the planification of the CVJF, one of the main driving factors for the creation of the aforementioned GVC. From the perspective of this public official, integration with China should have been one of the foundations of the new economic structure in Venezuela, one that would go beyond reliance on oil revenues. In this sense, Giordani and his team, during their years in the Ministry of Planning, organized different strategies to reduce the dependence on oil resources and, at the same time, to invest the money obtained from the CVJF in the industrial sector. In other words, his main goal was to promote the creation of an upgrading process that would bring economic growth to the country.

This plan was implemented in general terms during the Chávez administration, but over the years the new government headed by

Table 3. JVs Established by Chinese and Venezuelan Companies (2000-2023)

Area/Sector	JV´s name	Chinese company (share %)	Venezuelan company (share %)	Year of establishment	Amount (MM/ US$)	Employment (created)
Telecommunications	Venezolana de Industria Tecnológica (VIT)	Inspur (49%)	CORPIVENSA** (51%)	2005	20	618
Oil Industry	Petrolera Sinovenezolana	CNPC* (25%)	PDVSA *** (75%)	2007	N/A	N/A
Oil Industry	Petrozumano	CNPC (40%)	PDVSA (60%)	2007	N/A	N/A
Telecommunications	VTELCA	ZTE Company	CORPIVENSA (51%)	2007	10	640
Oil Industry	Chinese Venezuelan Drilling Company (ICVT)	CPTDC**** (N/A)	PDVSA Industrial (N/A)	2008	150	144
Oil Industry	Sinovensa	CNPC (49.9%)	PDVSA (50.1%)	2008	N/A	N/A
Telecommunications	Orinoquia Telecom factory	Huawei (35%)	Telecom Venezuela C.A. (65%)	2009	65	141
Oil Industry	Petrourica	CNPC (40%)	PDVSA (60%)	2010	N/A	N/A
Manufacturing	Home appliances factory "HAIER"	Haier Group (15%)	CORPIVENSA (85%)	2010	287	1,500
Transportation	Yutong Bus Factory	Yutong Company (15%)	Ministry of Transportation (85%)	2015	278	5,200
All sectors		All JVs		2005-2015	810	8,243

Source: Own elaboration based on data from RED-ALC Infrastructure Monitor (2024), Chinese OFDI Monitor in LAC (2024), annual reports of Venezuelan ministries and information from Venezuelan journal sources.
* CNPC: China National Petroleum Corporation
** CORPIVENSA: Corporación Venezolana de Industrias Intermedia (Venezuelan Corporation of Intermediate Industries)
*** PDVSA: Petróleos de Venezuela, S.A.
**** CPTDC: China Petroleum Technology & Development Corporation

Nicolás Maduro has not been able to develop a long-term strategy to keep it functioning. In addition, it is possible to say that at least ten JVs were into operation between Chinese and Venezuelan companies during the period 2000-2023. Half of them were related to the oil industry, and the other half were related to telecommunications and transportation systems. In Table 3, it is possible to observe the name of these JVs, their initial capital in million USD and the number of jobs created in them; as a result, it is relevant to consider the creation of more than eight thousand employees after an investment of about 810 million USD (Dussel Peters 2024b). The Venezuelan partners in all these JVs were state companies or ministries, such as PDVSA, the Venezuelan Corporation of Basic Industries (CORPIVENSA) and the Ministry of Transport (Piña 2019c).

Regarding the economic impact of these JVs, it was only possible to obtain information on their impact and productivity during the period 2007-2015, in the case of the telecommunications companies, and between 2008 and 2014 in the case of the four JVs in the oil sector. Information on companies such as the Haier appliance factory, the Yutong bus factory and ICTV is contradictory and can only be obtained from secondary sources, which cannot be considered credible (Brandt and Piña 2019).

First, an explanation of the impact of the four JVs conformed by CNPC and PDVSA on the national oil production in Venezuela is warranted. In this regard, it has only been possible to collect official information from 2007 to 2014. During these years, these companies had an average production of 109 thousand barrels of oil per day (mb/d) (PODE, 2016). The most important of these companies was Sinovensa, which produced an average of 94 mb/d during this period. The other JVs, such as Petrolera Sinovenezolana, Petrozumano and Petrourica showed a shorter production than Sinovensa, only reaching averages around five to nine thousand barrels per day during these eight years.

While these numbers are relevant, the production of these four JVs was not a significant part of the country's total oil production, which averaged over two million barrels per day. This production has been important in attracting some Chinese direct investment to Venezuela. For example, in 2013, CNPC and CBD disbursed a 4 billion USD loan to increase production at Sinovensa, and in 2016, CNPC invested 549 million USD in an oil upgrader; these investments maintained important crude oil operations in Venezuela at the time (Dussel Peters 2024).

Figure 5. Crude Oil Production of JVs Established by CNPC and PDVSA (2007-2014)

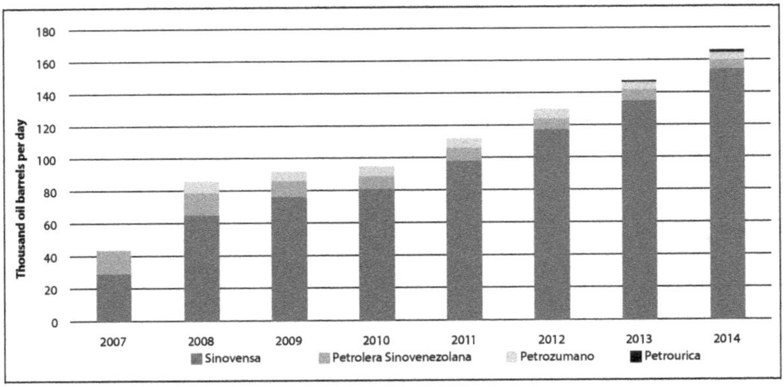

Source: Own elaboration with information from the Venezuelan Ministry of Oil (2008-2014).

Regarding the operation of these oil-based JVs after 2014, secondary sources such as the US Energy Information Administration (EIA) reported a 128 mb/d oil production in Sinovensa in 2017. For the rest of the JVs, this agency reported a production of 2 mb/d in Petrozumano, 0.8 mb/d in Petrolera Sinovenezolana and 0.3 mb/d in Petrourica (EIA, 2019). Years later, in 2019, Venezuelan President Nicolás Maduro indicated that Sinovensa was producing 110 mb/d (Reuters, 2019a). According to the latest available information, Sinovensa continues to operate in Venezuela, but the rest of these JVs are reducing their production in this South American country. According to different sources, the main problems that affected the production of these JVs were: 1) the oil embargo imposed by the United States against Venezuela, and 2) the delays in new investments to maintain production in the oil fields managed by these JVs.

The information about the Chinese Venezuelan Drilling Company (ICVT) suggests that this JV was created to increase and renew the drilling machinery used in the national oil industry in Venezuela. In this regard, the ICVT, which according to PDVSA hired 149 workers (44 from China and 105 Venezuelans), was to assemble and certify the drilling machinery purchased from China by the Venezuelan government (AVN 2011). As for its results, the only available information indicates that the joint venture successfully assembled 18 drilling machines by 2016 (Inventariando China 2016).

Regarding the productivity of the mobile phone's JVs such as Orinoquia (Huawei- Telecom Venezuela) and VTELCA (ZTE-Corpivensa), Figure 6 shows the evolution of the production of these factories during the period 2011-2015. According to the Ministry of Industry, the most successful and productive telephone company in the country was VTELCA, which assembled about 6.6 million mobile phones during this period. During these years, this company reached its production peak in 2012, a year in which the productivity per worker was 3,781 mobile phones per worker (MPPI, 2015); in 2015, this index decreased to 1,309 devices produced by each worker. In the case of Orinoquia, the total production during these years was around 4.3 million mobile phones, which also peaked in 2012, a year in which the productivity rate was around 6,571 devices per worker. Both JVs produced almost 10 million mobile phones, with the purpose of satisfying the demand for these electronic products in the country.

Figure 6. Number of Mobile Phones Produced by ORINOQUIA and VTELCA (2001-2015)

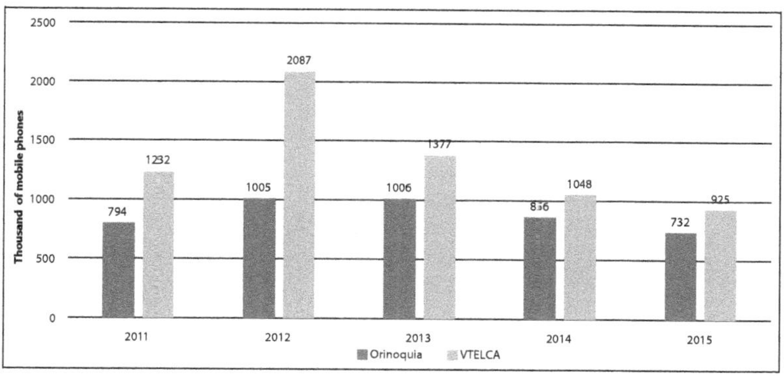

Source: Own elaboration with information from the 2015 Annual Report of the Venezuelan Ministry of Industry.

A similar path occurred with another JV called "Venezolana de Industrias Tecnológicas" (VIT), which was created with the aim of producing computers in Venezuela. As can be seen in Figure 7, this JV produced 994 thousand computers during the period 2011-2015. Contrary to what happened with VTELCA and ORINOQUIA, this JV had its production peak in 2013, a year in which this company reached a rate of productivity around the 407 computers per worker. After 2015, the only reference about the production in this JV took part in 2018, when its director confirmed the assembly of 1.35 million devices. Furthermore, it can be possible to consider at least 350 thousand more computers produced between 2015 and 2018 (YVKE 2018).

In the cases of these technological JVs, it is relevant to add the existence of technological transfers made by the Chinese partners such as ZTE, Huawei and/or Inspur. Despite the important production of these JVs described in figures 6 and 7, their board of directors publicly expressed the difficulty of continuing operations due to delays in the liquidation of foreign currency to maintain a minimum level of raw material imports (Hurtado 2016). Regarding this, it is important to add that most of the raw materials used during the period 2011-2015 were purchased with money

Figure 7. Number of Computing Devices Produced by the JV "VIT" (2011-2015) (thound units)

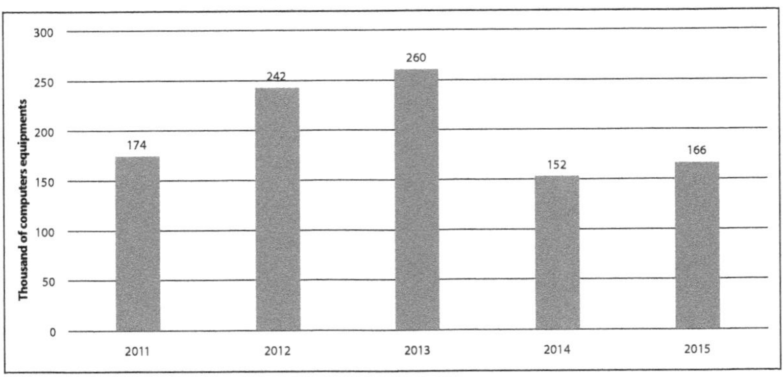

Source: Own elaboration with information from the 2015 Annual Report of the Venezuelan Ministry of Industry.

from the CVJF, which in practice represented a kind of subsidy for all these companies. In this sense, when oil revenues fell, the productivity of these companies, supported by public subsidies, reduced drastically.

Regarding the JV related to the transport system, as was the Yutong Buses factory, it is important to say that this factory, even when it was officially inaugurated in 2015, did not meet its initial production targets (Prensa MPPTTOP 2015). Four years after its inauguration, in 2019, the Venezuelan government approved about 4 million USD to repair about two thousand buses purchased with money from the CVJF. At that time, 13 million USD were also disbursed to complete the construction of this plant, located in the western part of the country (VTV, 2019). Regarding its capacity, a report by Claudia Smolansky suggests that the current spaces of this plant are used only to repair former transport units and, at the same time, to assemble prefabricated parts that come from China (Smolansky 2023).

Finally, JV having been oriented to the production of electronic products, the Haier Home Appliances Factory, has not been in operation since its construction was announced in 2010. Several reports have confirmed that this JV has not been completed by either the Haier Group company or the Venezuelan government. Most of these brand's products distributed in Venezuela were purchased directly with money from the CVJF in 2010 and 2015 (Infoabe 2010).

C) Microeconomic Level

At the microeconomic level, it is important to mention a study by Micolta and Piña, in which it was possible to identify the participation of at least 42 Chinese companies in Venezuela during the period 2000-2023. Most of them landed in this South American country since the creation of the CVJF, and Their participation can be categorized into three types of economic activities, such as 1) companies that participated in the construction of some infrastructure projects, 2) companies that participated in the conformation of joint ventures and, 3) companies that sold products and services to the Venezuelan government. The indicators about these three categories shows that the more relevant activities in which these companies participated were the infrastructure projects, followed by the sale of products and services, and ending with the creation of JV. Also in this study, it could be identified how the participation of these companies was especially focused on three sub-sectors such as: manufacturing, oil industry, and power energy. In addition, this research shows the participation of these companies in other subsectors such as health, security and defense, science and technology, housing, and food and agriculture (Micolta and Piña 2023).

Regarding the first group of companies, those that participated in joint ventures, their local impact in Venezuela has been explained within the "meso-economic" theory. And, regarding the purchase of consumer goods made for Venezuelan public entities from Chinese companies, it is possible to mention the following: household appliances (televisions, refrigerators, stoves, and washing machines), air conditioners, cell phones and other communication devices, as well as personal and mass transportation vehicles. These products have been distributed by both the Chávez and Maduro administrations during electoral processes to increase popular support for the ruling party (The Carter Center, 2012). The Chinese companies involved in these transactions were: Haier Group Company, Huawei, ZTE, Yutong, Chery Automobile, Sany Heavy Industry, China Petroleum Technology & Development Corporation (CPTDC), China's Bohai Shipbuilding Heavy Industry Company (BSIC), SINOMACH, China Aviation Industry Corporation (AVIC), and China Meheco Co. Ltd (MPPRE 2013).

Getting the specific number of beneficiaries of these direct donations is not an easy task due to the concealment of official figures, especially after 2016, but if we take in mind the information published by Haier, the main company that sold household appliances, it is possible to consider around three million people who received some kind of donation purchased with money from the CVJF, a mechanism created to channel resources from Venezuelan oil exports to China. If we add the information about the donations of vehicles, telephones and air conditioners, this number of three million increases. Thus, it can be considered that a large number of Venezuelan citizens have benefited from the creation of the new oil-based GVC consolidated by China and Venezuela between 2000 and 2020. For example, as has been mentioned, at least 10 million mobile phones were distributed by the JVs ORINOQUIA (Huawei), VTELCA (ZTE), and VIT (Inspur) (MPPI 2015).

It is also important to mention a brief analysis related to the technology transfer process initiated by the creation of the new oil-based GVC with China. The most important example of this situation was the Venezuelan purchase of three satellites manufactured in China. This equipment was launched in 2008, 2012, and 2017, respectively, and its purchase was part of a strategic agreement signed in 2005 between the Venezuelan government, represented by its Bolivarian Agency for Space Activities (ABAE, in Spanish), and the company China Great Wall Industry Corporation (CGWIC), a subsidiary of China Aerospace Science and Technology Corporation. As part of the agreement, both parties included a capacity building process for Venezuelan engineers who will oversee the satellites once they are in orbit. In addition, the investment made by the Venezuelan government created at least 93 new jobs (39 jobs in 2011 and 54 new jobs in 2013), which were located in the Aerospace Terminal Base in the state of Guárico (central Venezuela) (Observatorio de la Política China 2013).

Regarding the Chinese companies that participated in infrastructure projects in Venezuela during the twenty-first century, it can be possible to mention these were integrated in the local economy as part of the territorial development plan drafted by President Hugo Chávez. The following section explains the projects they participated in and their impact on variables such as employment, upgrading activities, and investment.

D) Territorial Analysis

Another level of analysis considered by Dussel Peters for studying the economic effects generated by the creation of a GVC is related to territorial analysis. In the case of the new oil-based GVC created by China and Venezuela, it is possible to consider at least two different plans aimed at creating a locally based productive upgrading. The first was the development of the "Deconcentrated Delocalization Project" planned during the government of Hugo Chávez and based on the division of five main territorial zones. The second, planned during the government of Nicolás Maduro, accompanied the creation of new Special Economic Zones (SEZ) in Venezuela. The following paragraphs will explain the fate of these two projects during the 2000-2023 period.

1) The Impact of Oil Exports to China in Hugo Chavez's Territorial Development Plan (1999-2013)

During his thirteen years in power, Hugo Chávez promoted a territorial development strategy as the basis of his economic policy. The main objective of this proposal, known as "deconcentrated decentralization," was not only to diversify economic activities from the north to the south of the country, but also to create a new industrialization process through massive public investments (De Lisio 2012). In addition, this strategy considered the strengthening of the living conditions of the people in each area, which meant that this plan also integrated the planning of housing projects, new highways, factories, and other types of construction such as agricultural plains.

In terms of its history, it is important to note that this plan was drawn up in the Ministry of Planning, which was headed for thirteen consecutive years, except for a few months, by Jorge Giordani, an academic from the Center for Development Studies (CENDES) at the Central University of Venezuela (UCV). In its first National Development Plan (2001-2007), the Venezuelan government considered some of the contributions made by CENDES and transformed them into public policies (De Lisio 2012). In this regard, five territorial areas were defined in order to develop the country's economy, such as 1) the North Coastal Axis; 2) the Western Axis; 3) the Eastern Axis; 4) the Northern Plains Axis; and 5) the Orinoco-Apure Axis (MPP 2001).

Figure 8 shows these areas on the map of Venezuela. "It is worth emphasizing that according to various public statements made by President Chávez, the most relevant of these areas in terms of connectivity was the "Northern Plains Axis", because it is the one that connects the most populated areas of the country (the North Coastal and the Western and Eastern Axis) with the less populated one, the Orinoco-Apure Axis (Delgado 2002). Chávez wanted to promote the economic development of this last zone to balance the economic growth between the north and the south of the country. In order to achieve success in this plan, the first step taken by the former president was to lay the foundations for a new national railway system while also financing various projects related

Figure 8. Territorial Development Regions Planned by the Government of Hugo Chavez (1999-2013)

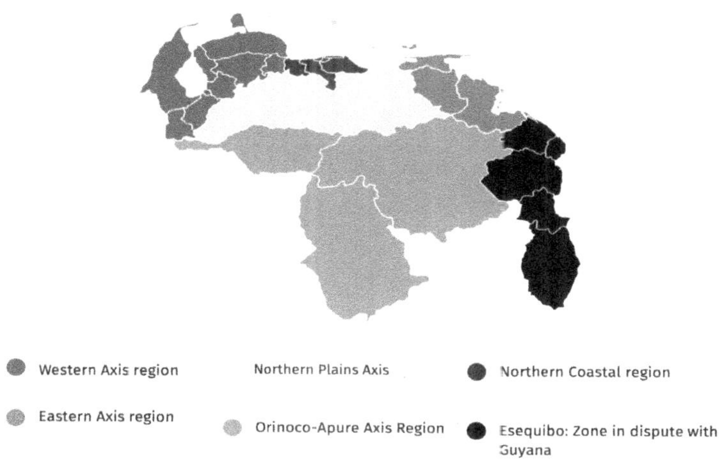

Source: Own elaboration with information from the Venezuelan Ministry of Planning.

to agriculture, housing and urbanism projects, the health system, and schools and universities.

To achieve the goal of increasing public investment in these areas, the former president had to take several steps. The first was to include in the new Venezuelan Constitution, approved in 1999, the commitment to promote a "territorial management policy" that considers "sustainable" standards (OAS 2024). The next step was the inclusion of the territorial management plan in the National Development Plan (2001-2007) and a reform of the Law of Special Assignments (LAEE, in Spanish), a legal strategy that allowed the simplification of several procedures to invest in each of the aforementioned areas. At the same time, Chávez began to use different strategies to obtain as many resources as possible and increase public investment in the five areas.

In parallel, Chávez tried to find new markets in which to sell Venezuelan oil, with China as a strategic partner for advancing this goal. As mentioned, in 2004, during one of his official visits to Beijing, the former Venezuelan president signed several sales and purchase agreements (SPA) to export crude oil and some of its derivatives to China (MPPRE 2010). At that time, both countries also agreed that Chinese companies would land in Venezuela to build some infrastructure projects in the Northern Plains Axis. Specifically, the Venezuelan leader pointed to the participation of the China Railway Construction Company (CRCC) in one of the first railway projects developed by his government, such as the "Puerto Cabello-Barquisimeto-Acarigua" tranche (Todo Chávez 2004). A year later, in 2005, Chávez announced that the Chinese CITIC group had signed an agreement to build 20,000 houses in Barinas, a province located near the Orinoco River; in 2006, the Venezuelan president agreed with the CAMCE company to build the third irrigation system in the state of Guárico, located in the center of the country, specifically in the Northern Plains axis.

These projects were developed at a time when, as mentioned above, the two countries were negotiating the creation of the CVJF, the loans-for-oil program through which Venezuela secured advance payments for its oil sales to China. In 2007-2008, the two main legal instruments formalizing the creation of the CVJF were signed (EFE 2007); after these events, the Venezuelan government used the money earned from oil exports to China to make greater advances in the development of both the North Plains Axis and the Orinoco-Apure Axis. In the first case, Chávez and his Minister of Planning decided to boost the construction of the National Railway System. In the second case, the former Venezuelan president financed housing, agricultural and electrical projects.

Regarding the National Railway System project, it should be pointed out that the Tinaco-Anaco tranche, which was the largest planned by the Chávez government, with a 468-kilometer extension through three different states which also contemplated the construction of ten different stations (Prensa IFE 2009). This project had an initial budget of 7.5 billion USD and began operations in 2009, managed by the China Railway Construction Company (CRCC). According to PDVSA, the Venezuelan National Oil Company (NOC), during the first two years of this project, disbursed about 2.4 billion USD (PDVSA). Also, according to the Venezuelan National Railway Institute (IFE, in Spanish), this project has created 9,550 jobs (7,200 jobs directly involved in the construction process and 2,350 jobs related to the operation and/or management of the machinery) (IFE 2013).

After 2013, this project suffered a lot of labor and social claims, which caused an important delay in its construction (El Nacional, 2018). Later, this project also suffered a considerable lack of financing because of the oil price crisis that affected the oil revenues obtained by Venezuela, including those that were destined for China. Another problem was related to the scarcity of some products, such as cement or iron boxes, which did not allow the construction process to continue (Segovia, 2021). All these things made the new Venezuelan government, headed by Nicolas Maduro, unofficially decide to stop this project.

Two other rail projects in these two regions (Northern Plains and Orinoco-Apure Axis) were also financed with money from Venezuelan oil exports to China, such as the San Juan-San

Fernando tranche (252 kilometers) and the Chaguaramas-Cabruta tranche (201 kilometers) (IFE, 2013). The available information on these projects indicates that they have never been completed by the government and its partner, CRCC; in fact, the most recent data shows progress of only 30 % and 22 %, respectively. In terms of investment, only the amount of the initial budget for the Chaguaramas-Cabruta tranche is known, which was approximately 2.1 billion USD and created approximately 4,750 jobs (3,960 in construction and 790 in operation and management) Regarding the San Juan-San Fernando de Apure railway tranche, there is information on the creation of 4,803 jobs (3,960 in the construction process and 843 in the operation and management process). It is important to note that for both projects, both the CRCC and the Venezuelan Ministry of Transportation faced significant financial constraints for completing the construction process. Nevertheless, during the construction period, thousands of jobs were created for the local population, even if these jobs were not highly qualified.

Other railroad tranches were initiated by Hugo Chávez' government during his thirteen years in power with oil revenues from China. These were the Puerto Cabello-La Encrucijada tranche (north coast axis) and the Puerto Cabello-Barquisimeto-Turén tranche (North Coastal and Western axis). In total, these projects guaranteed investments of approximately 500 million USD and created approximately 9,422 new jobs (IFE, 2013). In the case of the Puerto Cabello-Barquisimeto-Turén tranche, construction began in 2004, when President Chávez signed a contract with CRCC to rebuild this railway system, which had been abandoned in 1996. According to official sources, the first stage of this section, from Puerto Cabello to Barquisimeto, was completed, but the remainder of the section was not finished (AVN 2012).

The strategic approach to the national railway system was undeniable during the Hugo Chávez administration. For example, with the Tinaco-Anaco rail tranche, the main intention was to integrate the eastern and western regions of the country. The Chávez government also approved the construction of a new irrigation system in the Guárico River along some of the ten stations planned for the project, as well as a comprehensive agricultural plan in the town of Tiznados (Prensa MAT 2012). The irrigation system implied the disbursement of 370 million USD and the creation of 576 new jobs, while the Tiznados project implied an investment of 570 million USD (it was not possible to determine the number of jobs created in this project) (Dussel Peters 2024)

Regarding the San Juan-San Fernando de Apure section, it is also possible to consider a strategic planning approach. For example, San Fernando de Apure is one of the largest cities in southern Venezuela, but it is also connected to the Orinoco River. Its strategic location allows it to be considered an important market for the sale of livestock products that could be sold in the north of the country. In this sense, the connection with San Juan was totally strategic, because this city is located in the center of Venezuela, only two and a half hours by road from Caracas, the main metropolitan area of Venezuela. In addition, President Chávez's idea for this tranche was that it would connect San Juan by train to Caracas, the country's capital, and to Puerto Cabello, the second most important port in Venezuela.

Also, along the way between San Juan and San Fernando de Apure, there are some relevant cities such as Calabozo, a place with not only one of the largest drums in the country, but also a research operational center that has been prepared to manage the first and second Venezuelan satellites, which were purchased from a Chinese company. It should be said that the Venezuelan officials who managed this center were trained in the Chinese Academy of Aerospace. According to official sources, at least 91 Venezuelan engineers started to work in this center during the 2008-2013 period (OPCh 2013). It can be seen how the new oil-based GVC with China has also created high-value jobs in this area.

The Chaguaramas-Cabruta were even more important to the Chávez government in connecting the northern plains with the Orinoco-Apure axis. The city of Cabruta is the main river port along the Orinoco River, which gives it a strategic location to integrate the south of the country with the southwest and southeast. Also, Cabruta represents a middle point between the cities of San Fernando (southwest) and Guayana City (southeast); this last is the place where the most important heavy industrial center of the country is located, which produces iron, aluminum, coal and other type of materials necessary to supply the raw material to a large number of factories or companies in the main populated zones of the country.

In this regard, the Venezuelan idea around Cabruta was to transform this place into an important hub to dynamize the commercial relations in the south of the country. For this purpose, the construction of an oil refinery was planned, but never started, and the Chinese company China Petroleum & Chemical Corporation (SINOPEC) would build it. At that time, President Chávez used the money from oil exports to China to start the construction of the Third Bridge over the Orinoco River, which would connect the city of Cabruta with Caicara, a city on the other side of the river. According to the information published by the government authorities, the Third Bridge had an initial budget of 2.5 billion USD and created about 12,190 jobs (Prensa RNV 2011). Unfortunately, this bridge has not been completed, neither by the Chinese company CRCC nor by the Venezuelan public companies in charge of it. The last reports about it estimated a lack of economic resources (financing) to finish it, partly due to the financial problems the country had during the period of oil price collapse in 2014-2016 (World Bank 2018).

In this context, it is also important to mention that the investment plan of the Orinoco-Apure axis continued more to the west, specifically in the aforementioned city of Guayana. Here, the Venezuelan government invested a huge amount of money from the CVJF, the mechanism of selling oil to China in exchange for an advance payment. Some of the projects built in this zone were the following: 1) the modernization of the Palúa port terminal (112 million USD) (RNV 2017); 2) the second iron ore pellet production line in the company Ferrominera- Orinoco (425 million USD and 8400 jobs) (Últimas Noticias 2020); 3) the construction of an extrusion plant in Alcasa (Alluminum Orinoco) (403 million USD and 400 jobs created) (MPPI, 2013); 4) the modernization of the

Tocoma-Uribante energy plant (1.3 billion USD and 300 jobs created); and 5) Dredging of the Orinoco River (116 million USD) (Crooks 2011).

All these projects had the purpose of increasing the productivity in the "Heavy Industries" in Venezuela; nevertheless, a lack of long-term planning. However, a blockage in the national energy system in 2011 forced the Venezuelan government to decide to divert the energy transmission, conventionally used in the operational processes of these industries, to residential consumption in the main urban centers of the country. The damage that this decision made in the heavy industries in Venezuela continues to the present days, creating the necessity to get more investments to recover their former productivity.

The Chávez government also invested the oil revenues generated by exporting oil to China in several projects in the southeast of the country. One of the most important was the Santa Inés Industrial Hub in the state of Barinas. This project sought to generate new value chains in the region through the establishment of a series of manufacturing plants, but also the construction of new housing projects, an energy plant and an oil refinery. In this regard, the Chinese company CITIC Group was contracted to build 5,360 houses near this site and Sinohydro was contracted to build a power plant (300 million USD and 3572 employees) (Zerpa Guerrero 2016). Also, the Chinese oil company Wison Energy, in alliance with the Korean Hyundai Engineering and Construction, signed a contract to build a new oil refinery in this industrial complex. Finally, near this place, the Chávez government built a corn processing plant called "Leander", which has not only been completed but is active at the moment this chapter is being written (Ciudad Caracas 2022).

In the north of the country (North Coastal Axis), it is also possible to trace and confirm several public investments made with funds from the CVJF. These investments were made according to the National Territorial Development Plan, but with a different logic, a focus on the idea of improving the interurban means of transportation and consumption of goods. In this regard, the

Chavez government advanced in the modernization of the subway lines in the three major cities of the country such as Caracas (the capital city), Valencia (Central north) and Maracaibo (East). In addition, two interurban rail projects were built in the suburbs of Caracas, such as the Caracas-Los Teques and Caracas-Cúa metro lines. In addition, two cable lines were built in the east of Caracas, a place that is overpopulated and has many problems with its transport system.

It is important to note that these projects were planned with a view to their integration with the National Railway System mentioned before. Since they are the most populated places –but also the center of business, consumption of goods, and, last but not least, the main financial and political power centers of the country– the idea was to connect these places with the rest of the country. In addition, President Chávez thought of creating several factories in the cities around the capital's metropolitan area to supply some products to this zone. In this sense, the Venezuelan leader used the CVJF to finance the construction of an electronic equipment factory in Yare, a small town in the state of Miranda (Central North), in collaboration with the Haier Group Company, aiming to assemble approximately 850,000 electronic products, including refrigerators., washing machines and air conditioners. To build this plant, the Venezuelan government invested 287 million USD and created 4,584 jobs (Herrera 2021). In addition, a dairy plant was inaugurated in the same city, which cost 50 million USD and created 31 jobs (Ministry of Agriculture 2014). Elsewhere, in Aragua, a state two hours from Caracas, the Ministry of Industry, with the support of the Chinese company CATIC, has set up a cement plant. In Carabobo, the CVJF financed two energy plants and the modernization of the Puerto Cabello port terminal.

In summary, the "Deconcentrated Decentralization" plan drafted by Hugo Chávez in 1999 was the core of his economic plan during his thirteen years in power. These ideas were officially published in the new Venezuelan Constitution, approved in 1999, and in the National Development Plans for 2001-2007 and 2007-2013, respectively. This plan divided the country into five regions and allowed the government to focus its efforts on the development of the south and central region of Venezuela through a comprehensive plan to connect this area with the rest of the country. This strategy also focused on the creation of other economic activities that would not only improve the living conditions of the inhabitants of the less populated areas but would also integrate them economically with the main economic centers, which are generally located in the north of Venezuela.

Furthermore, the explanation of how Chávez and his government invested the money that the country received from the oil exports to China allows us to understand a high-level coordination of the Ministry of Planning with the rest of the government offices, following a path to progress in line with the national development goals. In this sense, behind each construction/project built there was a clear idea of integrating itself in the achievement of the national economic system. An important part of the 50.3 USD billion that came from the CVJF were invested to achieve this goal, especially between 2008 and 2012.

However, despite the initial idea behind this National Development Plan, the results of these investments have left some chiaroscuros in Venezuela. On the one hand, it is undeniable that this strategy improved the economic indicators in some regions of the country, especially in the south, a place that previous administrations did not historically focus on. Also, this idea really incorporated a national plan with local governments; the objective was to unify the local economic activities with the national outreach. To achieve this, the first and most important construction was related to the national railway system. Finally, Chavez created a business model that would allow the integration of several Chinese companies in the construction of some of these projects, especially those that implied the construction of railway systems, energy plants, irrigation systems and/or the modernization of some heavy industry factories.

Chavez once expressed an idea behind the attraction of Chinese companies to Venezuela: his intention was to transform his country into a Chinese hub for re-exporting high-quality goods and services to other Latin American countries. Unfortunately, this could never happen. Nevertheless, for a middle-income economy like Venezuela's, this comprehensive plan also presented many challenges. Initially, the revenue from oil exports to China, while important, was not enough to cover a long-term infrastructure plan like the one implemented by President Hugo Chávez. Also, part of the 50.3 billion USD that Venezuela received for this concept was invested in the purchase of goods and other services, which means that not all this money was directed to the infrastructure projects. It is important to remember, as mentioned before, that some of these projects could never be completed due to the lack of economic resources, but also due to economic decisions that prioritized investments in other economic activities. For example, Nicolás Maduro, Chávez's successor, decided to invest the money from the CVJF in the maintenance of oil wells in order to keep the industry functioning.

Another problem associated with these projects was the lack of materials for building them. Some of the most important constructions that Chávez tried to build required materials such as iron ore, iron pellets, cement, and some heavy industrial machinery. The former Venezuelan president tried to supply them with the national production; however, as mentioned, the iron ore and pellets –the heavy industries in Venezuela– suffered a lack of production due to a massive energy lockdown in 2011. In that year, Chavez ordered the closure of the energy plants from these industries and the redirection of the spare capacity to satisfy the residential demand in the country's main cities.

Chávez also tried to increase the national production of cement by promoting the nationalization of existing plants in the country. Hence, in the short term, the new state-owned companies effectively increased the production of cement; also, the Venezuelan government pushed two different modernization and expansion projects in collaboration with the Chinese company CATIC in order to further increase this production. Nevertheless, in the medium and long term, these factories were badly managed, and their productivity was felt. In addition, there were failures in planning the final use of the cement produced in these companies, especially because between 2010 and 2013 the country launched a massive and unplanned housing project that required most of the output of these factories. As a result, the government had to import more of this raw material, a situation that collapsed and stagnated infrastructure construction in the country when the oil revenues that Venezuela received decreased dramatically after the 2014-2016 oil price plunge.

In addition, there was an important factor that affected the fulfillment of the national development goals sought by Hugo Chávez: the deterioration of Venezuelan institutions and, consequently, the rise of corruption cases related to the construction of these infrastructure projects. During his two terms in office, the former Venezuelan president undermined the system of checks and balances in the country, paving the way for public officials to try to engage in corrupt activities during the construction of several projects, a situation that, in most cases, affected their completion. Recently, an important study carried out by Micolta and Piña showed that at least 60 % of the projects financed by the CVJF showed some kind of irregularities or cases of corruption in their construction process (Micolta and Piña 2023). These irregularities include cost overruns, lack of planning, failures in the accountability process, and/or failures in the construction process.

Finally, one of the most important issues surrounding the National Development Plan drafted by Hugo Chávez was its extreme dependence on oil revenues. At the beginning of his presidential term, this was a good approach, while the price of oil was in the middle of an upward trend, as it happened during the period 2000-2013. However, putting the trust of such a national development plan only on a single commodity exposed the whole country's economy to the commodity cycle, as it happened during the 2014-2016 oil price collapse. This was perhaps the biggest mistake in the design of this plan, which brought mixed results to the country during those years.

2) Nicolás Maduro (2013-2024): The New Special Economic Zones (SEZ)

In 2013, Hugo Chávez died and his successor, Nicolás Maduro, presided over a new six-year period in Venezuela. During his first two years in power, Maduro kept some of the territorial plans developed by Chávez, especially some of the major constructions around the country, such as the national railway system, some factories in the Guayana region or the massive housing policy, following the scheduled investments included in the 2012 national budget. Also, Maduro disbursed money from the CVJF to build a new bus factory in Yaracuy (west), which was supposed to be an investment of 278 million USD and the creation of around 5,000 jobs. Other major projects initiated by the new government include the second line of a cement plant in the southwest of the country, the modernization of several highways in the Caracas metropolitan area, and the creation of a new program to modernize and repair old houses called "Barrio Nuevo, Barrio Tricolor". The new president also continues to purchase goods from China, including vehicles, buses, electronic equipment, heavy industrial machinery, and drilling equipment to be used in the oil industry.

However, since 2016, Nicolás Maduro had to face several problematic situations. The most important was related to the collapse of oil prices between 2014 and 2016, which reduced the country's oil revenues, but also motivated the government to considerate new strategies in order to adjust the national economy. The most problematic situation was caused by the massive public investment expenditures made during the Chávez administration, which created a huge economic deficit in the public accounts. In addition, the decline in oil revenues experienced during those years led to a reduction in public investment in Venezuelan oil fields and a subsequent decline in the production of the natural resource.

Amid this, as mentioned above, the Chinese government continued to purchase oil from Venezuela and granted a new 15 billion USD loan for oil, divided into three tranches. In addition, the government of Xi Jinping, in strict agreement with Maduro, lent money to keep its four JVs with PDVSA in operation. As can be seen, one of the priorities during the first Maduro's term (2013-2018) was to direct the oil revenues to keep the oil industry functioning and to secure the oil spending in order to ensure the public support for the ruling party. During this period, some reports assure that the Gross Domestic Product (GDP) decreased 44 % (World Bank, 2024).

Amid this context did Nicolás Maduro could not focus on investing too much money in a massive infrastructure plan aimed at creating territorial development. In addition, the new Venezuelan leader fired Chávez' former Minister of Planning and replaced him with an official named Ricardo Menéndez, who had another idea to promote the economic growth in Venezuela, such as: the creation of the new Special Economic Zones (SEZs). According to this official, the SEZs is a more effective way to territorialize the economic activities and industrial policy in the country, integrating the national, regional and local levels (MPPP 2021).

In 2014, the Ministry of Planning proposed the creation of three SEZs, such as: 1) the Paraguaná SEZ, located in the west

Figure 9. Venezuela: Location of SEZs Proposed by Nicolás Maduro's Government in 2014

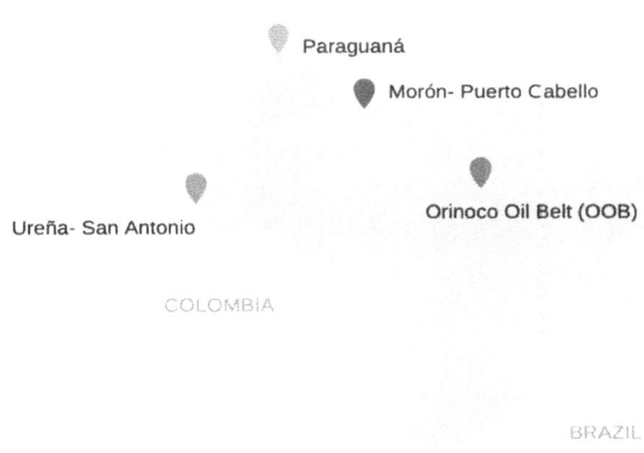

Source: Own elaboration with information from the Venezuelan Ministry of Planning.

of the country, specifically in a traditional tax-free zone; 2) the Ureña-San Antonio SEZ, located on the Venezuelan border with Colombia; and 3) the Puerto Cabello- Morón, a place located around the second most important port in the country (Puerto Cabello). Its objective was also to integrate the Orinoco Oil Belt (OOB) as a development pole in the country. This idea came from the geostrategic use of this area by Hugo Chávez with the purpose of attract investments to this part of the country.

As can be seen on the map, these SEZs are located far from each other. This practically means that the new initiative does not try to connect the country economically through a real economic engagement; in fact, the Maduro government tried to create zones where foreign companies felt attracted to invest in greenfield projects. In this sense, the government offered some incentives such as: 1) the 100 % exemption on the payment of income taxes to the established companies that imported all the necessary machinery to produce a specific product in the SEZs; 2) total exemption on the tax income payment during the first five years of operation in the SEZs and 3) if a company exports at least 70 % of its production after five years, it can maintain a 75 % exemption on the tax income payment. These incentives are contained in three laws: 1) the Foreign Investment Law, 2) the Comprehensive Regionalization to Improve Productive Development Law, and 3) the Public and Popular Planning Law (MPPP 2021).

Over the years, this was the legal framework for attracting foreign investment. However, the results were not what the Venezuelan government expected. None of these SEZs finally became operational or received any kind of significant investment. In general, the period 2013-2018 was one in which the country faced an economic crisis, and the government delayed the necessary measures to adapt the country to the new reality characterized by the decline in oil prices. Moreover, the Maduro government's top priority during these years was to maintain the oil industry, the country's main source of income. In this regard, it can be said that during this period the oil revenues were invested in projects that did not generate modernization activities or promote territorial development.

During his subsequent term, Nicolás Maduro continued to face more problems at the macroeconomic level. Oil revenues fell even more dramatically between 2019 and 2023, after the United States imposed an oil embargo on Venezuela. The impact of this measure also led to the stagnation of Venezuelan oil exports to China, at least officially (Moleiro 2019). Despite this, the idea of promoting the SEZs has remained in force, due to the special interest shown by the president's son, congressman Nicolás Maduro Guerra. He has expanded his relations with China over the years and has been one of the promoters of the approval of the new law on special economic zones, sanctioned in August 2022. After this event, President Maduro announced the creation of four new SEZs such as Paraguaná (in the west), La Guaira (in the central north), Aragua (in the central north), La Tortuga Island (in the Caribbean) and Margarita Island (in the east) (NTN24 2023).

Moreover, in his visit to China in 2023, President Nicolás Maduro was interested in expanding the cooperation with China in order to improve the operational aspects of these mentioned new SEZs (La Jornada 2023). As a result, the Chinese government agreed to consultative cooperation in this regard, even if the landing of massive investments from this Asian country in the new SEZs has not been confirmed. In general, the Maduro administration has indicated its interest in following the Chinese path in this type of development projects. Nevertheless, Venezuela's economic conditions differ significantly from those of China during its reform period in the 1980s and 1990s.

The practical results of this renewed bet on the SEZs have been unsuccessful for the Maduro government, especially because it has not created the conditions to move the country forward on a new path of economic development (source). It's true that there are several external factors that do not allow the SEZ plans to succeed. One of them is the economic sanctions imposed by the United States against the Venezuelan government, but there is also a strong consensus about the deterioration of the rule of law in the country, a situation that has been accompanied by a growing political instability (source). This last reason reinforces the idea of the lack of legal certainty/security on Venezuelan soil, a necessary condition to create a favorable environment to attract new foreign direct investment.

In summary, during Nicolas Maduro's term in office, there is no evidence of the implementation of a successful territorial development plan. The SEZs seem more like a strategy to circumvent the American sanctions against the country's economy than a plan to integrate different economic entities into a whole integrated system that works to promote national development goals. In this sense, it is also necessary to say that the oil revenues from China have been used both to keep the Venezuelan oil industry in operation and, during the period 2013-2016, to continue investing in some projects that were designed or started during the administration of his predecessor Hugo Chávez.

4. Conclusions and Policy Recommendations

Once the explanation of the creation and consolidation of the new oil-based GVC between China and Venezuela has been made, the first conclusion that can be highlighted is that in the twenty-first century, Sino-Venezuelan relations have been influenced by the key role of oil, which has been consolidated as the main driving factor to engage not only the bilateral political-diplomatic relations, but also the economic integration between both countries. In this regard, the creation of the new oil-based GVC is the result of a Venezuelan foreign policy approach aimed at improving and connecting with the rest of the world through its main commodity, but also a consequence of the Chinese interest in securing its access to this strategic raw material, which is considered necessary to maintaining the functioning of its industrial sector.

All of this progress has been possible thanks to the political relationship developed by both countries, which has allowed them to advance in the integration of their economies, creating a long-term cooperation scheme based on Venezuelan oil exports and, at the same time, on Chinese exports of capital and high value-added products to this South American country. To consolidate this in the early years of the twenty-first century, both the Chinese and Venezuelan governments signed a series of agreements covering all economic aspects related to the oil business, such as: trade, direct investment in upstream and downstream activities and, finally, financial cooperation.

An important turning point came in 2007, when both countries decided to create a loans-for-oil mechanism called the Chinese Venezuelan Joint Fund (CVJF). This mechanism was the final step in building a new oil-based GVC. Venezuela secured a new market for its oil exports, generating new revenues and diversifying its oil business by reducing its dependence on the U.S. market. The money received by the CVJF, approximately 50.3 billion USD, was invested in several infrastructure projects, the purchase of consumer goods from China, the creation of joint ventures in manufacturing and oil industry activities, and in social programs.

The economic impact of the new oil-based GVC has been significant over the years; at the macroeconomic level, Venezuela has been able to obtain millions of dollars to invest in its main territorial development plan, the "Deconcentrated Decentralization", which consisted of building massive infrastructure projects to connect the different regions, generate upgrading activities and create new value chains. The advance payments received by Venezuela through the CVJF thus allowed the country to obtain financing in a context in which the international credit market posed some difficulties to the country after the nationalization process of several foreign assets. Despite the initial advantages, the collateralization of debt in oil reserves and production has affected Venezuela since 2014, at a time when international oil prices collapsed, the country had to prioritize the payment of its debt obligations to China (only 10% of the total) over the rest of its creditors, a situation that generated high pressure on the local financial system.

Venezuela also took advantage of the economic integration with China to propose a business model that not only increased the trade relations between both countries but also stimulated the landing of new Chinese OFDI in Venezuela. To consider the importance of Chinese OFDI in Venezuela, in this research it was possible to identify that this indicator represented about 14.5% of the total OFDI received by Venezuela in 2018. The form in which these new OFDI transactions arrived in Venezuela were basically two: 1) investments in joint ventures with Venezuelan partners, and 2) investments made exclusively by Chinese companies.

This chapter also examined the local impact of establishing ten joint ventures between Chinese and Venezuelan companies. The main conclusions on this topic were the following: 1) these ten JVs were involved in four sub-sectors such as: oil, telecommunications, transportation and household appliances; 2) the participation of Chinese companies in these JVs was aimed at offering a technology transfer to their Venezuelan partner, but also at creating the conditions for their brand to obtain a greater market share than other foreign companies present in this South American country; 3) the results of their participation were ambiguous. On the one hand, most of these joint ventures were successful during the period 2007-2015, showing a significant advance in their productivity and gaining important customers in the country; moreover, these JVs generated around 8,200 jobs after an investment of US$ 810 million. On the other hand, after 2015, the Venezuelan partners in these JVs faced many financial problems due to the fall in oil prices in 2014-2016, a situation that did not allow them to comply with the financing plans assigned to them.

At the microeconomic level, it was important to recognize the participation of at least forty-two Chinese companies in Venezuela during the first two decades of the twenty-first century. Their participation was expressed in three different ways, such as: 1) companies that participated as partners in the formation of joint ventures; 2) companies that participated in the construction of infrastructure projects financed by the Venezuelan government; and 3) companies that sold consumer goods to Venezuela and later established their local factories in the country. Part of the explanation of the impact of these companies was explained in the meso-economic analysis (in the case of the JVs) and in the territorial analysis (in the case of the construction of infrastructure projects).

Regarding the companies that sold consumer goods to Venezuela, it could be identified that at least three million people benefited from the donations of cell phones, air conditioners, refrigerators, stoves, washing machines, cars, buses, etc. These donations were made by the Venezuelan government and were part of a business model strategy that consisted of first buying many products and introducing them to the Venezuelan market, in order to later promote the establishment of companies that would produce them on Venezuelan soil. As a result, Chinese companies such as Haier, Yutong, Chery Automobile, ZTE, Huawei and Inspur, just to mention the most important ones, not only gained recognition but also an important part of the Venezuelan markets in their respective sectors.

For its part, the most relevant contribution of this chapter was related to the territorial analysis of the new oil-based GVC between China and Venezuela. Along this explanation, it was possible not only to describe, but also to identify the territorial plans and objectives designed and proposed by President Hugo Chávez for using the revenues of said GVC. This plan divided the country into five different regions in order to prioritize investments in infrastructure in the south of the country, the less populated region and the one with more problems in terms of connectivity and industrial development.

The two regions in which the Venezuelan government focused its investments were the North Coastal Axis and the Orinoco-Apure Axis; the main plan for both was to invest in the National Railway System, which was designed to connect these regions with the most populated areas of the country. Along with these new routes, the idea was to create development poles that would be realized in industrial factories, housing projects, agricultural systems, refineries and power plants, and technology and research centers. In order to advance these projects, this research could identify at least twenty-five infrastructure projects developed during the two terms of Hugo Chávez, which involved an investment of around 17 billion USD and created 81,445 jobs. Even if most of these jobs were not highly qualified, it is important to say that they dynamized the economy in the North Coastal and Orinoco-Apure axis.

During the period 1999-2013, President Hugo Chávez promoted the construction of these territorial projects as much as possible. Despite the important progress made in some of them, most were not finished and their investment processes had to be completed in the following years. However, Nicolás Maduro, Chávez's successor, not only did not have enough money to accomplish this goal, but he also designed another territorial plan, the Special Economic Zones (SEZs), which made it impossible to continue Chávez's efforts. Two other problems affected the territorial plan developed by Hugo Chávez, such as 1) the lack of institutionalization to advance in the control of the resources invested; and 2) the excessive concentration on oil revenues to finance most of these infrastructure projects.

In conclusion, it could be said that the new Sino-Venezuelan oil-based GVC has had a real impact on the main economic indicators of this South American country, creating jobs, promoting foreign direct investment, diversifying oil markets, securing the country's access to new international debt, and encouraging the participation of new companies in the Venezuelan oil industry. Nevertheless, it is also important to add that Venezuela has based all its economic relations with China around the oil industry, which at the end of the period 2000-2023 contributed to an increase the country's economic vulnerability to possible countercyclical processes, as seen during the period of low oil prices between 2014 and 2016.

Policy Recommendations

1. One of the main criticisms of the new Sino-Venezuelan oil-based GVC is the lack of vision and plans to create long-term value-added activities in Venezuela. A review of the

available information shows that this is not entirely true, at least during the two terms of Hugo Chávez, a period in which Venezuela developed a territorial plan designed to create value-added activities in the country. This plan, even if it was logical, redoubled the dependence of the territorial development plan on oil revenues. For the future, the Venezuelan authorities could consider designing and proposing a different territorial plan that does not depend only in the revenues generated for the oil exports. In fact, it could be considered a mixed strategy that includes partnerships with private capital. China could be a partner in this sense.

2. Another major failure of the Chávez era was the lack of institutions to prevent corruption or irregularities in projects like those under the 'deconcentrated decentralization' plan. The Venezuelan authorities should take this situation into account in order to promote more efficient management of the resources generated by oil exports.
3. Over the years, Venezuela has become increasingly dependent on oil revenues to maintain the functioning of its entire economy. This process has affected the industrialization of the country, creating the conditions for a reprimarized economy. For the future, Venezuelan policymakers should consider planning a real industrial policy that would allow the country to take advantage of the creation of new GVCs with China.
4. Venezuela could also try to diversify its economic relations with China. The comparative advantages of Venezuela could be far from the historical oil industry approach to integrate with different countries around the world, including, and especially, China. For example, this South American country has great potential in the agricultural sector, but also in heavy industry.
5. Most of the Chinese FDI transactions in recent years have been carried out under the joint venture model. Looking at the results from the 2000–2024 period, it is reasonable to consider this model a failure. Looking ahead, a shift in the

model–one that includes diverse options for attracting new FDI beyond the public-led framework–could have a more positive impact on Venezuela's economic indicators.

References

AVN (Agencia Venezolana de Noticias). 2011. "Empresa Chino-Venezolana desarrolla taladro petrolero para Faja del Orinoco". *Petróleo América*, November 11.

AVN (Agencia Venezolana de Noticias). 2012. "Chávez: Tramo ferroviario Barquisimeto-Yaritagua-Acarigua ya está listo". *Aporrea*, January 18.

Anguiano Roch, Eugenio. 1997. *China, de las reformas recientes a la era pos-Deng*. El Colegio de Mexico: Mexico.

ANC (Asamblea Nacional Constituyente). 2024. *Constitución de la República Bolivariana de Venezuela 1999*. ANC: Caracas.

Asamblea Nacional de la República Bolivariana de Venezuela. 2013. Ley del Plan de la Patria. Segundo Plan Socialista de Desarrollo Económico y Social de la Nación 2013-2019. *Asamblea Nacional de la República Bolivariana de Venezuela*: Caracas.

Aizhu, Chen, Chu, Mei, and Parraga, Mariana. 2021. "Venezuelan oil, masked as Malaysian, rushes into China before fuel tax". *Reuters*, June 3.

Reuters. 2019. "CNPC y la estatal PDVSA reinician operaciones de mezcla de crudo. Banca y Negocios". *Banca y Negocios*, October 10.

Brandt, Carlos and Piña, Carlos E. 2019. *Las relaciones Venezuela-China (2000-2018): entre la cooperación y la dependencia*. Friedrich-Ebert-Stiftung Venezuela: Caracas.

Brandt Carlos. 2020. "China's "health diplomacy" in Latin America: facts, figures and strategic dilemmas". *Asia Power Watch*, June 10.

Brewer-Carías, Allan. 2008. *La "Estatización" petrolera en 2006-2007 con la terminación unilateral y anticipada de los contratos operativos y de asociación respecto de las actividades primarias de hidrocarburos.* Blog Personal.

CVECH (Centro Venezolano de Estudios sobre China). 2019. *China y Venezuela: una asociación estratégica integral. Informe sobre las relaciones bilaterales 2018-2019.* CVECH: Caracas-Beijing.

CNPC (China National Petroleum Corporation). 2013. *CNPC in Latin America.* CNPC: Beijing.

Ciudad Caracas. 2022. "Planta Procesadora Leander produce harina de maíz en Barinas". *Ciudad Caracas,* November 21.

Connelly, Marisela and Cornejo Bustamante, Romer. 1992. *China-América Latina. Génesis y desarrollo de sus relaciones.* El Colegio de Mexico: Mexico.

Crooks, Nathan. 2011. "Venezuela signs Chinese accords to boost iron output, AVN says". *Bloomberg,* September 6.

D´Elia, Yolanda and Cabezas, Luis F. 2008. *Las Misiones Sociales en Venezuela.* Instituto Latinoamericano de Investigaciones Sociales (ILDIS): Caracas.

De Lisio, Antonio. 2012. "La ordenación territorial en la Venezuela Bolivariana. Entre la catálisis sustentable y la desaceleración petro". *Terra Nueva Etapa,* 28(43), pp. 1-43.

Delgado de Bravo, María. T. 2003. *El desarrollo del eje Orinoco-Apure: ¿alternativa de desconcentración territorial?* Universidad de Los Andes: Merida-Venezuela.

DoS (Department of State). 2024. "Rapprochement with China, 1972. Office of the Historian." *DoS* (at: https://history.state.gov/milestones/1969-1976/rapprochement-china).

Diez, Pablo. 2006. "Chávez pone a la revolución China como modelo ante el capitalismo". ABC, August 24.

Dussel Peters, Enrique (edit.). 2018. *Cadenas globales de valor metodología, teoría y debates* (1st ed.). Universidad Nacional Autónoma de México: México.

Dussel Peters, Enrique. 2024/a. *Monitor de la OFDI China en América Latina y el Caribe 2024.* Red ALC-China: Mexico.

Dussel Peters, Enrique. 2024/b. *Monitor de la Infraestructura China en América Latina y el Caribe 2024.* Red ALC-China: Mexico.

EFE. 2007. "Venezuela y China crean fondo de inversiones por 6.000 millones de dólares". *El Economista*, November 6.

El Nacional. 2018. "Obra de ferrocarril Tinaco-Anaco tiene ocho años parada". *El Nacional,* January 3.

Giacalone, Rita and Briceño, José. 2020. "The Chinese–Venezuelan OilAgreements: Material and Nonmaterial Goals". *Wiley Periodicals, Inc.*

González Urrutia, Edmundo. 2006. "Las dos etapas de la política exterior de Chávez". *Nueva Sociedad 205, pp. 159-171.*

Hurtado, Jesús. 2016. "Sequía de dólares frenó la producción de vergatarios". *El Interés*, March 4.

Infobae. 2010. "Chávez anunció el programa ´Mi casa bien equipada´". *Infobae,* September 15.

Todo Chávez. 2004. "Intervención del comandante presidente Hugo Chávez durante conferencia dictada en la Universidad de Beijing". *Todo Chávez,* December 24.

Todo Chávez. 2007. "Firma de instrumentos jurídicos entre la República Bolivariana de Venezuela y la República Popular China". *Todo Chávez,* March 26.

IESA (Instituto de Estudios Superiores de Administración). 2014. *El Plan Siembra Petrolera.* IESA: Caracas-Venezuela.

IFE (Instituto de Ferrocarriles del Estado). 2013. *Plan Socialista Nacional de Desarrollo Ferroviario.* Consejo Suramericano de Infraestructura y Planeamiento (COSIPLAN).

Inventariando China. 2016. "Ministro Del Pino: Venezuela y China en integración perfecta". *Inventariando China*, August 11.

Jingjing, Ma. 2019. "China pulled US out of 2008 financial crisis: expert". *Global Times*, November 21.

La Jornada. 2023. "Pactan Venezuela y China cooperación en zonas económicas especiales". *La Jornada*, September 10.

Micolta, María and Piña, Carlos. 2023. *Seguimiento de los Fondos Conjuntos Chino Venezolanos*. Fundación Andrés Bello: Bogotá.

MENPET (Ministerio del Poder Popular de Petróleo). 2016. *Petróleo y otros datos estadísticos. Quincuagésima quinta edición 2014.* MENPET: Venezuela.

MPP (Ministerio del Poder Popular para la Planificación). 2001. *Líneas generales del Plan Nacional de Desarrollo Económico y Social de la Nación 2001-2007*. MPP: Venezuela.

MPP (Ministerio del Poder Popular para la Planificación). 2021. *Zonas Económicas Especiales de la República Bolivariana de Venezuela. Un modelo revolucionario para la economía*. MPP: Venezuela.

MPPCYT (Ministerio del Poder Popular para Ciencia y Tecnología). 2024. "Venezuela y China conmemoran 50 años de relaciones bilaterales" *MPPCYT*, June 28.

MPPI (Ministerio del Poder Popular para las Industrias). 2014. *Memoria 2013*. MPPI: Venezuela.

MPPI (Ministerio del Poder Popular para las Industrias). 2016. *Memoria 2015*. MPPI: Venezuela.

MRE (Ministerio del Poder Popular para las Relaciones Exteriores de Venezuela). 2001. *Memorando de Entendimiento entre el Ministerio de Energía y Minas de la República Bolivariana de Venezuela y la Comisión Estatal de Planificación y Desarrollo de la República Popular China sobre la Cooperación Energética Decenal (2001-2011)*. Embajada de Venezuela ante la República Popular China: China.

MRE (Ministerio del Poder Popular para las Relaciones Exteriores de Venezuela). 2013. *Memoria 2012*. MRE: Venezuela.

MRE (Ministerio del Poder Popular para las Relaciones Exteriores de Venezuela). 2010. *Acuerdos suscritos entre la República Bolivariana de Venezuela y la República Popular China. (Registrados por la embajada en Beijing al 25 de marzo de 2010)*. Embajada de Venezuela ante la República Popular China: China.

MOFCOM (Ministry of Commerce), NBS (National Bureau of Statistics) and SAFE (State Administration of Foreign Exchange). 2021. 2019 *Statistical Bulletin of China's Outward Foreign Direct Investment*. MOFCOM, NBS and SAFE: Beijing.

Moleiro, Alonso. 2019. "China National Petroleum paraliza sus inversiones en Venezuela". *El País*, September 5.

Molina Medina, Norbert. 2018. "Las relaciones diplomáticas Venezuela-China (1974-1999)" *Humania Del Sur 25*, pp. 79–102.

NTN24. 2023. "Maduro crea cuatro "zonas económicas especiales" y niega la recesión". *NTN24*, August 11.

Observatorio de la Política China. 2013. "Venezolanos recibirán capacitación en China sobre ingeniería satelital". *Observatorio de la Política China*, June 23.

Paredes, Andrey. 2022. *Impacto de la deuda china en Venezuela.* Transparencia Venezuela: Caracas.

People's Daily News. 2001. "Go Global investment strategy needed for Chinese enterprises". *China.org*, September 12.

PDVSA (Petróleos de Venezuela, S.A.). 2010. "Reservas probadas de Venezuela ascienden a 211 mil 173 millones de barriles". PDVSA, March 18.

PDVSA (Petróleos de Venezuela, S.A.). 2016. *Informe de Gestión Anual 2016.* PDVSA: Venezuela.

Piña, Carlos. 2019/a. "Chinese financing in Venezuela (2000-2018). Joint funds and loans-for-oil". In, Dussel Peters, Enrique (edit.). *Chinas Financing in Latin America and the Caribbean.* Universidad Nacional Autónoma de México (UNAM): Mexico, pp. 337–371.

Piña, Carlos. 2019/b. "Chinese OFDI in Venezuela (2000-2017). Conditions, challenges, and policy proposals". In, Dussel Peters, Enrique (edit.). *China´s Foreign Direct Investment in Latin America and the Caribbean. Conditions and challenges.* Universidad Nacional Autónoma de México (UNAM): Mexico, pp. 211-229.

Piña, Carlos. 2019/c. "Inversiones y préstamos chinos en el sector petrolero venezolano (2000-2018)". *Cuadernos de Trabajo del Cechimex 1*, pp. 1-18.

Piña, Carlos. 2024. "China: a silent ally protecting Venezuela's Maduro". CADAL, July 22.

Prensa IFE. 2009. "Se inician obras ferroviarias del tramo Tinaco – Anaco". *Aporrea*, October 14.

Prensa MAT. 2012. "Proyecto Integral de Desarrollo Agrario Río Tiznado cultivó 10 mil hectáreas de cereales". *Prensa MAT*, May 22.

Prensa MPPTTOP. 2015. "Inaugurada en Yaracuy primera planta de autobuses Yutong del continente". *Prensa* MPPTTOP, December 2.

Prensa PDVSA. 2006. "Gobierno venezolano pone fin a la producción de Orimulsión". *Aporrea*, September 25.

Prensa RNV. 2011. "2.500 millones de dólares invierten en el tercer puente del Río Orinoco". *Aporrea,* June 21.

RNV (Radio Nacional de Venezuela). 2017. "Aprueban ampliación del muelle Palúa de Ferrominera del Orinoco. Radio Nacional De Venezuela. RNV, January 29.

Reuters. 2014. "ICSID: Venezuela must pay Exxon $ 1.6B for Nationalizations". *Voz de América,* October 9.

Reuters. 2014. "Venezuela negocia con China periodo de gracia para préstamos de crudo". *El Economista,* June 14.

Reuters. 2019. "Venezuela expande capacidad de producción de petrolera conjunta con China". *Reuters*, August 8.

Reuters. 2022/a. "US to let Eni, Repsol ship Venezuela oil to Europe for debt: Sources". *The Economic Times*, June 6.

Reuters. 2022/b. "Chinese Defense Firm Has Taken Over Lifting Venezuelan Oil for Debt Offset, Sources Say". *Voz de América,* August 26.

Reuters. 2023. "China, Venezuela upgrade ties to "all-weather strategic partnership," state media report". *Reuters*, September 13.

Ríos, Xulio. 2009. *China y Venezuela: una amistad con reparos.* Instituto Galego De Análise E Documentación Internacional (IGADI): Galicia-España.

Romero, Simón. 2000. "World Business Briefing: Americas; Venezuela- China fuel deal". *The New York Times,* April 18.

Segovia, María. 2021. "El tren chino del progreso descarriló en los Llanos venezolanos". *The Dialogue Earth,* March 3.

Smolanski, Claudia. 2023. "Las promesas sobre la fábrica de autobuses Yutong se cobraban como si se cumplieran". *Fundación Andrés Bello*, May 17.

Stiglitz, Joseph. 2016. *¿Cómo hacer que funciones la globalización?* Penguin Random House: Barcelona.

SWI Swissinfo.ch. 2019. "Embargo de EEUU al petróleo de Venezuela deja a China y Rusia como salvavidas" SWI, April 25.

The Carter Center. 2012. *Misión de Estudio del Centro Carter Elecciones Presidenciales en Venezuela el 7 de Octubre de 2012. Informe Final.* The Carter Center: United States.

UN (Últimas Noticias). 2020. "Asociación Venezuela-China elevará capacidad productiva del país". *UN*, January 3.

UNCTAD (United Nations Commission for Trade and Development). 2024. *Foreign direct investment: Inward and outward flows and stock, annual.* UNTACD: Geneva.

EIA (U.S. Energy Information Administration). 2019. Background reference: Venezuela. EIA.

YVKE Mundial. 2018. "VIT ha ensamblado 1 millón 350 mil equipos desde su creación". YVKE *Mundial*, February 26.

Vyas, Kejal. 2012. "Venezuela venderá un 10% de Petroplar a la china Citic". *The Wall Street Journal*, February 28.

VTV (Venezolana de Televisión). 2019. "Gobierno Nacional aprobó recursos para ampliación de fábrica de autobuses Yutong en Venezuela". VTV, March 21.

World Bank. 2024. *World Integrated Trade Solution*. Washington, D.C.: World Bank.

Zerpa, Ivan. 2016. "Programa de viviendas en Venezuela con respaldo chino, ejemplo de cooperación Sur-Sur". *China Hoy*, May 30.

3. The Impacts of Chilean Exports to China of the Cherry Global Value Chain

Dorotea López, Andrés Bórquez and
Juan E. Serrano-Moreno

1. Introduction[1]

Since the end of the twentieth century, the bilateral relationship between China and Chile has been strengthened mainly thanks to bilateral trade, as both countries joined the Asia-Pacific Economic Cooperation (APEC) in 1991 and 1994, respectively, as well as the World Trade Organization, which Chile joined in 1995, later supporting the entry of the People's Republic in 2001. The rapprochement between the two allowed Chile to become the first country in the Latin American region to sign a Free Trade Agreement (FTA) with China in 2005, with entry into force in October 2006. The agreement was promoted to foster bilateral trade and cooperation and made China Chile's leading trading partner, increasing trade fivefold in the first ten years since its implementation. Today, China is the leading destination for Chilean exports –over one-third of its total– of which around two-thirds are copper and derived products. In 2015, the suppression of ex-

1 The authors thank the editor for his detailed comments on an earlier version of the manuscript and gratefully acknowledge the financial support for this study by the National Agency of Innovation and Development of Chile (ANID) through the Millennium Science Initiative Program NSC2022 053 and project Fondecyt Regular n. 1240664.

port tariffs on agricultural products from Chile to China ignited a "cherry boom" with significant effects on the Chilean economy.

Chile has a significant advantage among the leading cherry producers as the country harvests and processes the fruit just in time for the Lunar New Year, the biggest celebration in Chinese culture. In the last decade, cherries have penetrated Chinese consumption habits and have become a highly symbolic milestone for the urbanized middle class, who see this sweet red fruit as a sign of prosperity, affection, trust, and even social distinction. This phenomenon created a lucrative opportunity for Chilean agribusinesses, who rapidly concentrated resources on producing and commercializing the fruit. Nevertheless, as noted by the recent case report prepared by the Chilean research center ICLAC (Montt *et al.* 2024), the Chilean cherry industry is highly exposed to global and local factors, especially agricultural worker shortage, water scarcity due to climate change, and the impact of geopolitics on trade and foreign investment. For this reason, it is necessary to rethink its future development to reduce risks and develop sustainable competitive advantages (Olavarrieta and Ellinger 1997).

One frequent criticism of the increasing trade between China and Chile is that it has perpetuated the recommodification pattern within the export sector between the central and peripherical economies in which the former exports to the later raw materials with no added value. Indeed, scholarly work in political economy has consistently highlighted the increasing economic dependence of Latin American countries on China, with Chile being a prominent example, primarily due to deindustrialization and insufficient economic diversification (Ahumada 2019:177-181; Jenkins 2018:655-656; Gallagher 2016:99-105; Hung 2015:108-111). It is also theorized that commodity upgrading can be relevant for those countries that produce commodities, which can offer development opportunities but also entail risks that must be carefully managed by producing countries. In other words, natural resources can be both a blessing and a curse for developing countries. However, if adequately managed, resource-rich countries can avoid falling into the commodity dependence trap (Collier 2007).

The case of Chilean cherry exports to China shows there is room "to move from low-value to relatively high-value activities in global production networks" (Gereffi, Bamber and Fernandez-Stark 2022:6-7). Thanks to the Chinese demand, Chile is today the global leader in the cherry business. This leadership would only have happened with the sophistication of the production and distribution developed by Chilean companies. Since Chile accounts for 45.3 % of global cherry exports, working on economic upgrading would strengthen value added in production and thus strengthen the national industry. Hence, analyzing the strategy of Chilean cherry producers and exporters contributes to understanding how the Global Value Chains (GVC) are governed nowadays. For this, we borrow Gary Gereffi's theoretical proposal on the study of GVCs adopting a "systematic approach to economic development that combines broad analyses of global industry structures and trends with detailed mapping of national value chains and with local economic clusters, based on existing economic statistics from interviews and field research involving lead firms and intermediaries, national suppliers and institutional participants" (Gereffi 2018:13).

This study analyses the advantages, lessons learned, and upgrading challenges identified in the cherry GVC, focusing on the production, processing, distribution, marketing, and consumption stages. Our objective is to analyze the wider economic implications of the cherry trade for Chile, including its role in job creation and income generation and its influence on bilateral relations between Chile and China. The study relies on an exploratory analysis that examines publicly available documents produced by Chilean authorities, specialized media, companies, and business associations. This work is enriched with data on international trade and interviews with experts and stakeholders in the cherry industry.

Based on the academic literature, the first section of this study presents the long-standing relationship between Chile and China, looking at critical events and diplomatic exchanges that have shaped their relationship over time. The second focuses on bilateral trade, specifically the trade dynamics in cherries, analyzing data from Chile's Undersecretariat of International Economic Relations (*Subsecretaría de Relaciones Económicas Internacionales*) and Chile's Office of Agricultural Studies and Policies (*Oficina de Estudios y Políticas Agrarias*). The third section, interviews with farmers, exporters, and trade officials, will be analyzed in light of the cherry GVC stages, along with the content of specialized press in the Chilean agroindustrial sector, such as Simfruit, SmartCherry, and Cerezos Chile. Finally, the findings culminate in actionable insights and overall conclusions.

1. Overall Socioeconomic and Historical Relationship Between Chile and China

Over the last fifty years, Chile and the People's Republic of China have undergone significant political, economic, and cultural transformations. These changes, often radical, have taken place in a relatively short period within a framework of integration and openness towards an increasingly globalized world. In this context, beyond periods of closeness and ideological distancing, both nations have decided to establish a solid relationship based on the principles of state policy, prioritizing continuity, non-intervention in internal affairs, and the search for mutual benefits based on economic complementarity (Bórquez, López and Muñoz 2021).

The formal start of diplomatic relations between Chile and China dates back to December 1970, when Chile, under the government of President Salvador Allende, became the first South American country to establish ties with the People's Republic of China (PRC) and recognize its 'one China' policy. This rapprochement was ideologically motivated, as in the case of Cuba (Matta 1991). Three years after relations were established, the Allende government was overthrown, which led Chile into a period of military dictatorship. In the context of the Cold War, many believed that relations between Chile and China would cool. Nevertheless, both countries kept diplomatic channels open (Matta 1991). This behaviour is testimony to the pragmatism that has characterized

Chinese diplomatic relations, in which nations of ideologically opposed regimes seek a relationship that transcends their differences. China's re-entry into the United Nations in 1971 and President Richard Nixon's official visit to Beijing in 1972 marked the beginning of a more pragmatic approach to Chinese foreign policy (Kissinger 2017). During this decade, several Latin American countries, including five linked to the Alliance for Progress, established diplomatic relations with Beijing, reflecting the growing pragmatism in international politics. When faced with the dilemma of maintaining ideological consistency or avoiding isolation, Chile chose the latter, identifying China as a promising destination for its mineral exports with the purpose of strengthening a tactical partnership on the global stage (Fermandois 1985). This pragmatism was evident when, after Augusto Pinochet's rise to power, China reaffirmed its support for Chilean sovereignty in Antarctica (Compa 2001).

In the mid-1980s and with greater force in the early 1990s, Chile and China initiated a policy of international insertion that marked a significant change in their diplomatic relations. To attract foreign investment and promote international trade, both nations implemented unilateral tariff reductions and invested significantly in road infrastructure to ease the flow of goods. These dynamics, together with Chile's return to democracy, laid the foundations for a new direction in Sino-Chilean relations (Gachúz 2012).

The new insertion stage in the international economy was consolidated in 2002, when China, in a rapprochement with Chile during the APEC Leaders Summit held in Santiago in 2004, proposed negotiating an FTA –the first of its kind negotiated by China with a Latin American country. Chile had demonstrated its support for China's insertion into the world trading system, actively participating in its accession process to the World Trade Organisation (WTO) and recognizing it as a market economy. After a pragmatic negotiation, the FTA was signed in 2005 at the APEC Leaders Summit in Busan, Korea. Although the treaty did not cover all the typical provisions, Chile was privileged in the trade relationship with China. The agreement has been periodically revised and further developed since then, particularly in 2018.

The political aspect of these relations has taken on a prominent role, reflected in official visits and the creation of consultation mechanisms. Since the return to democracy, all Chilean presidents have made at least one official visit to China, regardless of their political ideology. On the Chinese side, the last three presidents have also visited Chile, demonstrating a sustained bilateral interest in strengthening ties. In the last ten years, bilateral relations between Chile and China have been marked by new impulses that, unlike in previous decades, have taken on a multidimensional character. This change was formalized in 2016 when both countries reaffirmed their commitment to becoming "comprehensive strategic partners," the highest level of bilateral cooperation for Chinese foreign policy (Bórquez and Bravo 2021). Although this is not a binding agreement, it reinforces a multidimensional cooperation framework that includes science and technology cooperation, city-to-city collaboration, and ongoing consultation processes. Later, in 2018, Chile signed a memorandum of understanding with China to jointly advance the Belt and Road Initiative, which was expected to improve the connectivity between the two countries by attracting Chinese foreign direct investment and encouraging the participation of Chinese companies in public procurements to build infrastructures (Serrano-Moreno 2024). However, rising tensions between the major Western powers and China have forced middle powers, such as Chile, to navigate and make strategic decisions in a scenario where mistrust and strategic competition leave less room for cooperation in key areas such as public infrastructures and technology (Kuik 2024; Montt, Chan and Serrano-Moreno 2023).

The export of copper and other minerals from Chile to China has been progressively complemented by other products, such as wood pulp, cellulose, and fruit (see Table 1). However, this growth has posed new challenges, such as establishing new administrative offices to manage these trade relations effectively. An important aspect is the criticism of Chile's growing dependence on its natural resources and specialization in a single market, China. This issue has become one of the main concerns in the economic relationship as diversifying the export basket becomes crucial. In 2019, after a joint evaluation of the FTA, both countries began a deepening phase focused on increasing investments in both directions and diversifying the commercial offer (López, Bórquez and Serrano-Moreno 2023).

2. Significance of the Country's Trade with China

2.1. Bilateral Trade General Characterization

After the China-Chile FTA entry into force in October 2006, trade flows took little time to improve since between 2003 and 2005 Chile's average exports to China were 3.8 billion USD, while by 2007, the figure reached 10.5 billion USD (Figure 1). This situation was strengthened by the increase in the diversification of exports, mainly in the chemical and agricultural sectors. In addition, the FTA considered the immediate tariff relief of 92 % of the products to be exported, accompanied by progressive decreases for up to ten years. Thus, in 2015, zero tariffs on agricultural products between Chile and China were reached (Reyes 2021:11). This fact is of great relevance for agricultural trade since, by the following year, fruits and vegetables exported from Chile reached a growth of 55.5 % in the Chinese market (OEC 2024).

Notably, this is the first FTA between China and a Latin American country to undergo a deepening process. In 2019, new productive sectors were negotiated, making the Sino-Chilean free trade zone the most open in the People's Republic. This treaty became a key milestone in establishing China as Chile's primary trading partner. In this sense, during 2023, China reached 39 % of Chile's exports (Central Bank of Chile 2024). On the other hand, in the same period, Chile positioned itself as China's second-largest trading partner in Latin America, preceded by Brazil. The Sino-Chilean trade growth reached a sustained growth of 7.9 % between 2018 and 2023 that, even with the covid-19 pandemic, was not affected, in addition to an 11.1 % growth in non-mining and non-cellulose products (Subrei 2024/a), reaching in 2023 37,449 million USD exported to China and 27,100 million USD imported from that country (Figure 1).

Figure 1. Total export trade between China and Chile (2005-2023) (billions of USD)

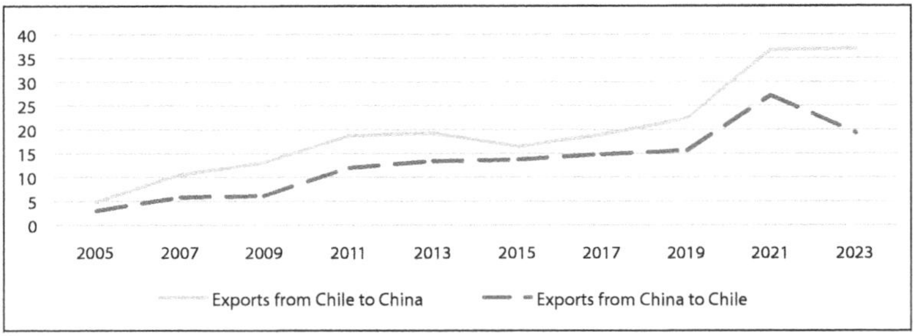

Source: Compiled from Subsecretaría de Relaciones Económicas Internacionales de Chile (2024).

As noted (López and Muñoz 2021), the Chilean export basket to China is heavily concentrated in copper and derivatives, which represent 66.6 % in 2023 of total exports (Table 1) (Central Bank 2023). However, after the disappearance of the tariff for the entry of Chilean agricultural products in 2015, a possible trend towards diversification of this basket could be observed (Serrano-Moreno *et al.* 2021). This "green shoot" was not confirmed in subsequent years due to the persistent high demand for minerals from the Chinese industry and the concentration of agricultural exports in cherries.

Between 2010 and 2022, the share of cherries in Chile's agricultural exports increased significantly, from 4.83 % to 25.26 %. This growth suggests that both production and demand for cherries have increased considerably, reflecting an evolution in the preferences of mainly Asian consumers and the sophistication of Chilean agribusiness production and commercialization (Table 2 and Figure 2).

Table 1. Chile: Main products exported to China in 2023 (billions USD).

	Description	Export (Dollars)	Percentage of Total Exports to China
Copper ore and concentrates	Chile produces 25.3 % of the world's total. They are used in the technology and construction industry.	17.4 billion USD exported to China.	47.03 % of Chile's total exports to China.
Cathodes and sections of refined copper cathodes	Chile is the world's leading exporter, generating 21 % of global exports. They are used in the electrical industry.	6.072 billion USD exported to China.	16.41 % of Chile's total exports to China.
Lithium carbonates	Chile is the world's top exporter, generating 79.9 % of lithium carbonate. They are used in high-precision technology.	3.245 billion USD exported to China.	8.77 % of Chile's total exports to China.
Fresh cherries	45.3 % of the world's cherry production is in Chile. Since 2015, there have been zero tariffs on cherry exports to China.	2.11 billion USD exported to China.	5.7 % of Chile's total exports to China.
Iron ore fines and concentrates, non-agglomerated	A large part of production is exported to Asia, with 73 % going to China.	1.19 billion USD exported to China.	3.22 % of Chile's total exports to China.
Chemical wood pulp, soda or sulfate, semi-bleached or bleached, coniferous	Chile is the world's fifth-largest producer; Asia is the leading import partner. Used for making boxes or Kraft paper.	880 million USD exported to China.	2.38 % of Chile's total exports to China.
Lithium sulfate	This product has gained importance in international trade for use in electric vehicles and lithium-ion batteries.	709 million USD exported to China.	1.92 % of Chile's total exports to China.
Chemical wood pulp, soda or sulfate, semi-bleached or bleached, eucalyptus	Small production worldwide. Used for fine paper like magazines, newspapers, and sanitary products.	637 million USD exported to China.	1.72 % of Chile's total exports to China.
Copper anodes with copper content equal to or greater than 99 % and thickness less than 10 mm	Highly pure, small product with a high percentage of copper. They are used in electrical and industrial applications.	559 million USD exported to China.	1.51 % of Chile's total exports to China.

Source: Subsecretaría de Relaciones Económicas Internacionales de Chile (2024).

Table 2. Vegetable and other vegetable exports (2010-2022) (Billions of USD)

	Grapes	Cherries	Apples	Cranberries, Bilberries & Similar Fruits	Avocados	Other vegetable products
2010	30.9 %	5.7 %	14.7 %	7.9 %	4.4 %	36.4 %
2011	29.3 %	7.2 %	13.5 %	8.0 %	4.4 %	37.7 %
2012	28.6 %	7.5 %	14.4 %	7.9 %	3.5 %	38.2 %
2013	28.4 %	7.0 %	15.0 %	8.0 %	3.6 %	38.1 %
2014	26.2 %	10.2 %	13.1 %	9.3 %	4.7 %	36.5 %
2015	24.9 %	9.3 %	10.1 %	9.7 %	4.4 %	41.6 %
2016	22.9 %	13.6 %	11.5 %	10.5 %	6.6 %	35.0 %
2017	21.3 %	9.7 %	11.4 %	8.4 %	9.1 %	40.1 %
2018	18.6 %	16.9 %	11.1 %	9.6 %	5.2 %	38.5 %
2019	17.9 %	22.9 %	8.8 %	8.1 %	5.9 %	36.4 %
2020	15.6 %	23.5 %	8.8 %	8.2 %	4.7 %	39.2 %
2021	13.5 %	23.8 %	8.9 %	8.5 %	4.6 %	40.7 %
2022	14.8 %	28.6 %	8.0 %	6.5 %	3.6 %	38.5 %
Total	21.7 %	15.3 %	11.2 %	8.5 %	5.0 %	38.3 %

Source: Subsecretaría de Relaciones Económicas Internacionales de Chile (2024).

Figure 2. Proportion of Cherries in Main Vegetable Exports from Chile (2010-2022) (Billions of USD)

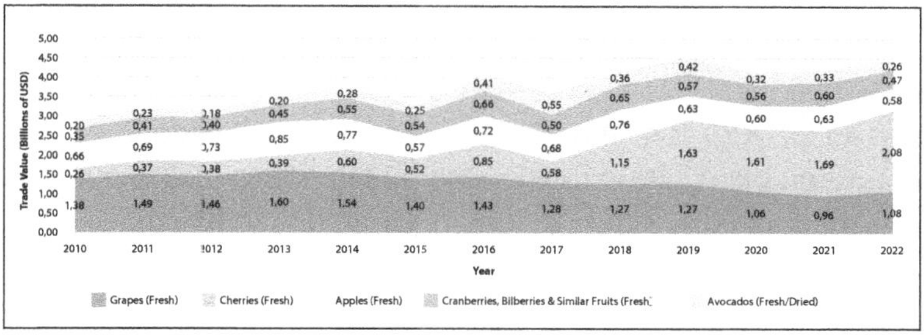

Source: Own elaboration based on data from the Observatory of Economic Complexity, regarding exports for products in HS2 06 (Vegetable Products) from Chile for 2022 (latest data available and consulted on September 28, 2024).

2.2. Chilean Cherries Exports

The recent export of Chilean cherries to China is crucial for understanding the Chilean export model. This model selects products to diversify its export basket based on the logic of comparative advantages. At the same time, it takes advantage of the preferential access provided by the FTA between the two countries, strengthening competitiveness in an expanding market such as the Chinese one. Cherries are Chile's third main non-mineral export, reaching 2,346.3 million USD, and are preceded by the export of salmon, trout, and cellulose (Servicio Nacional de Aduanas 2023).

Chile produces several cherry varieties; however, the most exported are *prunus cerasus*, the most acidic fruit, and *prunus avium*, the traditional sweet cherry. China is the world's fifth largest importer of *prunus cerasus*, followed by Germany, Russia, Qatar, and Singapore; it is also the leading importer of *prunus avium*. Together, both strains account for the 2.09 billion USD that Chile exported to the Asian country in 2023 (Subrei 2024/a).

Chile is the world leader in cherry production, with 413,979 tons of cherries exported in the 2023-2024 season, of which 377,000 tons went to China (Smartcherry 2024/a). In 2022, Chile produced 45.3 % of global cherry exports, followed by Hong Kong

(28.1 %), the United States (7.51 %), Turkey (3.16 %), and Spain (2.4 %) (Table 3). Chile leads cherry production in South America, representing 95.7 % of the total export supply from the southern hemisphere. During the 2021-2022 season, it exported 356,345 tons, making it the region's top exporter, followed by Argentina, Australia, New Zealand, and South Africa (Garrido 2023). In Latin America, Chile is also the leading exporter, with 380,000 tons exported, of which the Andean country currently exports 99 % (Smartcherry 2024/b). However, this leadership hides a strong dependence on the Chinese market, which in the 2023-24 season received 91 % of total Chilean cherry exports.

Table 3. Which countries export cherries (fresh)? (2022) (Billion of USD)

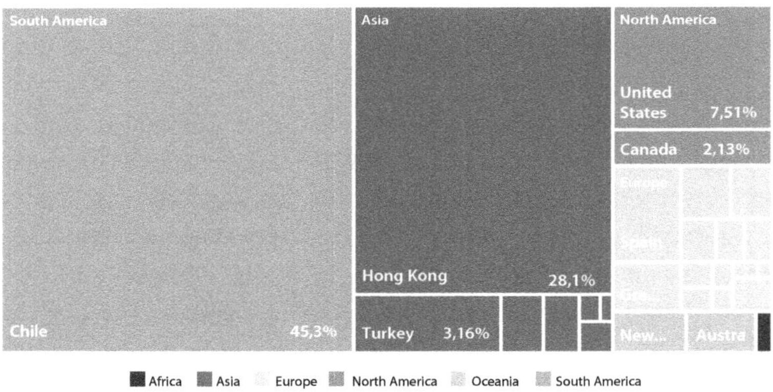

Source: Compiled from The Observatory of Economic Complexity (2024).

During the recent 2023-2024 season, cherries in Chile reached a historic figure, representing 40 % of the country's fruit exports and an increase of 1,555 million USD during January 2024 exports (ProChile 2024/a). This significant growth in the industry compared to the situation twenty years ago; in 2004, Chile exported $ 1,848 million FOB, while today, the figure is more than surpassed with $ 5,065 million FOB, with shipments reaching 88 international markets. The fresh cherry market is expected to grow and expand the destination markets since Asia, as the leading destination, currently accounts for about 94 % of exports. More hectares are being allocated to cultivation in the country, occupying 16.4 % of the fruit-growing areas to generate more extensive production, while the value of the fruit is increasing, to the detriment of other fresh fruits exported by the country, such as blueberries, grapes and peaches (Briceño and Méndez 2024).

During the 2023-2024 season, Asia remains the leading importer of fresh cherries from Chile, receiving 388,171 tons, while the United States imported 13,977 tons, the Latin American region 7,296 tons, Europe 3,850 tons, and Canada 685 tons. It is worth mentioning that there were decreases in all regions except East Asia, where the figures remained relatively similar, with a growth of 1.5 % (SmartCherry 2024). In this sense, among the leading importers of Chilean cherries –besides China– the United States stands out with 15.91 % of imports in 2021, Japan with 7.65 %, South Korea with 4.94 %, and Brazil with 4.55 % (The Atlas of Economic Complexity 2024).

The case of Hong Kong is noteworthy, as fresh cherries represent Chile's main export to this market, reaching 8.4 million USD in 2024 (Subrei 2024/b). Chile's 2012 Free Trade Agreement with Hong Kong eliminated tariffs on various products, including cherries. The "high administrative autonomy" of the Hong Kong region, enshrined in the Constitution of the People's Republic of China and the Basic Law of the Region, allows the region to have its own customs union and a limited international legal personality that allows it to conclude FTAs with third countries (Sun, 2008; Serrano-Moreno, 2021). As a result, Hong Kong has developed as an easily accessible trade center, with FTAs with the People's Republic of China, New Zeland, EFTA (Iceland, Liechtenstein, Norway, and Switzerland), Chile, Macao, ASEAN, Australia, and Peru (Yeung 2024; WTO n.d.).

As shown in Table 3, Hong Kong is the second largest exporter of cherries worldwide, exporting 99.9 % of the fruit to the People's Republic of China In 2022. However, 88.1 % of the cherries imported to Hong Kong came from Chile (The Atlas of Economic Complexity, 2024). Since the region does not have the necessary geography to harvest this fruit, it has positioned itself as a "re-export" center thanks to its geographical position and high-end services in the distribution, financial, and logistics sectors. Hence, Hong Kong represents a privileged platform for Chilean exporters to reach the Guangdong market, one of China's wealthiest (Simfruit 2024). Thus, from the export of cherries, they generate 1.29 billion USD, equivalent to 1.14 % of their total exports, from the 42.3 billion USD of cherries imported from the Chilean market, as shown in Table 3 (OEC 2024).

Locally, Chilean cherry export growth has positively impacted the economy, creating jobs and fostering development in the producing regions. The remaining problem is that more and more producers are attracted by the "cherry boom," generating a new concentration and dependence cycle. Therefore, studying the different GVC stages offers valuable insights for economic development and formulating trade strategies that promote sustainable and balanced growth.

3. Impact of Exports to China in the Cherry GVC

The global value chain (GVC) refers to a product's various stages, from conception to its final delivery to the consumer. In particular, it pays attention to how economic actors, such as governments, companies, workers, or entire regions, develop activities that generate low value added to those that generate higher value. Value chain scaling is crucial because it enables countries and companies to improve their competitiveness and sustainability. This process is neither linear nor predictable; it can be complicated and face several challenges, such as the need for investment in skills, infrastructure, and technologies (Bamber and Fernandez-Stark 2016; Gereffi, Bamber and Fernandez-Stark 2022).

3.1. The Stages of the Chilean Cherry GVC

The Cherry GVC is composed of four main stages, which are detailed below. The basis used to identify these stages was extracted from two publications: "Global Value Chains in Agriculture and Food," published by OECD (2020), and "Fresh Cherry Industry in Chile" by Bamber and Fernandez-Stark (2016). The development of these steps for the cherry case is also based on the analysis of interviews and review of official documents.

1. Production: This stage involves the cultivation of cherry trees, selection of cherry varieties, agronomic management practices, and harvesting of cherries at the right time to ensure quality.
2. Processing: After harvest, the cherries undergo a series of processes that include obtaining the necessary permits, grading the fruit based on quality and size, and packaging it appropriately for distribution.
3. Logistics: Effective logistics are critical to maintaining the freshness of the cherries. This includes transporting the harvested cherries from the orchards to the distribution centers while ensuring proper refrigeration throughout the journey.
4. Marketing and final consumption: The final stage includes both wholesale and retail activities that can take place in local markets, grocery stores, supermarkets, and export channels. Various marketing strategies increase brand awareness and drive sales, catering to consumer preferences and market segments.

3.1.1. Production

The cherry planting season in Chile is divided into two periods: during the winter, a one-year-old plant from the nursery is planted, while in the spring (between October and November), a three-month-old plant that already has growing leaves is planted. Throughout the fall and winter, the cherries are grown, and weather conditions play a crucial role in the optimal development of the fruit. The topography of central and southern Chile provides an ideal environment for cultivation, and various production techniques are used, such as outdoor cultivation in greenhouses, vertical systems, or high tunnels. With the arrival of spring, harvesting begins and lasts from October until 80 % of production is reached between December and January. This period is critical, so it is expected to outsource labor. Experts indicate that the demand for seasonal workers is increasing due to the expansion of cherry plantations. It is estimated that by the 2025 season, around 469,000 seasonal workers will be needed to meet the high demand from November to January, which coincides with the period leading up to the Chinese New Year. Finally, there is a selection process in which the fruit that meets the technical and phytosanitary requirements for export is selected. It should be noted that the cherry plants produce fruit in the third year.

One of the characteristics of the production stage highlighted in the interviews is the high degree of collaboration between the different participants. This collaboration is because shared learning serves to grow the business. As one interviewee explains:

> *Cherries are highly perishable and delicate, and their main market, China, is the farthest from Chile. Nearly 90 % of the harvest is shipped there. Therefore, every factor is meticulously taken care of, and everything has to do with the care of the fruit, from planting the tree until the fruit is available in the market to be sold in China. For example, the cherry, in particular, in the harvesting process, has a characteristic that you do not see in other fruits, and that is that it is harvested early in the morning so that the heat does not affect it. Harvesting typically runs from 11:00 to 11:30 AM. It is intentionally limited to avoid working during the peak heat of late November, December, beginning of January* (Interview n.1)[2].

2 Interviewee profile: Executive of the business association Frutas de Chile, interview conducted in October 2024.

According to the business association *Frutas de Chile*, records are expected to be broken in the 2024-2025 season, with a 59% growth over the previous year. This translates into 131,587,007 boxes of fresh cherries of 5 kilos, equivalent to 657,935 tons (EMOL 2024). This expansion responds to the high Chinese demand and has been supported by developing an integrated structure between producers and exporters to optimize the supply chain. The leading export companies are San Francisco Lo Garcés, Copefrut, Dole Chile, Exportadora Rancagua, and Frutera San Fernando.

3.1.2. Processing

International sanitary and phytosanitary standards are essential for preserving the quality of the product during transport. As an agricultural exporting country, Chilean authorities have developed a complex compliance system with sanitary and phytosanitary measures. Chile's Agriculture and Livestock Service (SAG) conducts quality inspections according to international phytosanitary standards; some guidelines are related to the appearance of cherries, crop pest control, and soil quality. It has defined guidelines for the export of cherries to China that involve measures at the orchard level, pest control, establishment level, packaging, and sanitary and phytosanitary records.

Interviews with key actors indicate that the packinghouse industry has gone hand in hand with the cherry industry in terms of manufacturing better and better machines to ensure their good arrival to the market. Here, a process is developed in which knowledge and services are generated to control temperature during harvest, transport, and inside the plant. A cherry plant must be fully refrigerated, i.e., with the ambient temperature inside the plant at a low level. Most of the packing is imported from France and New Zealand; however, these processes have more and more Chilean content.

3.1.3. Logistics

In cherry logistics, it is essential to maintain the cold chain and not handle the cherries during transport from Chile to the final destination. Cherries are delicate and perishable products requiring special packaging and controlled conditions to guarantee quality. This aspect was highlighted in all the interviews conducted:

> *The cherries leave Chile fully finished. It is a delicate and highly perishable product, which has to go in special bags that have, in fact, a controlled atmosphere, in special boxes, in trucks, in special containers, by ships that are refrigerated. The truth is that the cold chain is fundamental, and not touching the product is fundamental until the final destination is reached* (Interview n.1.).

Most fresh cherries are exported by sea, with 93.3 % reaching international markets via maritime transport. For this purpose, shipping lines offer specific services for the high export season. Among them, the leading service is "Cherry Express," launched in 2019 by Hapag-Lloyd after purchasing several state-of-the-art ships, creating a fleet composed today of 17 ships. As a result, the duration of the maritime trip was reduced from 30 to 21 days (Mundomaritimo 2019; Cooperativa 2024).

The San Antonio International Terminal (STI) is the port that concentrates these exports. The remaining volume is shipped by air (5.5 %) and land (1.2 %). In the latter case, to closer markets, mainly Brazil. The beginning of the Chilean cherry export season in mid-November represents a critical period for delivering the fruit in optimal conditions in its biggest market, China. The transport by air to China is concentrated at this time when the product reaches its highest price. Aerosan and China Eastern Airlines are the major companies providing this service. The latter has been transporting Chilean Cherries to Shanghai Pudong International Airport since 2014, reaching a capacity of 76 tones per flight that is 24 hours long (China Daily 2024).

Optimization has allowed ships to arrive on the other side of the Pacific Ocean in approximately 21 days. Furthermore, ensuring an unbroken cold chain is essential for the fruit to retain its freshness upon arrival at the destination port. Thus, while packing the cherries, local companies carefully arrange them in refrigerated trucks that transport the containers by land to the port of San Antonio or Valparaiso, where they are loaded onto the Cherry Express ships (Logistec 2023). This specialized service is the fastest in the industry and was planned by the Fresh Pass team in coordination with Maersk, including the transfer, booking, documentation, and constant checking of the products during the trip.

Upon arrival in China, the main ports receiving cherry shipments are in the Pearl River Greater Bay Area: Hong Kong, Shenzhen, and Guangzhou. At this stage, Maersk Customs House takes care of inter-port clearance so that the cargoes are cleared within three hours to other ports, such as the Port of Nansha in Guangzhou, where it is easier to distribute them inland. However, in 2024, for the first time, the Cherry Express route arrived at the port of Tianjin, which shortened transfer times to Beijing, improving logistics by reducing inspection and transfer times to the interior of the country, in addition to the costs of entry into the Chinese market (ProChile 2024/b).

3.1.4. Marketing and Consumption

The Chilean exporters have identified four zones or consumption centers for Chilean cherries in mainland China. Zone one, which covers 26 % of China's total population, is the Guangdong province, the most densely populated province in China, with 127 million inhabitants. Hong Kong, Nansha, Shekou, and Yantai ports are in this zone, through which 66 % of Chile's cherry exports entered last season. Zone two is located in the central-eastern area and covers 31 % of the Chinese population. This area includes the port of Shanghai and the Jiangxi and Shanghai markets. Zone three, located in the northern part of the East Coast, represents 15 % of the total population. The cherries arrive at the port of

Dalian before being transported to Beijing and other cities in the area. Finally, zone four, which covers 11 % of the population, is a developing area for the imported cherry market but is becoming more and more relevant. The attractiveness is due to the province of Sichuan, the Chengdu airport that receives direct shipments, and the cities of Chengdu and Chongqing. The latter has access to the Yangtze River, which connects it with the major cities of Yichang, Wuhan, Nanjing, and Shanghai. It is also connected by land to zone one and two to supply cherries from Chile.

Selling price is a crucial indicator of the level of competition in the global cherry market, underlining the importance of quality and value-added to achieve better prices in international trade. In this context, Chile is in a favorable position. The average value per kilo of cherries exported from Chile is 5.64 USD, slightly above the global average price of 5.22 USD. Since cherries are seasonal fruit sold mainly in the Chinese market, assessing Chile's competition

Figure 3. Global Trade of Fresh Cherries 2023: Quantity Sold Relative to Price per Kilo (USD)

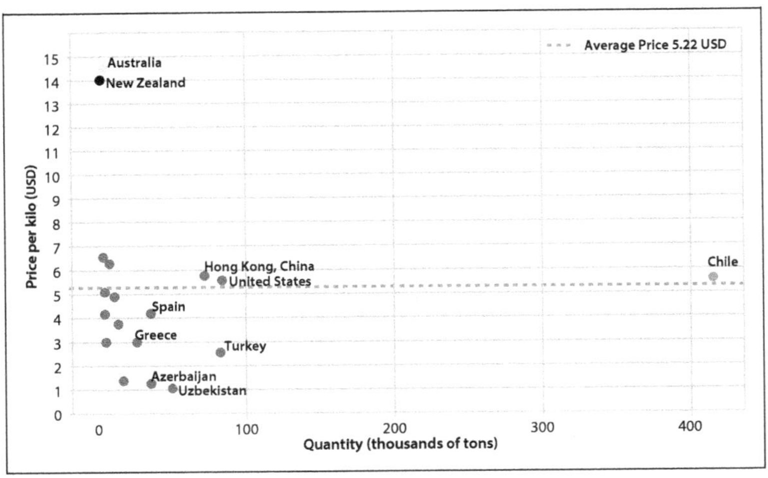

Source: Figure elaborated by Fabián Pino (2024) regarding global cherry exports with data for 2023 obtained from the World Bank in WITS. Only the top 20 producers were considered in terms of quantity.

from countries that can produce during the last three months of each calendar year is crucial. As with other fruits, these competitors tend to be from the southern hemisphere, mainly Argentina, South Africa, Australia, and New Zealand. The latter two achieve prices per kilo that significantly exceed those of Chile; however, their production volume is considerably lower, being well below the cargo exported by Chile.

The relatively high selling price of Chilean cherries in the Chinese market is due to a combination of key factors. First, seasonality plays a crucial role, as Chilean cherries are harvested when local Chinese cherries are unavailable, generating strong demand and making consumers willing to pay more for the product. In addition, the quality of Chilean cherries is internationally recognized, as their flavor, freshness, and size characterize them. This contributes to the perception of a high-quality product in the market, which increases its attractiveness to Chinese consumers. Also, cherries must meet strict sanitary standards and certifications to export to China, increasing production costs and, therefore, the product's final price. Logistics also play a role: transport costs, cold storage, and handling of cherries from Chile to China are significant, as reflected in the selling price.

Despite competition from other producing countries such as the United States, New Zealand, and Australia, Chile's harvest season advantage allows its cherries to occupy a unique niche in the market. However, from the Chilean perspective, the marketing and consumption of the cherry GVC could be improved in terms of economic upgrading. Once the fruit reaches Chinese ports, Chilean companies add little further value, as their participation in local marketing and retail services is minimal, as we explain in the next section.

3.2. Local Impacts of the Cherry Exports to China

Based on economic data and the perceptions of key actors in the cherry industry, we identified five major areas impacted locally by the evolution of the GVC due to its access to the Chinese market:

employment, innovation, and technology in production, technological changes in packaging and logistics, collaborative strategy development, and new sales strategies.

3.2.1. Impacts on Employment

The evolution of the GVC has led to labor shortages, as the Chilean cherry harvest lasts only four to five months –from late October to early February– and takes place in sparsely populated regions. Also, picking cherries from the trees implies a more intense labor force than other crops harvest because the fruit's fragility leaves little room for mechanization. By 2024, more than 400,000 workers will be harvesting and packing the 130 million boxes planned for the season. In the Maule and Bernardo O'Higgins regions, companies attract workers with special incentives like car raffles and cash prizes. Unlike other crops, such as apples, cherry producers face increasing competition for labor.

> *The cherry crop in the (Maule) region has had more incidents. In the south, it may be different; that is, in the end, cherry attracts many people, and I think they use these incentives of 'we are going to raffle a car among the people who have participated,' 'we are going to raffle, I don't know, two million pesos,' in their own words, and a lot of extra things. Other crops that needed people at that time had to adapt, as I was saying in the example of apple trees* (Interview n.2)[3].

3.2.2. Innovation and Technological Changes in Production

The increasing demand for cherries has generated profound changes in production processes in the last decade. Chile has the advantage of having a Mediterranean climate ideal for growing this fruit, with cold winters necessary for optimal growth. Indeed,

3 Interviewee profile: Official of Coquimbo Regional Government, logistic expert. Interview conducted in September 2024.

the cherry needs many hours of cold in winter so that Chile can produce between 15 and 18 tons per hectare (EMOL 2024). Unlike Peru, which competes in other fruits, such as blueberries and grapes, Chile is the only country in the region to produce high-quality cherries. In addition, local agribusinesses have invested in genetics and packaging technology to meet increasing quality and productivity challenges. This allowed for the increase in the cultivation of land surface and the adaptation to the demands of the global market and has had a positive impact not only on the shipment of cherries but also on other products, such as plums:

> *Fewer companies are making different formats, that is, formats of 2 kilos, a larger box than 3 of 2 kilos, and the total is 6 kilos or bulk boxes of 9 kilos, those are the minorities. I would say that this standard has even had repercussions and has begun to impact other items. I mean, today we have Sugar Plants, for example, which are plums because plums from there are adopting the same format, and cherries from the United States or Australia are adopting the same format we have in China. So, I think the industry is very mature and moving towards the same formats, which also helps everything. It's the entire value chain because whoever has a different format finally shoots himself in the foot because he has fewer sales channels in China* (Interview n.4).[4]

Another aspect that stands out is the commitment to sustainability. Chile has been promoting new standards in agricultural development regarding renewable energy and water use. We observed significant progress in adopting clean energy sources and irrigation practices, which has allowed for a more efficient use of water resources in agricultural production. However, more efforts will be needed to solve the water scarcity in the short and mid-term. Water scarcity is the biggest challenge for the whole Chilean agricultural sector, considering the increasing droughts provoked by climate change. Indeed, agriculture is the economic

4 Interviewee profile: General Manager of a leading cherry producer, commercialization, and consumption expert. Interview conducted in September 2024.

activity that consumes the most water in Chile and concentrates the largest of water use rights. Around 70 % of the freshwater available in the country is used for crop irrigation (Montt 2024:19). Despite the need to improve water use efficiency, the market still needs to align with this demand fully.

> *Chile is a country that has an attribute such as sustainability that is very much its own. That is, and I will give two examples, the use of energy in Chile is world-class. In other words, Chile is a world leader in conventional and non-conventional renewable energy. That, on the one hand. Secondly, water use: Chile has a much higher percentage of irrigation than the countries with which it competes, which goes back a long time. In fact, nowadays, the market does not ask for much sustainability. That is to mean, the consumer does not say, 'I am going to choose this product from this country because it is sustainable.' We have not yet reached that point. The consumer is not yet asking for that and is not yet paying for that either. Therefore, Chile has been advancing in several aspects of sustainability. Fruit growing, of course, has been advancing in that direction on its own. Because producers see it as a desirable attribute* (Interview n.1).

Concerning production growth, the hectares of plantations have grown exponentially in the last twenty years. According to the executive director of the business association *Frutas de Chile*, the country registered 16,242 hectares planted with cherry trees in 2013. In 2023, this number had increased to 63,494 hectares (EMOL 2024), representing a growth of more than 290 %. This expansion of production also translates into new plantations throughout the country. Although most cherry harvests are in the O'Higgins and Maule regions (approximately 80 %), crops have been opened in the central-northern zone, where, thanks to the climate, the fruit is harvested earlier and arrives first each year in the Asian market. Also, the Bio Bio region is expected to increase its production in the new year as its climate becomes more and more Mediterranean (Figure 4).

Figure 4. Cherry Trees Production by Region in Chile

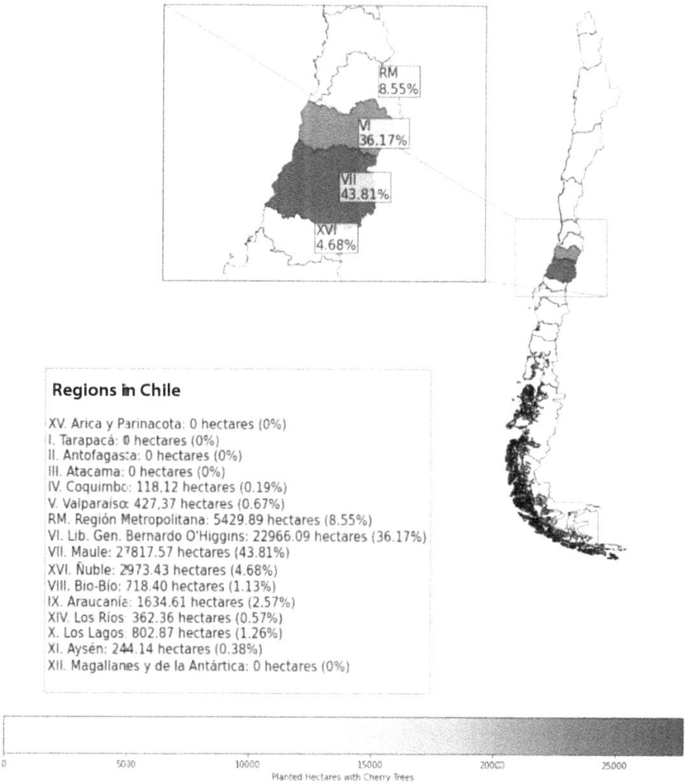

Source: The map prepared by Fabián Pino (2024) shows the number of hectares of cherry trees harvested in Chile at the regional level, using data obtained from ODEPA.

Reducing the arrival date to China is crucial to reach the highest sale prices. Some producers in the north-central zone are achieving prices of more than USD 20. This has sparked growers' interest in identifying new locations to obtain an earlier harvest. Although these shipments are smaller in volume than those in the south-central zone, they are eligible for air transport and higher prices. In any case, the three main markets maintain a price above 10 USD during the crucial dates of the Chinese New Year.

Figure 5. Average Weekly Prices of Chilean Cherries in Chinese Wholesale Markets (2023-2024) (USD)

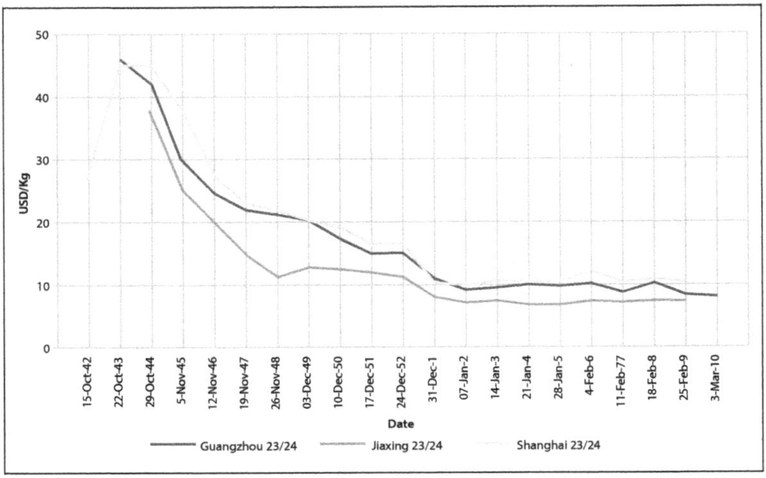

Source: Figure prepared by Fabián Pino (2024) and adapted from the original graphic in "Anuarios de Mercado 2024: Cerezas"; iQonsulting (2024).

Due to several interrelated factors, the price of cherries in China can experience drastic fluctuations from week to week during the Chinese New Year. First, demand for cherries increases significantly at this time, as they are considered a symbol of good fortune and happiness, and consumers buy them for celebrations and as gifts during the holidays. The sharp increase in demand can cause prices to skyrocket. In addition, the supply of fresh cherries is also important. The Chilean cherry harvest coincides with this season, but weather conditions and variations in production can affect availability. Prices can remain relatively stable with a good crop and a stable supply. However, prices can increase rapidly if problems such as excessive rains, pests, or other factors reduce supply.

Finally, people's buying and consumption patterns during the Chinese New Year, which often include massive purchases and stockpiling of fruit, can cause prices to spike at certain times, as retailers and wholesalers adjust their prices in response to significant demand and anticipated purchases.

3.2.3. Technological Change and Innovation in Packaging and Logistics

Significant progress has been made in the packaging process, and technology has been transferred. Previously, the bags from the United States were modified atmosphere bags, which involved injecting nitrogen to reduce oxygen.

> *The issue of the bags, which also started there, between CopeFrut and Garcés, in 1998, more or less. In the past, the bags were brought from abroad, from the United States. Biofresh was the company. They used atmosphere bags; we called them 'modified atmosphere bags.' You had to inject nitrogen to sweep out the oxygen and seal it. You had a modified atmosphere, where you were looking for 8 or 10% oxygen and 4 or 6% CO2, and that was done through a nitrogen sweep, which had a special machine that injected the nitrogen to sweep out the oxygen and achieved those concentrations* (Interview n.3).[5]

Now, thanks to developments in Chile, optimal storage conditions have been created without the need for nitrogen injection. In the packing houses, advanced technology is used to ensure uniform quality and size of the cherries, using robotic equipment and photoelectric cells for sorting. Currently, a photoelectric cell sorts the fruit according to color, flavor, and size. The entire process is robotized. This high level of technification has been fundamental for Chilean cherries to gain prestige in the international market.

> *Then there are all the other things, box-type materials, little boxes, or pins, most of which are local producers who have the business. Now, much innovation beyond what we have already achieved is rather limited because the bags are already very technological, let's say, the bags, what many people think is that we export almost raw material, and that is not so real, that is, to export fresh fruit, you cannot export it fresher*

5 Interview profile: Export technical manager and production expert at a cherry production company. Interview conducted in September 2024.

than what we already do, with the technologies we have today. That is, today, we travel 30 days or 40 days, and the fruit is still fresh, and that is allowed because of the technology that exists in the cold containers, in the bags, which allows extending the post-harvest of the fruit, which allows the gases to leave the bag. However, no new oxygen enters the product, which is pure technology. One doesn't seem to see it, but the export of fruit and cherry has much technology behind it, specifically on the subject of bags (Interview n.4).

The interviews report a rapid technologization of the sector, which initially depended on imported technology. They highlight a significant evolution in production, and technological innovations, such as the transition from mechanical machinery to advanced electronic systems for packaging, have accompanied this growth. These innovations were brought to Chile thanks to the vision of pioneering entrepreneurs such as Hernán Garcés, making the company a benchmark in the industry.

I was part of that. The largest product in Chile is Hernán Garcés, and the largest fruit exporter is Agrícola Garcés, Garcés Fruit. I have worked with them for 12 years, since 2001, when they made 135,000 boxes. Today, they make around 4 million boxes, which gives you an idea of 5 kilos. And in 2006, before 2006, we had American machines, which were mechanical, where they had a divergent caliber separator, there were two divergent tubes, from larger to smaller, and the fruit passed through there. When the divergent tube was opened, the fruit fell because of size, which was very complicated; it had a lot of wrong calibrations and many other things. In 2006, it was my turn to go to Spain through Garcés, let's say, and there they were just testing the first Unitec in the world for cherries, and we participated in that development. I told Hernán Garcés how good the machine was, and he, being the visionary that Hernán Garcés is, brought the machine to Chile. He was the first to bring the machine to Chile in this style. An electronic system of quality that made all the color issues already in electronic form, and there everything started. Hernán Garcés was a reference for using this technology, and they all later began to import the machine.

> *This was in 2006 when the big change was from mechanical to electronic* (Interview n. 3).

Although many packing houses are of foreign origin, the value of Chilean intellectual property in agricultural techniques is also highlighted, which generates a debate on the added value of technology in the local context and its origin. This virtuous circle of innovation and marketing has been key to the sector's growth.

> *I would say that (technology) is foreign at the packaging level. The big packing companies, such as Italian, French, and New Zealand, are foreign. However, also at the field level, intellectual property has been created here, which has to do with production methods, such as agricultural techniques. There is Chilean material. I think an old discussion is important for what you are doing. Some people emphasize who owns the technology and consider that it is of greater added value than the country from which it comes* (Interview n. 1).

Although Chile imports much technology, it has gradually become a benchmark in generating standards for packing export fruits.

> *The New Zealanders, who are also an agro-exporting power, come to Chile to see what we do regarding adaptability (...) I have also traveled to Spain to different parts of the world, and this year, there was a seminar in Italy, and one of the professors, who is a well-known Italian, said, 'In the past, the Chileans came here to Europe to learn from us, and today we are learning from the Chileans.' (...) Today, we are a global reference for our post-harvest technology, handling, and production to reach distant destinations with a good product. This is so important that, in several other products, for example, today in Europe. However, today, they have 8 days of travel, from when it is packed until it reaches the supermarket. Today, they look at which varieties in Chile work, which are good, and which are travelers to have them in Europe because they know that they will have the best post-harvest life in the showcase, in the Trade Life. They know that if a fruit works well in*

> *Chile, it will work very well for them too because they will have a better post-harvest life* (Interview n. 1).

Transport logistics have also been profoundly transformed to match the needs of the Chinese market. Keeping the cherries fresh after weeks of travel to Asia is crucial. In the 1990s, cherries could only be transported by plane due to their high perishability. However, a key innovation allowed the product to arrive by ship without losing its freshness: the modified atmosphere bag that absorbs oxygen and releases CO_2, allowing the cherry to last between four and six weeks. Our interviewees commented that freight dropped from20 USD per box by air to only 2 USD per box by ship.

Also, transportation lines have become more sophisticated by creating a unique premium service called "Cherry Express" in the high season. This service uses fast ships that allow direct trips to be made in approximately 22 days, facilitating the rapid arrival of fresh cherries to the Chinese market.

3.2.4. Development of Collaborative Work

Collaboration in agricultural markets is crucial. The fragile nature of exports and tight timeframes have driven the development of important cooperative efforts:

> *Collaboration is key in the background. In the fruit business, there are many actors who all contribute and are key at some point. It has been quite dynamic, how it has moved, how the crop has grown here in Chile. This has been accompanied by significant commercial potential. There have been good collaborations from the public, private, and academia and research; in the background, important efforts are being made in several regions. As I say, it is a crop that arouses a lot of interest and participation from different regional actors; we are seeing it, too; these collaborations are taking place. People come from the central or southern zone to understand how the fruit is produced here and share their experience, which has been very positive* (Interview n.2)

In this regard, there are mechanisms for collaboration between the public and private sectors. The Cherry Committee of the Exporters Association (Asoex) and foreign affairs and agriculture ministries are exploring new Asian markets. These dynamics emphasize the strategy of forming commercial alliances to expand export opportunities.

> *Another work that the Cherry Committee and Asoex are also doing, as today we depend on China, we are in principle 90 or 92% of exploring a new market. There is the whole issue of alliances. Recently, there was a tour, during the August tour to India, where the Minister of Foreign Affairs and the Minister of Agriculture went, where an agreement was signed in which we are going to establish a business agreement, precisely to strengthen this market, cherries and other products that can enter* (Interview n. 3).

The associative work focuses on establishing commercial alliances and developing marketing strategies to promote the "Chile" brand internationally. The collaboration between Chilean authorities and business associations has improved the image of Chilean cherries in China, creating its own brand and providing the local producers with designs to be used, for example, in their packages

Figure 6. Cherries from Chile registered brand logo

Sources: www.fruitsfromchile.com ; https://www.cherriesfromchile.cn/

(Figure 6). Also, the state export promotion agency (ProChile) brings Chilean producers to China to participate every year in commercial fairs –"Chile Week China"– in Beijing, Hangzhou, Chengdu, and Guangzhou, for which it also hires local online influencers (Montt *et al.* 2024:11; ProChile 2019).

Also, the actors conduct market research to understand consumers better. This reflects a strategic approach to market segmentation and tailored marketing campaigns aimed at boosting cherry exports and capitalizing on rising production volumes.

> *In that sense, we have an exporters association, and within that association, there is a branch called the Cherry Committee, where alliances are made at a commercial level, especially, where a marketing issue for the Chile brand is being raised, where it accepted a consumer study work. The Committee has even managed, for example, to characterize who buys in China, who is the one who makes the purchase decision in China, for example, it was determined that it is a woman, let's say, between 28 and 32 years old, that she is the one who makes the purchase decision to do that...* (Interview n. 3).

3.2.5. Export Challenges

While the Chilean cherry industry has positioned itself as the leading exporter in Asia, it still faces significant challenges in diversification, coordination with state actors, and maintaining competitive prices.

Although Chile leads exports in four varieties, Chilean producers are exploring new varieties to diversify the offer. However, this process is long-term, as it requires time to validate that these new varieties are well accepted by consumers and maintain good quality after harvest.

> *So, today, especially the producers, we are especially concentrated on four varieties representing around 80 % of the cherry volume, which are Lapins, Santina, Regina, and Sweetheart. Today, 80, 75, and 70 % of the fruit volume is concentrated in those four varieties, and we are already*

trying to introduce some new varieties, but that is... it is long-term, let's say. We have to validate the varieties, that the market likes them, and that they have a good post-harvest life. So, there is a lot to deal with, but today, we are mainly concentrated on four varietiew (Interview n.3).

While collaborations exist between public and private actors in the cherry industry, the state export promotion agency (ProChile) must be modernized and adapted to a constantly changing commercial environment.

Prochile is an institution that has been operating since 1980 with the same objectives, doing the same things year after year. It has not adapted to new times, technologies, or ways of doing business. If you look at the competition, you look at the Australians, the New Zealanders, and the Americans; they have a completely different approach. We continue using the same playbook that we have been using since 1980, with certain small changes, but not substantive ones (Interview n.4).

The selling prices of cherries fluctuate depending on the volume exported each season. In this sense, the industry risks facing a highly variable market, such as the agricultural market, whose price variability is well known.

However, sales prices fluctuate considerably between seasons due to variations in exported volume. (...) Last year, you could get 4 USD (per kilo) from a Lapins; the year before, it was closer to 3 USD. Production was lower in years with higher prices, which raised the market value. So normally, you can have an income of around 30,000 USD with a direct cost of 15,000 USD, and you will eventually have around 15,000 USD left in your pocket, but then you have to pay back the investment plus the interest rate you made at the beginning (Interview n. 3).

4. Conclusions and Policy Suggestions

4.1. Conclusions

Over the last two decades, China and Chile have deepened their relations, leading to expanded bilateral trade that has played a key role in sustaining Chile's economic growth. Although copper and some derivatives are the leading products exported from Chile to China, cherries have been taking a fundamental position since the end of tariffs on agricultural products in 2015. The booming export of Chilean cherries is a relatively recent phenomenon that has completely reshaped the cherry GVC with profound international and local impacts. The Andean country has exploited its geographical and climate comparative advantages that permit harvest timing to align perfectly with the Lunar New Year. The combination of China's strong demand and advancements in Chile's agribusiness, production, and logistics has positioned the latter as the world's leading cherry producer. Nevertheless, the cherry GVC is highly disaggregated, and Chilean producers exploit the less lucrative stages. Additionally, we observe three crucial challenges that need to be addressed to ensure the sustainability and upgradability of the cherry GVC: limited local labor, water scarcity, and dependence on one single market.

The production stage of the cherry GVC has experienced substantial upgrades thanks to private investments in transport, harvesting techniques, and variety selection technology. The sustained growth of the production capacity since 2015 and the competitive price of the Chilean cherries prove it. However, the impacts on labor and water resources bring new challenges.

Chile's expanding cherry industry has driven job creation, though most roles remain low-skilled, low-wage, and seasonal, tied to the harvest. Nevertheless, it is becoming more challenging every season for the producers to find enough workers to satisfy the Chinese demand. Labor scarcity represents a limit for the expansion of cherry production in the mid and long term. Also, the competition among local agribusiness companies to hire workers during the spring and summer seasons displaces traditional crops such as apples and grapes.

With droughts becoming more frequent and intense, water scarcity jeopardizes the sustainability of the cherry industry in the short and mid-term. Companies must invest heavily in state-of-the-art irrigation systems that maximize water-use efficiency by importing technology from countries such as Spain or Israel.

Logistics presents the most significant upgrade among all the stages of the cherry GVC due to reduced transport duration and packaging innovations that guarantee the cold chain until the product arrives at Chinese ports. The duration of the maritime trip has been reduced since 2019 from 30 to 21 days thanks to robust private investment in state-of-the-art ships. Also, Chile is a benchmark in generating standards for fruit-packing exports. The country's long history of fruit exports has provided invaluable experience, enabling the development of robust systems to ensure that high-quality produce reaches international markets. Companies have invested heavily in advanced technologies and practices for packing and transportation. Techniques such as temperature-controlled storage, modified atmosphere packaging, and biodegradable materials help preserve fruit quality, extending shelf life and ensuring freshness upon arrival at destinations.

Moreover, the Chilean fruit industry is characterized by continuous improvement and adaptation. Stakeholders regularly update packing standards based on international market trends and feedback, allowing Chile to respond effectively to changing consumer demands and regulatory requirements. This adaptability ensures that Chile maintains its competitive edge in various markets. These advancements enhance the quality of the exports and bolster the country's reputation as a supplier of premium fruits.

In contrast to the upgrades in production and logistics, we observed a slight improvement in the processing and marketing stages. Processing is largely reliant on imported technologies, such as packinghouse machinery, primarily sourced from Europe and New Zealand. Also, the processing is limited to fruit selection and includes no product transformation. Local industries could be developed to produce cherry-derived products with high added value, such as essential oils, juices and concentrates, jams, jellies, snacks, and frozen and dried cherries.

From the Chilean point of view, marketing and final consumption are arguably the weakest stages of the cherry GVC. These stages rely intensely on Chinese service providers. Associative work between producers and Chilean authorities has contributed to expanding the "Cherries from Chile" brand in China and celebrating yearly trade fairs. However, these actions do not allow for the effective participation of Chilean agribusiness in the marketing and consumption stage. In other words, the value added to the product by the Chilean producers stops when the cherries arrive at the Chinese ports.

On top of that, there are concerns about the concentration of the exports in one destination: around 91 % of Chilean exported cherries are destined for the Chinese market. The public-private associative work is exploring new markets in East and South Asia, but more ambitious work needs to be done to penetrate them.

The study stresses the need to diversify markets and products to lessen overreliance on the Chinese market, improve water use to adapt to climate change effects, and address technological and infrastructural challenges. Although cherry represents an export of primary goods, it includes a GVC with upgrading potential. Investing in the processing and marketing stages is essential to maximize the profitability and sustainability of cherry production and commercialization, benefiting all actors involved.

4.2. Policy Suggestions

Chilean authorities need to focus on three goals to address the challenges of the cherry GVC and obtain economic upgrades: diversifying the export destinations, improving the water use efficiency, and optimizing the labor force. To achieve this, we suggest these public policies:

- Market development: Encourage research and diversification in international markets, such as the United States, European Union, and other East Asian economies that demand cherries, especially ASEAN emerging economies such as Vietnam and Indonesia. Indeed, these are countries that also celebrate the Lunar New Year. Seeking new alliances and trade agreements is vital for facilitating access to new markets and reducing tariff barriers for Chilean cherries. Official trade missions and participation in international fairs should be encouraged. Although China will continue to be the primary destination market for our cherries, it is necessary to continue to diversify our exports to other markets of interest within and outside Asia because of the risk of depending on a single market that is highly noted in the literature.
- Analysis of consumption trends: The business association should invest in conducting regular studies on consumption trends in target markets, such as ASEAN countries and in China's wealthiest provinces and cities, to anticipate changes in demand and adapt to consumer preferences, especially within the educated urban middle-class and young generation.
- Expectation management: It is vital to raise awareness among exporters that the value currently being paid has characteristics that make them assume it is accurate, temporary, and non-replaceable. In a perfect market economy, abnormal returns are corrected over time when more actors enter production. In the case of cherries, a "bubble" will burst sooner or later, strongly affecting the business and its profitability.
- Import seasonal labor: The government should study the possibility of creating a special visa scheme for seasonal foreign workers, allowing them to access the country yearly to participate in the harvest. An agreement with the Peruvian government should be a priority. Also, the business associations and local producers should participate in this project,

assuming the costs of transportation and housing, at least partially.

- Investment in infrastructure and equipment: Improve logistics and local transport infrastructure, including the cold chain, to ensure that cherries reach markets in optimal conditions. Investments in roads, ports, packaging, and refrigeration during transport are needed. Packinghouses are needed in the Bio Bio region, which has the most significant potential to increase cherry production.
- Access to finance to upgrade: Facilitate access to finance for small and medium-sized producers who wish to expand their export capacity, including subsidies, soft loans, or support programs. Public policy should encourage investing in generating capacities to produce high-added-value products derived from cherries and importing state-of-the-art irrigation systems to improve water use efficiency.
- Research and development: Encourage university research into cultivation techniques, water use, and cherry varieties that improve resistance to pests, diseases, and changing climatic conditions. Collaboration between universities, business associations, and central and regional governments should focus on registering patents and creating farmer training programs.
- Sustainability: Implement sustainable practices that promote responsible agriculture and minimize environmental impact. Water use must be improved, as climate change is expected to affect Chile with regular droughts. These practices can also increase competitiveness in markets that value sustainably sourced products.

References

Agüero García, Javier. 2016. "América Latina Durante La Guerra Fría (1947-1989): Una Introducción". *InterSedes* 17(35), pp. 151–195.

Ahumada, José Miguel. 2019. *The Political Economy of Peripheral Growth. Chile in the Global Economy.* Palgrave Macmillan: Suiza.

Bamber, Penny and Fernandez-Stark, Karina. 2016. "Fresh cherry industry in Chile." In, Low, Patrick and Pasadilla, Gloria O. (edits). *Services in global value chains: Manufacturing-related services.* APEC: Singapur, pp.701-741.

Bórquez, Andrés, López, Dorotea and Muñoz, Felipe. 2021. *Relaciones entre Chile y China: un enfoque integral.* RIL Ediciones: Santiago.

Bórquez, Andrés and Bravo, Carlos. 2021. "Who are China's strategic economic partners in South America?". *Asian Education and Development Studies* 10 (3), pp. 445-456.

Bórquez, Andrés. 2019. "Exploring the non-traditional foreign investment in Sino–Latin American relations: The Chilean case." *Competition and Regulation in Network Industries* 21(1), pp. 18–33.

Briceño, Constanza and Méndez, Raphael. 2024. "Destacado en prensa: Las cerezas superan el 40 % de las exportaciones frutícolas del país." *ProChile.*

Carmagnani, Marcello. 2011. "*El otro Occidente. América Latina desde la invasión europea hasta la globalización*". Fondo de Cultura Económica and El Colegio de México: México.

China Daily. 2024. "China Eastern Airlines celebrates decade-long Chilean cherry imports". *China Daily*, November 21.

Cooperativa. 2024. "Cherry Express en camino: Partió primer embarque de Chile a China de esta temporada". *Cooperativa*, November 18.

EMOL. 2024. "Ruta de la cereza: Las explosivas cifras de un negocio que moverá casi medio millón de empleos esta temporada.". EMOL, November 2.

Fermandois, Joaquín. 1985. "Ideología y Pragmatismo en la política exterior chilena durante la crisis del sistema político 1970-1975." *Revista de Ciencia Política* 7(2), pp. 169-178.

Figueroa, Juan Pablo. 2021. "Necesitaremos otros 55.000 temporeros a diciembre de 2025". *Agrilink*, October 12.

Gachúz, Juan Carlos. 2012. "Chile's Economic and Political Relationship with China." *Journal of Current Chinese Affairs* 41(1), pp. 133-154.

Gallagher, Kevin. 2016. "*The China Triangle: Latin America's China Boom and the Fate of the Washington Consensus.*" Oxford University Press: New York.

Garrido, Andrea. 2023. "Chile sigue siendo el número 1 en exportación de cerezas." *Smartcherry,* May 23.

Gereffi, Gary. 2017. "Políticas de desarrollo productivo y escalamiento: la necesidad de vincular empresas, agrupamientos y cadenas de valor." In, Dussel Peters, Enrique (edit). *Cadenas Globales de Valor. Metodología, teorías y debates.* Universidad Nacional Autónoma de México: Mexico, pp. 13-44.

Gereffi, Gary, Bamber, Penny, and Fernandez-Stark, Karina (edits). 2022. *China's New Development Strategies: Upgrading from Above and from Below in Global Value Chains.* Palgrave Macmillan: Singapur.

Hung, Ho-fung. 2015. *The China Boom: Why China Will Not Rule the World.* Columbia University Press: New York.

Jenkins, Rhys. 2018. *How China is Reshaping the Global Economy: Development Impacts in Africa and Latin America.* Oxford University Press.

Kissinger, Henry. 2017. *China.* Editorial Debate: Barcelona.

Kuik, Cheng-Chwee. 2024. "Southeast Asian Responses to U.S.-China Tech Competition: Hedging and Economy-Security Tradeoffs". *Journal of Chinese Political Science* 29, pp. 509–538.

Logistec. 2023. "Cherry Express: Una cadena de frío integrada es fundamental para el éxito de las exportaciones". *Revista Logistec,* April 27.

López, Dorotea, Bórquez, Andrés, and Serrano-Moreno, Juan Enrique. 2023. "Chilean Overseas Foreign Direct Investment to China". In, Enrique Dussel Peters (edit). *Latin-American and Caribbean Overseas Foreign Direct Investment to China in the Twenty-First Century.* Lynne-Rienner and Red ALC-China: Boulder, pp.177-210.

López, Dorotea and Muñoz, Felipe. 2021. "China's trade policy towards Latin America: an analysis of free trade agreements policy". *Asian Education and Development Studies* 10 (3), pp. 399-409.

Matta, Javier. 1991. "Chile y la República Popular China: 1970-1990." *Estudios Internacionales* 24(95), pp. 347-367.

Montalva, Juan and Navia, Patricio. 2006. "Chile and China: Building Relations Beyond Trade?" *China-Latin America Task Force* 14, pp. 1-14.

Montt, María, Serrano-Moreno Juan Enrique, and Chan, Carol. 2023. *Empresas e inversión de China en Chile: aportes para una discusión balanceada*. ICLAC. Núcleo Milenio Impactos de China en América Latina y el Caribe: Santiago.

Montt, María, Urdinez, Francisco, Aguirre, Italo and Matamala, Gonzalo. 2024. *El auge de las cerezas chilenas y el desafío del mercado chino*. ICLAC. Núcleo Milenio Impactos de China en América Latina y el Caribe: Santiago.

MundoMarítimo. 2019. "Hapag-Lloyd lanza 'Cherry Express' para atender la temporada de cerezas en Chile". *MundoMarítimo*, October 28.

Pino, Fabián. 2024. "Situación de las Cerezas en Chile ¿problema de concentración?". Tesis de Magíster. Facultad de Economía y Negocios, Universidad de Chile.

Portal Portuario. 2024. "Hong Kong establece récord para contenedores de cerezas chilenas descargados en una sola escala." *Portal Portuario*, February 7.

ProChile. 2019. "Con divertido concurso en parejas Cherries From Chile y JD.com celebran el Súper Cherries Day". *Prochile*, January 21.

ProChile. 2024/a. "Cerezas chilenas logran récord de envíos durante enero de 2024, con montos por US$ 1.555 millones". *ProChile*, February 2.

Prochile. 2024/b. "Tianjing recibe por primera vez el Cherry Express: cerezas chilenas debutan con ruta directa a puerto estratégico de China." *ProChile*, January 19th.

Reyes, Angeli. 2021. "Comercio silvoagropecuario entre China y Chile en 50 años de relaciones diplomáticas". ODEPA. Chile.

Serrano-Moreno, Juan Enrique. 2021. "La aceleración de la integración jurídica y política de Hong Kong en la República Popular China". *Estudos Internacionais* 9(3), pp. 96-113.

Serrano-Moreno, Juan Enrique. 2024. "Latin America and the Caribbean: How the Belt and Road Initiative Diminished the United States Influence." In, Regilme, Salvador (edits). *The United States and China in the Era of Global Transformations: Geographies of Rivalry*. Bristol University Press: Bristol, pp. 138-159

Serrano-Moreno, Juan Enrique, Pérez, Alejandra and De Abreu, María Gabriela. 2021. "Beyond copper: China and Chile relations." *Asian Education and Development Studies* 10 (3), pp. 359–373.

Servicio Nacional de Aduanas. 2023. *Anuario Estadístico 2023*. Servicio Nacional de Aduanas de Chile.

Simfruit. 2024. "Hong Kong: Chile y Tailandia principales proveedores de frutas frescas". *Simfruit*, January 29.

SmartCherry. 2024. "Chile exportó 413.979 toneladas de cerezas durante la Tp. 2023-2024." *Smartcherry*, March 14.

Subsecretaria de Relaciones Económicas Internacionales de Chile. 2024/a. "Ficha país: Chile-China." *Subsecretaria de Relaciones Económicas Internacionales de Chile*. (et al: https://www.subrei.gob.cl/docs/default-source/estudios-y-documentos/fichas/china-anual10c2b0cc88be48bca8b90595a01e5f11.pdf?sfvrsn=69595d55_5)

Subsecretaria de Relaciones Económicas Internacionales de Chile. 2024/b. "Ficha país: Chile-Hong Kong SAR, China." *Subsecretaria de Relaciones Económicas Internacionales de Chile*.

Sun, Zhichao. 2008. "The special status of the Hong Kong Special Administrative Region in the international community". *The Comparative and International Law Journal of Southern Africa 41*(2), pp. 205–220.

The Atlas of Economic Complexity. 2024a. *HarvardGrwthLab*.

The Observatory of Economic Complexity. 2024. At: https://oec.world/en.

Yeung, Cherry. 2024. "Economic and Trade Information: Hong Kong". HKTDC *Research*, January 28.

Organization for Economic Cooperation and Development (OECD). 2020. "Global value chains in agriculture and food: A synthesis of OECD analysis", OECD *Food, Agriculture and Fisheries Papers*, No. 139. OECD Publishing: Paris.

World Trade Organization (WTO). s.f. "Regional trade agreements. Hong Kong". WTO.

4. The Brazil-China Oil Relationship: Impacts from a Local Perspective

Pedro Henrique Batista Barbosa[1]

Introduction

Recently the petroleum sector has been one of the most dynamic and thriving in Brazil-China economic relations. From almost nonexistent ties a few decades ago, Brazil is nowadays the seventh supplier of crude to China, which as of 2024 the main destination of Brazilian oil exports. PRC's oil companies are also heavy investors in Brazil, especially in the highly productive upstream pre-salt projects.

The fast growth of petroleum commerce and investment numbers has raised concerns about possible regional effects in Brazil, particularly in the state of Rio de Janeiro, which is the main oil exporter to China and is where Chinese oil firms invested and established local branches. Much has been speculated about impacts on employment, suppliers, work conditions, technology transfers, new socioeconomic conditions, environment, potential tensions and others, but little has been written about these topics, aside from sparse media coverage. There is a growing literature on

1 The opinions expressed by the author in this article do not necessarily reflect those from the Brazilian Ministry of Foreign Affairs.

Brazil-China petroleum ties, but not from a regional perspective and not focusing on localized effects.

This paper aims to bridge this gap. Making use of multiple sources, it tries to shed some light on some of these above-mentioned topics. In the first section, it is presented the past and the current state of bilateral political relations. Brazil and China celebrated the 50-year anniversary of diplomatic ties in 2024 in a moment of expanding cooperation initiatives and increasing high-level contacts.

In the second section, the focus is on economic relations, precisely trade, investments and infrastructure projects. It is shown that bilateral commerce has reached a historical record in 2024, with Brazilian exports to China showing strong vitality. Additionally, the PRC has become an important investor in Brazil, especially in the energy sector. Some sources put Brazil in the fourth destination of Chinese investments in the world.

The third section discusses the case of oil in Sino-Brazilian relations. It argues that complementary conditions –one being the fifth-largest exporter and the other the largest importer (as of 2023)– have been a key factor in the rapid growth of oil exports to China in recent years. Moreover, it claims that the discovery of new untapped petroleum resources in Brazil has attracted the four major Chinese oil corporations to Rio de Janeiro. The cases of each firm, namely Sinopec, Sinochem, CNPC and CNOOC, are debated separately.

The fourth part of this paper is dedicated to analyzing the possible regional impacts of Brazilian oil exports to China and of Chinese investments in Brazil's oil sector, especially in the state of Rio de Janeiro. Drawing from multiple sources, it presents the revealed effects, their extent, where they occurred, and how China's experience in Brazil may differ from others.

The paper ends with a conclusion that tries to wrap up the main points discussed over the text and offers some policy suggestions.

1. Brazil-China Political Relations

Brazil and China celebrated the jubilee of their diplomatic relationship on August 15th, 2024. The date did not go unnoticed. The governments of both countries organized events to commemorate the fiftieth anniversary, while their presidents exchanged letters to mark this historic occasion.

In this past half century, bilateral relations have undergone different phases, but somehow have continuously evolved until the present day. Brazil and China have developed from distant, sparse and erratic past interactions to an increasingly dense and diverse current agenda. While relatively less significant in 1974, binational ties today are founded on deep economic complementarity (China is Brazil's main commercial partner, and Brasilia is Beijing's top provider of agricultural goods) and growing diplomatic interaction bilaterally and multilaterally. High-level visits and meetings are frequent and recurrent. In international fora, there are several venues where common interests emerge and mutual support happens under a South-South solidarity spirit.

Fifty years ago, Brazil and China established a relationship that, for many, was somewhat unlikely, since the political systems of both countries were diametrically different. However, the circumstances of that moment made the improbable, probable. China was seeking to break out of the global isolation experienced in previous decades and gain international recognition. Brazil was implementing the then called diplomatic policy of "Responsible and Ecumenical Pragmatism" and was more open to maintaining relations with ideologically distant nations. Economic reasons also played a role. On the one hand, the first Oil Crisis prompted Brazil to look for new oil suppliers. Heavily dependent on imports to satisfy domestic needs, Brasilia was interested in buying Beijing's then petroleum production's surplus. On the other hand, China wanted to diversify its economic partnerships, find new sources of foreign currency–which were scarce at the time–and desired to purchase Brazilian iron ore (Barbosa 2024).

The years that followed the establishment of diplomatic ties were lackluster, both politically and economically. Things began to change in the 1980s with Brazil's re-democratization and China's policy of "reform and opening up". The first exchange of high-level visits happened at that time: president Figueiredo went to Beijing in 1984 and prime-minister Zhao Ziyang was in Brasilia, in 1985. Both governments started to cooperate under the banner of fostering development and South-South collaboration. The first experiment in bilateral rapprochement was in science and technology –the CBERS joint satellite program was launched in 1986.

The fruits of the rapprochement that began in the 1980s began to appear in the following decade. In 1993, Brazil and China established a Strategic Partnership, the first experiment among developing nations. The rationale behind the verdict was their growing similarities: both are large countries with sizable populations seeking a more active role in the international system. Both states were equally interested in learning from each other's development strategies across various sectors, including infrastructure, agriculture, telecommunications, and energy (Biato 2010). The PRC, for instance, wanted to study Brazil's expertise in the construction of huge hydro dams. Itaipu hydroelectric barrage was a reference for China's Three Gorges project (Barbosa 2020:41).

The election of President Lula in late 2002 inaugurated a new phase in the bilateral political relationship. Ideologically aligned, Sino-Brazilian diplomatic relations were thrilled with increasing bilateral interactions and growing common interests in the international arena. In his inaugural speech on January 1st, 2003, President Lula announced his desire to promote dialogue and cooperation with the global south and, more specifically, with "big developing nations." China was singularized, alongside with Russia, India and South Africa. Among the objectives was to expand the voice of developing states in the international arena and to reform existing multilateral organizations, such as the UN, IMF and World Bank, in their favor (Biato 2010:145). The creation of the BRICS and the G20 in the following years happened under the background of close alignment of interests between Brazil and China.

During Lula's first and second terms, two pillars of the bilateral diplomatic relationship, which remain relevant today, began to emerge: frequency of political meetings and institutionalization of governmental interactions. For instance, Lula went to Beijing, in May 2004, a visit that was reciprocated by Hu Jintao in November of that year. Afterwards, the Brazilian president went to PRC twice, in August 2008 and in May 2009. Hu Jintao visited Brazil again in April 2010.

Institutionally speaking, one of the results of Lula's 2004 visit was the creation of the Sino-Brazilian High-Level Commission for Consultation and Cooperation (COSBAN, as it is overtly known). To this day, the binational mechanism has played a leading role in fostering bilateral cooperation through its 11 subcommittees –including one for energy cooperation– and 16 working groups, all under the guidance of both countries' vice presidents.

Diplomatic relations kept a high-profile during Dilma Rousseff's presidency. She went to China in April 2011 and received visits from President Xi Jinping in July 2014 and from Prime-Minister Li Keqiang in May 2015. The chiefs of state and government of both countries also met on several occasions on the sidelines of multilateral events, such as during the Rio+20 Summit in Rio de Janeiro, in June 2012. This meeting was a landmark: diplomatic relations were elevated to Global Strategic Partnership, the Global Strategic Dialogue between the Ministries of Foreign Affairs was launched, and the Brazil-China Ten-year Cooperation Plan (2012-2021) was signed.

Less bilateral diplomatic intensity was seen in the following years, in part caused by the political turbulent years experienced in Brazil and by the COVID pandemic. The fact that President Michel Temer stayed less time in power has influenced bilateral interactions. There was only one bilateral high-level visit during his term: his state visit to Beijing in September 2017. During President Jair Bolsonaro's administration, despite the lack of ideological affinity, bilateral ties initiated under predictable terms, with the visit of

Vice-President Hamilton Mourao in May 2019 and an exchange of presidential visits in October (Bolsonaro) and November (Xi Jinping) of that year. The advent of the COVID pandemic changed the perspective of political exchanges not only between Brazil and China, but also among all countries, and the few high-level contacts afterwards were restricted to virtual gatherings, such as the sixth plenary session of COSBAN in May 2022. In this meeting, the Sino-Brazilian Executive Plan (2022-26) and the Strategic Plan (2022-2031) were launched.

Lula initiated his third presidential term in early 2023 with China high on its agenda. The Asian country was one of his first international destinations, with which the official objective was to "relaunch" bilateral relations (Gv.Br 2023). Top leadership interactions gained a new impulse. After the mission led by President Lula in April 2023, in the period of a bit more than one year, three more Brazilian leaders paid a visit to the PRC: the President of the Chamber of Deputies Arthur Lira (October 2023), the Vice-President Geraldo Alckmin (June 2024), and the president of the Supreme Federal Court Luis Barroso (July 2024). President Xi Jinping went to Brazil in November 2024 to participate in the G20 Leaders' Summit and made a state visit to celebrate the jubilee of Sino-Brazilian diplomatic relations, which were rebranded as "Brazil-China Community with a Shared Future for a More Just World and a More Sustainable Planet".

2. Brazil-China Economic Relations

2.1 Trade

Brazil-China commerce has shown extraordinary growth over the last decades. According to Brazilian numbers, between 1974 and 2024, bilateral trade grew an extraordinary seven thousand times. In 1974, only 0.24% of Brazilian exports went to China, and only 0.02% of the Latin American country's imports came from the Eastern country. The PRC was Brazil's 50th largest trade partner and 75th source of imported goods (Prazeres 2024). In 2024, the People's Republic absorbed 28 % of Brazilian foreign sales and was the origin of 24 % of its purchases from abroad. As of 2024, China is Brazil's main trading partner and provider of products (since 2009), and Brazil, in turn, is the PRC's tenth partner (Hong Kong excluded, Taiwan included) –ahead of France, India and the United Kingdom, for example.

Table 1. Brazil-China trade (2000-2024, US$ million)

	Exports	Imports	Balance	Total trade
2024	94,411.1	63,579.7	30,831.4	157,990.8
2023	104,324.8	53,175.8	51,149.1	157,500.6
2022	89,427.8	60,744.0	28,683.8	150,171.7
2021	87,907.9	47,650.9	40,256.9	135,558.8
2020	67,788.1	34,778.4	33,009.6	102,566.5
2019	63,357.5	36,028.3	27,329.2	99,385.8
2018	63,929.6	35,157.2	28,772.3	99,086.8
2017	47,488.4	27,554.0	19,934.5	75,042.4
2016	35,133.3	23,349.9	11,783.4	58,483.2
2015	35,155.4	30,714.1	4,441.3	65,869.4
2014	40,611.9	37,349.5	3,262.4	77,961.4
2013	46,023.2	37,325.5	8,697.7	83,348.7
2012	41,225.8	34,244.7	6,981.1	75,470.6
2011	44,304.6	32,786.2	11,518.4	77,090.8
2010	30,747.6	25,591.5	5,156.1	56,339.0
2009	20,994.9	15,904.6	5,090.4	36,899.5
2008	16,520.0	20,035.4	-3,515.5	36,555.4
2007	10,776.7	12,596.3	-1,819.6	23,373.1
2006	8,398.2	7,975.4	422.8	16,373.6
2005	6,826.9	5,337.3	1,489.6	12,164.1
2004	5,438.6	3,703.5	1,735.2	9,142.1
2003	4,531.2	2,143.1	2,388.1	6,674.3
2002	2,516.6	1,549.0	967.6	4,065.6
2001	1,901.3	1,320.1	581.1	3,221.4
2000	1,084.9	1,219.2	-134.3	2,304.1

Source: Own elaboration based on MDIC (2025).

Trade expansion was uneven in the first two and more decades after the establishment of diplomatic ties. However, since the beginning of this century, it has experienced unprecedented evolution. Brazilian exports towards China have substantially augmented since then. They expanded from US$ 1 billion to the historical record of US$ 104 billion between 2000 and 2023 (Table 1). In 2023, for the first time, Brazil has exported more than US$ 100 billion to a trade partner.

As seen in table 1, there were some negative fluctuations in 2012, 2014, 2016 and 2019. The first two years are included, by most scholars, in the period that marked the end of what became known as the "commodities super cycle", of which Brazil was one of the main beneficiaries. Brazilian exports to China are highly concentrated in three products –soybeans, crude oil and iron or–, whose percentage of the total has hovered around 70 % over the last years. In 2024, soybeans lead the exports and represented 33 % of the total.

It is worth mentioning that Brazil is China's main trading partner in an extremely important sector, agriculture, since it is China's main supplier of agrarian products. Of all the food the PRC imports, nearly a quarter comes from Brazil, a figure that significantly exceeds that of the country in second place, the United States, which accounts for nearly 14 % of China's agricultural imports (as of 2023). Besides soybeans, Brazil delivers great quantities of corn, meat, sugar, and other commodities.

Imports followed the same upward trend, although numbers have oscillated more over time, as shown in table 1. They expanded from US$ 1.2 billion in 2000 to US$ 63.5 billion in 2024. From 2007 on, the growth trend started to accelerate and reached a historical record in 2024. The import basket is more diverse and includes much more items, such as electronic equipment and parts, telephones, machines etc. None of them has more than 10 % of the total imports. China, indeed, is Brazil's largest source of capital goods.

The remarkable growth of bilateral commerce has boosted total trade numbers. In 2024, they reached the historical record of US$ 158 billion and consolidated China's position as Brazil's main trade partner and concurrently top destination of exports and first provider of imported goods. The exponential expansion of Brazilian exports, often outpacing the growth of imports, has led the South American nation to accumulate trade surpluses over the years (with the recent exceptions of 2000, 2007 and 2008). The difference between what is sold and what is bought from China reached the historical height of US$ 51 billion in 2023. Brazil is one

Table 2. Brazil's global trade and Brazil-China trade relations (2000-2024, US$ million)

	BRAZIL-WORLD TRADE				% CHINA			
	Total exports	Total imports	Total trade balance	Total trade	Total exports	Total imports	Total trade balance	Total trade
2000	54,993	56,976	-1,983	111,970	2.0%	2.1%	6.8%	2.1%
2001	58,032	56,569	1,463	114,601	3.3%	2.3%	39.7%	2.8%
2002	60,147	48,275	11,872	108,422	4.2%	3.2%	8.1%	3.7%
2003	72,777	49,307	23,470	122,084	6.2%	4.3%	10.2%	5.5%
2004	95,122	63,814	31,308	158,935	5.7%	5.8%	5.5%	5.8%
2005	118,598	74,692	43,906	193,290	5.8%	7.1%	3.4%	6.3%
2006	137,581	92,531	45,050	230,112	6.1%	8.6%	0.9%	7.1%
2007	159,816	122,042	37,774	281,858	6.7%	10.3%	-4.8%	8.3%
2008	195,765	174,707	21,058	370,472	8.4%	11.5%	-16.7%	9.9%
2009	151,792	129,398	22,394	281,189	13.8%	12.3%	22.7%	13.1%
2010	200,434	183,337	17,097	383,771	15.3%	14.0%	30.2%	14.7%
2011	253,666	227,970	25,697	481,636	17.5%	14.4%	44.8%	16.0%
2012	239,953	225,166	14,786	465,119	17.2%	15.2%	47.2%	16.2%
2013	232,544	241,501	-8,957	474,045	19.8%	15.5%	-97.1%	17.6%
2014	220,923	230,823	-9,900	451,746	18.4%	16.2%	-33.0%	17.3%
2015	186,782	173,104	13,678	359,887	18.8%	17.7%	32.5%	18.3%
2016	179,526	139,321	40,205	318,847	19.6%	16.8%	29.3%	18.3%
2017	214,988	158,951	56,037	373,940	22.1%	17.3%	35.6%	20.1%
2018	231,890	185,322	46,568	417,212	27.6%	19.0%	61.8%	23.7%
2019	221,127	185,928	35,199	407,055	28.7%	19.4%	77.6%	24.4%
2020	209,180	158,787	50,393	367,967	32.4%	21.9%	65.5%	27.9%
2021	280,815	219,408	61,407	500,223	31.3%	21.7%	65.6%	27.1%
2022	334,136	272,611	61,525	606,747	26.8%	22.3%	46.6%	24.8%
2023	339,696	240,793	98,903	580,489	30.7%	22.1%	51.7%	27.1%
2024	337,036	262,484	74,552	599,520	28.0%	24.2%	41.3%	26.3%

Source: Own elaboration based on MDIC (2025).

of the few states that have a trade surplus with PRC; its amount in 2023 was the third largest.

From a broader Brazilian perspective, the importance of trade ties with China is emphasized. The growth of Brazil's global commerce of the last few years was accompanied by the expansion of Sino-Brazilian trade numbers. In other words, the more Brazil exported to the world, the more it sold to China; the more it bought from outside, the more it bought from the PRC. Therefore, the participation of China in Brazil's external trade has increased over time, occupying spaces once held by other countries. As table 2 indicates, in 2000 only 2 % of Brazil's total trade was done with China. In 2024, the participation raised to 26 %. The People's Republic is now the destination of 28 % of Brazil's exports and the origin of nearly 24 % of its imports. More remarkably is the stake of China in Brazil's global surplus, which reached 41 % in 2024. In previous years, the percentage was even higher, such as 78 % in 2019.

Figure 1. Percentage of Brazilian exports to China by region and by state (2024, US$)

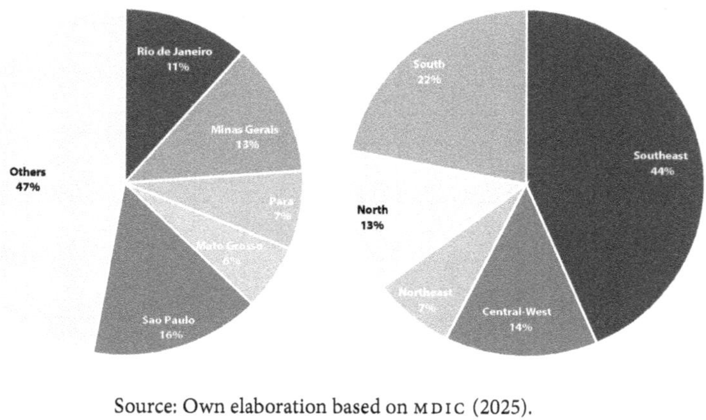

Source: Own elaboration based on MDIC (2025).

From a regional angle, Brazil-China trade ties are unequally distributed over the Brazilian territory. As of 2024, the Southeast region concentrated almost half (44 %) of the total bilateral trade (figure 1), a share twice larger than the second place, which is occupied by the Southern states (22 %). From a provincial perspective, the state of Sao Paulo (SP, 16 %) ranks first in terms of commercial ties with the PRC, followed by Rio de Janeiro (RJ, 11 %) and Minas Gerais (MG, 12 %). Sao Paulo's top position is due to the fact that it was the largest importer of Chinese goods in Brazil, with imports exceeding exports, resulting in the second-largest deficit among the country's states. Although Rio de Janeiro was the third biggest provincial trade partner (behind SP and MG), it was the main exporter to China and one of the subnational entities that imported the least from the Asian country, thus experiencing the greatest surplus with the Asian country.

Over the last few years, Rio de Janeiro experienced a remarkable growth of its commerce with the PRC. Among the currently seven largest Chinese trade subnational partners in Brazil, Rio is the state whose exports expanded the most between 2000 and 2024, nearly 336 times, from US$ 49 million to US$ 16 billion. Rio surpassed Minas Gerais –a major exporter of iron ore and concentrates– in 2018 to become the leading exporter to China. However, it lost this position between 2020 and 2022, only to reclaim it in 2023. Conversely, it is the Brazilian state whose imports from China grew the least during the same period. Therefore, Rio enjoys the largest trade surplus with China among all states. Its numbers in 2024 were almost half of Brazil's total trade surplus with the Asian country (MDIC 2025).

2.2 China's outbound foreign direct investments (OFDI) in Brazil

Over the last decades, China has increasingly become a major source of investments, not only a chief receiver of foreign direct investments (FDI). According to UNCTAD statistics, the PRC was the second recipient of inflows and the third source of outflows in 2023 –not considering Hong Kong, which was in the fourth and fifth positions respectively (UNCTAD 2024).

One major destination for Chinese OFDI has been South America, where Brazil has been playing an important role. Different sources show distinct numbers for Chinese investments in Brazil. However, as a whole, they all highlight Brazil's position as one of the main destinations of Chinese capital flows.

According to the American Enterprise Institute (AEI), between 2005 and 2023, Brazil received no less than US$ 71 billion in investments, ranking fourth after the United States, Australia and Britain. This amount represents almost half of all Chinese FDI in South America. In 2021, for instance, Brazil was the top recipient of Chinese OFDI in the world, for the first time (AEI 2024).

Data collected by the Brazil-China Business Council (generally known as CEBC) shows a similar picture. Until the end of 2023, Chinese OFDI in Brazil reached US$ 73,3 billion, of which 75% was concentrated in the energy sector (CEBC 2024)

Brazilian official numbers provided by the Central Bank are lower. China is considered to be the fifth largest source of foreign investment in Brazil, with a total stock of US$ 36,7 billion as of 2022 (BACEN 2024).

Red ALC-China provides a database of Chinese FDI in Latin America where the role of Brazil as the main recipient of Chinese OFDI is also emphasized. Of the total of US$ 193 billion directed to the region over time, approximately US$ 65,5 billion went to the Federal Republic. Fortunately, the data is disaggregated by sector and state level. Almost half of the total was spent in energy related projects –US$ 30 billion, mostly M&A – and Rio de Janeiro received US$ 4,9 billion of this amount (Dussel Peters 2024/b).

Red ALC-China equally compiles information about the number of workers involved in Chinese investments in the region. Between 2000 and 2023, Chinese projects were responsible for more than 663 thousand jobs. Of this total, nearly one-quarter were in Brazil (161 thousand) (Dussel Peters 2024/b).

2.3 Chinese infrastructure projects in Brazil

Not only Chinese investors went to Brazil over the last decades, service providers also disembarked in the Latin American country so as to participate in infrastructure related construction projects.

The American Enterprise Institute and Red ALC-China compile data about these contracts.

According to the AEI, Chinese firms were involved in overseas construction projects that amounted to at least US$ 945 billion between 2005 and 2023. Differently to Chinese OFDI, Brazil's share in Chinese infrastructure services in the world is much lower, less than 1 % of the total (US$ 9 billion). Thus, Brazil ranks 32 among the main destinations of Chinese service contractors (AEI 2024).[2]

Red ALC-China estimates that Chinese firms have taken on US$ 113 billion in projects across Latin America between 2005 and 2023. Similarly, a smaller portion of these contracts, approximately US$ 16.6 billion, occurred in Brazil. Argentina is the Latin-American country that had more Chinese infrastructure projects, with US$ 29 billion. Interestingly, Chinese construction projects in Brazil created more jobs compared to other regional neighbors. Red ALC-China calculates that, during the 2005-2023 period, 774 thousand people were locally employed by Chinese corporations (268 projects), of which 187 thousand in Brazil (35 projects) and 96 thousand in Argentina (27 projects) (Dussel Peters 2024/a).

3. The case of oil in Sino-Brazilian relations

Brazil-China oil relations date back to the 1970s, when both countries established diplomatic relationship. At that time, China exported petroleum to Brazil. However, only in the 2000s, especially since the discovery of pre-salt oil provinces, bilateral relations have increasingly deepened and in a different direction: Brazil started to sell crude to China. More recently, oil ties began to diversify in four pillars: trade, investments, infrastructure

2 In the *Monitor of Chinese Infrastructure in Latin America and the Caribbean* 2024, Dussel Peters argues that CGIT records Chinese infrastructure projects in LAC without a clear definition, including announced projects and others that were never carried out. Therefore, the projects registered by the database for Latin America are lower than the Monitor (Dussel Peters 2024/b:2).

services, and finance (Barbosa 2024). In this paper, we focus on the first three.

3.1 Sino-Brazilian oil trade

The discovery of the pre-salt oil in mid 2000s was a watershed not only in the history of the global petroleum industry, but also in the evolution of Brazil's oil sector and –as seen after– of Brazil-China relations. Brazil's new reservoirs were not only huge in size, but also better in quality.[3] After that, crude oil has progressively occupied a larger share of Brazil's export basket, both globally and to China, with Brazilian petroleum becoming increasingly important in China's energy security plans. This situation undermarks a growing complementarity between both countries' oil sectors. On the one hand, Brazil has been gradually becoming a major producer and exporter of the commodity over the last years. On the other hand, China is still highly dependent on imports to satisfy its internal demand.

Between 2000 and 2023, the South American nation's domestic production almost tripled, expanding from 1,2 million barrels a day (mbd) to 3.4 mbd. Pre-salt oil was responsible for the majority of the recent growth, since extraction from onshore and pos-salt fields has been consistently shrinking over this time. For instance, onshore production decreased from 0,2 mbd in 2000 to 0,08 mbd in 2023. Pos-salt production experienced the same reduction path –from 1 mbd to 0,72 mbd in the period–, yet it first increased until 2010 to then start to retreat. On the contrary, pre-salt production, which formally started in 2008, grew to 2,6 mbd in 2023 and represented 76 % of the total (the same percentage of the pos-salt

3 Brazil is a historical producer of heavy oil (<22 API), which comes from post-salt basins. Pre-salt provinces presented a new reality, since its oil is lighter. Most of pre-salt petroleum has an API density superior of 28 API (medium), with some part having a gravity above 31 API, being then considered light (>31 API). This oil also has a low content of polluting substances, such as sulfur and nitrogen, a feature that enhances its market value (IBP, n.d.). In the case of China, Brazil's pre-salt oil fitted well in the needs of mid-size private independent refiners known as "tea pots," which are better suited to refine low sulfur oils (Barbosa 2020:7).

in 2013) (ANP, 2024). As of 2023, Brazil's share of world output (3.6 %) was more than twice the participation in the beginning of the century (1.7 % in 2000) (EnergyInstitute 2024).

Over this period, Brazilian production outpaced consumption and the external markets were the natural destination of exceeding petroleum. By 2023, the country was exporting almost half of its national output (48 %) and ranked ninth in the largest global exporters, with 3.3 % of the global exports (it had around 0.5 % two decades ago) (ITC 2024).

In an opposite situation, PRC's domestic production over the last decades was far outpaced by consumption, propelling the country to rely on imports to satisfy internal needs. For instance, in 2000, approximately one third of the national demand was dependent on imports; in 2023, nearly 70 % of the crude consumed came from abroad. This situation was due to a dual phenomenon: slow growth of internal production (from 3.3 mbd to 4.2 mbd, with negative oscillation in some years) and fast expansion of consumption (from 4.6 mbd to 16.6 mbd) (EnergyInstitute, 2024). As a consequence, imports boomed, ranging from 1,4 mbd to 11,3 mbd. In 2015, China became the world's number one importer of crude oil, overcoming the United States. As of 2023, its imports account for more than one-fifth of the world's total (ITC 2024).

Considering China's mounting appetite for petroleum in the last decades, the Asian country was a natural and growing destination for Brazil's mounting crude oil exports, as table 3 indicates. China was not a relevant buyer of Brazilian oil until 2009, when it imported nearly 14 % of Brazil's global oil exports. The picture has changed since then and China's percentage in Brazil's exports raised substantially. Between 2018 and 2020, for example, more than half of the total shipments went to the PRC. In the following two years, numbers went down, but regained strength in 2023, when the People's Republic consumed 46 % of Brazilian exports. Until 2023, the share of Brazilian oil in China's total petroleum imports has risen significantly, especially since 2015. From 4 % in that year, it increased to 7 % in 2023.

Table 3. Sino-Brazilian crude oil trade (2000-2023, mbd)

	Brazilian exports to the world	Brazilian exports to China	% of China in Brazilian exports	% of Brazil in Chinese imports
2000	0.02	0.00	-	0%
2001	0.11	0.00	4%	0%
2002	0.23	0.00	0%	0%
2003	0.24	0.00	1%	0%
2004	0.23	0.02	8%	1%
2005	0.27	0.04	13%	1%
2006	0.37	0.04	12%	2%
2007	0.42	0.04	10%	1%
2008	0.43	0.05	13%	2%
2009	0.53	0.07	14%	2%
2010	0.63	0.16	25%	3%
2011	0.60	0.14	23%	3%
2012	0.55	0.12	23%	2%
2013	0.38	0.11	30%	2%
2014	0.52	0.10	21%	2%
2015	0.74	0.25	34%	4%
2016	0.80	0.30	37%	5%
2017	0.99	0.42	42%	6%
2018	1.12	0.62	56%	7%
2019	1.17	0.74	63%	8%
2020	1.37	0.80	58%	8%
2021	1.36	0.64	47%	6%
2022	1.38	0.54	39%	5%
2023	1.63	0.75	46%	7%

Source: Own elaboration based on MDIC (2025) and ITC (2024).

From a regional perspective, it is not all Brazilian and Chinese provinces that are involved in bilateral trade. From a Chinese subnational perspective, as of 2023, bilateral oil trade (basically imports from Brazil) was concentrated in seven provinces and municipalities under the administration of the central government: Beijing, Zhejiang, Shandong, Hubei, Liaoning, Guangxi, and Guangdong. Beijing is Brazil's crude oil main entrance port, 85 %

of PRC's imports go there. It is followed by Shandong in a distant second place (9 %) (GAC 2024).

Only three Brazilian states export crude to China, namely Rio de Janeiro (RJ), Sao Paulo (SP) and Espirito Santo (ES). Rio is historically the major seller to China. In the recent past, the state was responsible for all Brazilian crude exports to China. Nowadays, its participation is 89 %, followed by Sao Paulo with 11 %. Espirito Santo was not always an oil export port to China and its share has always been minimal. Rio's trade with China is highly concentrated in oil, 88 % of its exports to the PRC is crude. Sao Paulo has a different mix, only 17 % of its exports is crude (second most trade), its main exported product is soybean (34 %) (MDIC 2025).

The predominance of Rio and Sao Paulo is not only because they have important port infrastructure, but also due to their participation in national crude production. Two of the country's most important oil basins are located there –Campos and Santos–, especially in Rio. Pre-salt provinces are also situated there. Rio accounted for 86 % of national output in 2023, whereas Sao Paulo provided 7 % and Espirito Santo 5 % (ANP 2024).

3.2 Chinese oil firms' investments in Brazil

The discovery of a vast untapped oil province and the fast expansion of Brazil's oil sector since then have attracted the attention of China's major oil companies. From 2010 on, the big four Chinese national firms –namely Sinopec, CNPC, CNOOC and Sinochem– all established branches in Brazil and started to participate in exploration and production projects, especially those in the pre-salt area.

Barbosa estimates that between 2010 –when the first Chinese oil related FDI happened– and 2023, no less than US$ 33 billion has been spent in Brazil by Chinese petrol companies. Of this total, US$ 20,4 billion entered the country through merger and acquisitions (M&A or brownfield), and almost US$ 9 billion were related to new projects (greenfield), including investments in research and development (R&D). Disbursements varied over time.

Brownfield transactions were concentrated in the first years, and greenfield projects were mainly announced recently. As a whole, the author emphasizes that China invested more in the Brazilian oil sector in times of high or growing oil prices. Exploration and production (E&P, "upstream") was the segment that received the majority of investments. From a global perspective, Barbosa argues that Brazil was the country that received the majority of Chinese oil investments, after Canada (Barbosa 2024).

Due to these heavy investments and important stakes in pre-salt projects, the output of Chinese local firms has increased over time. Between 2011 and 2023, data show that their production expanded an astonishing 13 times, far faster than the growth of other concessionaires in the same period (54%). As of 2023, Chinese petrol firms' total production in Brazil already jumped to the third position (Barbosa 2024).

3.3 Case studies

3.3.1. Sinopec

Sinopec was the first Chinese oil firm to disembark in Brazil, firstly as a service provider and then as an investor. It was one of the companies responsible for building the Southeast-Northeast Integration Gas Pipeline (GASENE), inaugurated in March 2010. In October of the same year, Sinopec made the first of its two largest investments in Brazil: buying 40% of the Brazilian branch of the Spanish corporation Repsol (which was rebranded as Repsol-Sinopec) in a transaction estimated in US$ 7,1 billion. One year later, the second one was announced: acquisition of 30% of the Brazilian branch of the Portuguese company Galp, Petrogal, disbursing at least US$ 5 billion.

Repsol and Petrogal were two of the largest investors in the Brazilian oil sector at that time and their participation in new local projects kept growing over the following years. As of 2023, these companies were, respectively, the fourth and seventh largest producers in Brazil. In previous years, they were correspondingly the third and fourth biggest ones.

This situation has made Sinopec become the Chinese firm most involved in E&P projects in Brazil. It was also the first to participate in pre-salt projects, since Petrogal was part of the consortium of the Tupi field. Moreover, for a long time, it was the Chinese oil corporation that showcased the largest oil produced in the South American country. Only in 2023 its output was surpassed by CNOOC, thanks to the rapid growth of production in the Buzios field.

3.3.2. CNPC

CNPC also bet heavily in Brazil and concentrated investments in pre-salt projects. Alongside CNOOC, it participated in two milestones of the pre-salt exploration history: the consortia to explore Libra (auctioned in 2013) and Buzios (2019), the world's largest deep-sea oil fields at the time of their auctions. Over time, it also acquired minority stakes at two other pre-salt projects (Peroba and Aram), once again in partnership with the Brazilian oil firm Petrobras.

Due to its stakes in pre-salt projects, CNPC's output in Brazil has expanded remarkably over a short period of time. In 2023, seven years since Libra's production started (2017), the firm was already the tenth largest producer in Brazil (yet the third one among Chinese corporations).

3.3.3. CNOOC

CNOOC is the Chinese company with the biggest stakes in pre-salt projects. Like CNPC, it is a member of the consortia exploring the Libra and Búzios fields. In the first one, in 2013, each Chinese firm has a 10 % participation, alongside Petrobras (40 %), Shell (20 %) and Total (20 %). It was the first time that Chinese oil corporations won an upstream concession through the Brazilian public bidding system. In the second one, in 2019, the two companies partnered with Petrobras and guaranteed a 5 % stake each. Showing confidence in future prospects of Buzios' production, CNOOC alone bought an additional 5 % share in the fields' consortium in 2021.

CNOOC also took other bold steps in Brazil. In 2017, it participated alone in a public auction and won the concession for a post-salt block in the Espírito Santo Basin, which it explores independently. In late 2023, another post-salt block was added to its basket, this time in the Santos basin, once again 100 % explored by the Chinese firm. Over time, CNOOC joined two other groups that are exploring pre-salt fields.

3.3.4. Sinochem

Sinochem was the first Chinese oil company to invest in Brazil. In May 2010, it bought stakes in two ongoing exploration projects, namely Peregrino and Pitangola. In January 2012 and August 2013, the firm acquired stakes in exploration projects in the Espírito Santo Basin from Petrobras and the Anglo-French company Perenco.

Due to its early entry into Brazil, Sinochem was the second-largest Chinese oil producer in the country until 2020. Its output expanded remarkably until 2019, but declined substantially in the next year, because of the interruption of production in the Peregrino field, in May 2020. In 2021, for example, its output was zero, but in the two following years, it restarted to expand again.

In September 2024, Sinochem announced the sale of all its assets in Brazil (Pitangola and Peregrino fields) to the Brazilian firm PRIO, in a deal that involved US$ 1.9 billion (PRIO 2024). The Nordish firm Equinor is the operator of the fields with a 60 % interest. The transaction received approval from local antitrust authorities (CADE) weeks later and, in December 2024 the conclusion of the transaction was publicized (PRIO 2024). According to information collected by the author in October 2024, the Chinese company was preparing the closure of its office in Rio de Janeiro.

It was not the first time that Sinochem traded assets in Brazil. In 2016, it left some ongoing projects in the Espirito Santo basin, which were bought in 2012.

4. Impacts of Chinese OFDI in Brazil and of Brazilian oil exports to China

China's outbound foreign direct investments have long attracted global coverage. This attention has grown in tandem with the sharp increase of numbers invested and the consolidation of the country as one of the major sources of capital in the world (not only a chief receiver).

The same exposure is true about commerce. PRC's fast economic growth has catapulted its exports and imports to and from abroad over the last years. Since 2009, it is the largest exporter and has become the second biggest importer in the world (after the United States) (Trademap 2024). Its emergence as an industrial powerhouse, responsible for almost one third of global manufacturing value added as of 2022 (World Bank 2024) has prompted rearrangements in global value chains. Impacts are seen in many countries and economic sectors.

Over this period, there have been basically two types of reactions to Chinese OFDI and the growing exports to the PRC. On the one hand, there are the optimists, who welcome Chinese disbursements and trade with the country looking through positive lens. Their arguments are generally related to the role of FDI to stimulate local development, build infrastructure, dynamize specific economic sectors, create jobs, bring new expertise and technologies and so forth and so on. On the other hand, there are the pessimists, who focus on possible negative spillovers of Chinese investments. They argue that some projects are associated with cases of closure or displacement of native industries, environmental impacts, clashes with local communities, worsening working conditions, augmented corruption, import of Chinese workers, trade deficit, economic dependency etc. (Blanchard 2024).

One of the main objectives of this study is to provide an analysis of the impacts of Chinese investments and of exports to China in the Brazilian petroleum sector, with a localized emphasis on the state and city of Rio de Janeiro. The reasons for choosing Rio are two.

The first one is Rio's predominant position in Brazil's oil segment. As of 2023, the state was responsible for 86 % of national production, more than 70 % of E&P investments and of the E&P related jobs and almost 80 % of national tax collection in the oil field (IBP 2024). Rio is equally the state with the largest proven oil reserves, with 8,5 billion barrels of equivalent oil (boe) in 2020, which represents 79 % and 63 % of national oil and gas reserves respectively. Rio alone has the world's 17th largest proven reserves, ahead of Angola, Mexico and Norway (IBP 2024). Not without reason all major oil companies and related governmental organs have offices in the Southern city. The headquarters of Petrobras and the National Agency of Petroleum (ANP) are located in Rio.

The second reason is that so far there is no comprehensive study that assesses the effects of Chinese investments and imports in terms of employment, suppliers, new socioeconomic conditions, potential domestic political tensions, learning processes, technology transfer, and environment protection. Specific research on these topics is also rare, mostly limited to media reports.

It is fair to say that this section does not aim to depict a complete picture of each of these topics. There are limitations in this paper. Two of them are data quality and availability. Quantitative information is sometimes scarce. For instance, none of the abovementioned Chinese oil firms has an operational website destined for Brazil, not to mention the publication of public annual reports. The only exception is the joint venture Repsol-Sinopec, whose webpage does not offer insights into many of the topics just raised.

Another limit is the impossibility to go to Rio de Janeiro to do field work. Moreover, not all impacts commonly raised in related academic research are considered here. Sometimes, the simple reason is that they do not apply, such as the fact that there are no reported big scale environment problems associated with PRC's oil corporations in Brazil.

As a remedy to these limits, the author has resorted to virtual discussions with professionals in the Brazilian oil sector and with staff of Chinese oil firms based in Brazil. Notwithstanding repeated efforts, not all companies responded to requests of online meetings. Interviews were few, but illustrative. The few informal conversations gathered were highly valuable in providing insights into various aspects of Chinese investments and oil exports to the PRC. In this process, some views were confirmed, other misperceptions were corrected.

4.1 Employment impacts

Employment effects of Chinese foreign direct investments have received global extensive attention over the last decades, not only from scholars, but also from governmental officials in recipient states. As a rule, Chinese FDI are welcomed in many countries. However, in recent years, media reports have revealed cases of overseas projects where local work traditions and regulations clashed with Chinese labor practices. Negative coverage involved examples of overtime culture, poor working conditions, irregular presence of Chinese workers, unbalanced percentage of locals versus Chinese workers, especially in executive and high-level positions, and so forth and so on.

There are few studies on the employment effects of Chinese investments in Brazil, especially in the oil sector. Here are some: Hiratuka argues that economic relations with China have resulted in a substantial growth in job creation. In the 2000-2017 period, 1.6 million China-related jobs were created in Brazil, most of them the result of net trade (1.5 million jobs). Chinese OFDI and infrastructure projects were responsible for less new employments, respectively 30,500 and 60, 100 jobs (Hiratuka 2018:171). Unfortunately, the author rarely mentioned the oil sector in its analysis. The only reference was to refined oil trade and not to Chinese upstream investments or Brazilian crude exports. Dussel Peters and Santillán (2023) converge at Hiratuka's argument that trade with the PRC had positive spillovers in terms of job creation. They assert that the net trade effect of Sino-Brazilian commerce has resulted in a surplus of 6.5 million new jobs in Brazil between 1995 and 2018 (Dussel Peters and Santillán 2023:5), of which 516,400come from energy exports (Dussel Peters and Santillán 2023:23). Although the petroleum sector is not specified in these estimates, considering that Brazil-China energy trade is dominated by oil, it is fair to predict that those half a million posts came from crude exports.

So far, the best references for job related research come from Red ALC-China and CECHIMEX. The *Monitor of Chinese Infrastructure 2024* reveals that Chinese construction contracts in Brazil have created over 184,000 jobs of this total more than 110,000 in the energy sector, of which 34,600 in the O&G segment (Dussel Peters 2024/a). The *Monitor of Chinese* OFDI *in 2024* indicates that around 161,000 jobs were related or generated by Chinese investments in the country, of which 30,000 were correlated to energy projects, of which over 10, 000 to specifically oil and gas ventures. According to the database, Rio has hosted almost half of them, or 4,900 (Dussel Peters 2024/b).

Besides data from the Red ALC-China and CECHIMEX, there is very few available information about job conditions and environment concerning Chinese oil companies locally established in Brazil and, more specifically, in Rio de Janeiro, where all four firms have opened offices. Searching LinkedIn could provide a glimpse of the number of employees working at these four companies in Rio. As of October 2024, the total number of individuals listing these companies as their current employer is 276, with 213 at Repsol-Sinopec, 44 at CNPC and its affiliates, 14 at Sinochem, and 5 at CNOOC. The possible reasons why Repsol-Sinopec had more staff are the lengthy time the Spanish firm is established in Brazil and the greater number of projects in which it is involved. Generally speaking, most of the workers seems to be locals. Browsing through CNPC's declared personnel, 11 seemed to be Chinese and 7 from other countries not Brazil.

Considering the amounts invested by these firms in recent years, it is reasonable to believe that these figures are mere estimates; the actual number is likely higher.

Conversations with workers in the Brazilian oil sector and with employees of Chinese oil firms in Brazil have shed some light on working conditions in those corporations. Interviewees highlighted that salaries and other benefits offered are according to local standards and sometimes higher, as a tool to attract qualified labor force. Since the firms are state-owned and thus must report to the capital (or receive instructions), some internal documents are written in Mandarin directedly. Managerial positions are typically held by Chinese nationals, while line positions exhibit a more mixed composition, with a predominance of local employees As a whole, the majority of the workforce is local or sometimes from countries other than Brazil and China.

4.2. Technology transfer/learning process

Technology transfer is a frequently asked question in relation to Chinese outbound investments. There is extensive literature on China's access of foreign technology through the acquisition of overseas companies. More recently, this issue has become more sensitive and therefore more exposed in the media, as many countries have progressively adopted restrictions on M&A transactions and even on greenfield projects in which Chinese corporations are involved. From the receiving country perspective, there is a pressuring request that Chinese FDI could generate some kind of tech transference that could benefit local firms' development.

Before analyzing the Sino-Brazilian oil relationship circumstances, it is worth setting the definition of technology transfer (TT). According to the World International Property Organization (WIPO), transfer of technology (TOT) is a "collaborative process that allows scientific findings, knowledge and intellectual property to flow from creators to public and private users" (WIPO 2024). Moreover, among the modes of TT, it is included sponsored research and R&D collaborations, institution-industry staff exchange, assignment and licensing of technology, and others (WIPO 2024).

Brazil's, and more specifically Petrobras' expertise in ultra-deepwater drilling, is considered one of the key factors driving Chinese oil companies' involvement in exploration projects in partnership with the Brazilian national petroleum corporation.[4] Indeed, as Barbosa argues, the discovery of pre-salt provinces was not by chance, but rather the result of continuous technological breakthroughs over time, some of them recognized by international awards (Barbosa 2024). Historically, Chinese oil companies have lacked expertise and technical knowledge in certain areas of offshore exploration, leading them to view partnerships with Brazilian firms as a means of gaining access to these skills (Husar and Best 2013).[5] Therefore, Chinese oil corporations have decided to join already established production consortia and participated in bidding processes alongside other technologically more mature oil companies (Alves 2013).

The Sino-Brazilian experience has shown that technology transfer *per se* might not have happened, instead Chinese petroleum firms may have absorbed the experience of Petrobras and other locally established companies in joint exploration projects. Relationships between partners in E&P consortia around the world are normally strictly regulated by joint operational agreements (JOA), whose contractual models are commonly offered by the Association of International Energy Negotiators (AIEN). Under these contracts, parties are not obligated to disclose proprietary technology to each other (AIEN 2023). Therefore, in legal terms, partnership in E&P projects did not give Chinese oil firms access to intellectual property.

4 The other three reasons behind Chinese investments in the Brazilian oil sector would be the presence of abundant oil reserves, availability of strategic assets and the existence of economic opportunities to Chinese engineering contractors and machinery companies. For more details, please refer to "Two Decades of Brazil-China Oil Cooperation: Investments and Infrastructure Projects" (Barbosa 2021).

5 According to Liu, the offshore technological capabilities of Brazilian firms were significantly more advanced than those of Chinese firms. For instance, in 2015, Brazil possessed 172 registered patents of deep-sea exploration technology, whilst China, only 9 (Liu 2015).

Nonetheless, in practical terms, Chinese technicians may have gained insight into Brazilian firms' deep-sea drilling expertise through mechanisms established under the JOAs, for example. For example, after the formation of E&P consortia, an operational committee is created to discuss procedural issues among technical staff from each party (AIEN, 2023). In these meetings, topics like geological analysis, drilling issues and others are examined. From explanations from technicians that operate exploration projects,[6] it might be possible to grasp some technical expertise.

The possibility of sharing exploration skills among consortium members is widely recognized and valued in the oil sector. This is one of the reasons that prompted PRIO to buy Sinochem's stakes in Brazil and thus partner with Equinor. Here is how Roberto Monteiro, CEO of PRIO, justified its firm new endeavor: "Here in Brazil, Equinor is doing a great job in Peregrino, so it is gratifying for us to be working alongside a good operator. (...) we will try to learn from them, from the point of view of maintenance, geology, reservoir, among other things. It is a two-way street" (PRIO 2024).

At the same that CNOOC has strengthened partnership with Petrobras in deep-water projects, it also progressed in offshore exploration projects in Brazil and over the Chinese coast. For instance, years after joining the pre-salt Libra consortium, CNOOC won a concession to explore oil fields in Brazil. Another example is China's recent progress in offshore drilling in its coastal waters. In March 2024, CNOOC announced PRC's first deep-water hundred-million-ton oilfield discovery (nearly 750 million barrels), which is located 300 kilometers from the coast of Guangdong province (Xinhua 2024). In August 2024, another milestone. The company revealed the detection of the world's first ultra-deep water and ultra-shallow gas field with 100 billion cubic meters (People´s Daily 2024). With the help of these recent findings and the continuous expansion of its reserve base, CNOOC presented record profits in the first-half of 2024. According to filings, in year-to-year terms,

---

6 In a consortium, one member is usually responsible for maneuvering oil production, while other parties just take yields.

net production rose 9.3 % and net profit increased 25 % (Howe and Aizhu 2024).

4.3. Projects setbacks

Not all Chinese projects in Brazil were successful. Two of them deserve attention: Shandong Kerui's construction project of GASLAB and Sinopec's UFN3 fertilizer unit.

Shandong Kerui's first and only project in Brazil was the contract to build the GASLAB natural gas processing unit at the former COMPERJ petrochemical complex,[7] installed in the city of Itaborai (state of Rio de Janeiro). In September 2017, it joined hands with the local firm Metodo Engenharia and won the bidding process to erect the unit. In March 2018, the US$ 590 million contract was signed (Petrobras 2018). Works commenced a month later and were expected to end in the second half of 2020.

GASLAB was designed to be the largest gas processing unit in the country with a clear strategic role: to expand the country's pre-salt gas offloading and processing infrastructure and to diminish the need for natural gas imports. Along with the processing unit, a 355 km-long gas pipeline, known as Route 3, was planned to connect the offshore pre-salt production structures in the Santos Basin to GASLAB (Petrobras 2018).

Nonetheless, the project was never finished by the winning consortium. Media reports exposed contractual obligations' breaches, construction delays and interruption of employees' payments (Barbosa, 2024). In January 2022, the construction firm Metodo filed for judicial recovery after a sharp rise in costs for materials, shipping, equipment and services. In July 2022, nearly 2,200 employees were laid off and works were halted (Petrobras 2022). Two months later, in September, the contract between Petrobras and the consortium Kerui-Metodo was terminated (Petrobras 2022).

7 Nowadays, it is called "Complexo de Energias Boaventura" and was reinaugurated in September 2024 (Machado 2024).

Sinopec has also undergone negative experiences in Brazil. As a service provider, its plan to erect, in partnership with Galvao Engenharia, a fertilizer unit named "Unidade de Fertilizantes Nitrogenados" (UFN-3) at the state of Mato Grosso do Sul (MS) ended before conclusion. After winning a R$ 3.1 billion bidding process ordered by Petrobras, construction works started in 2011. However, in December 2014, arguing the existence of contractual breaches, the Brazilian oil firm terminated the contract, although the unit was then nearly 81 % finalized. Once completed, the unit will have a projected urea and ammonia production capacity of 3,600 tons/day and 2,200 tons/day, respectively (Petrobras 2022).

In August 2018, Sinopec Petroleum do Brasil Ltda filed for judicial recovery due to labor and contractual debts that amounted to R$ 121 million at that time. The lawsuit was completed in June 2022, when the Chinese corporation was allowed to restart its business in Brazil (Ruddy 2022). Its local partner Galvao Engenharia also filed for judicial recovery, which ended in 2020.

In March 2024, the then president of Petrobras, Jean Paul Prates, declared in an interview that the national company was negotiating with Sinopec the possibility of selling a stake in the UFN-3 project. Sinopec would be a stakeholder, not a service provider (Datagro 2024). In the end of 2024, the resuming construction of the unit was included in Petrobras' Business Plan 2025-2029 (Petrobras 2024).

4.4. Suppliers

One phenomenon that marks the present Brazil-China oil relations is the emergence of Chinese shipyards and the concurrent decline of Brazilian shipbuilders in the provision of floating production storage and offloading (FPSOs) vessels to Petrobras. The discovery of the pre-salt province pressed the Brazilian giant firm into investing heavily in offshore drilling platforms. Initial plans involved the rebirth of Brazil's naval industry, where the new facilities –to be mostly owned by the state firm– would be partially or completely built.

Upcoming circumstances changed preliminary ideas. The outburst of the 2008 international financial crisis, the subsequent period of low and negative economic growth and the outcomes of the Lava Jato corruption investigations have pressed Petrobras to reconsider former plans. Some Brazilian shipyards became immersed in financial problems and some FPSO construction contracts were delayed and cancelled.

From 2013 on, novel contractual formulas and ownership possibilities were implemented and Chinese shipbuilders progressively assumed ongoing and new projects. The flexibilization of local content requirements has also helped the transfer of assignments to Chinese waters. Since 2014, almost all Petrobras's FPSO were in part or totality built or converted in China (Barbosa, 2020). Between 2000 and 2023, more than half of the FPSOs that the company contracted abroad were partially or totally built in PRC's shipyards (Barbosa 2024).

This transfer of roles in Petrobras' FPSO construction plans is related to the emergence of China as a global naval power. The Asian country is currently the largest builder of ships in the globe. It has also by far the largest naval fleet in world. As of 2023, China accounted for half of the global shipbuilding output, 55 % of the world's new deadweight tonnage, and 67 % of new orders were secured by Chinese shipyards (Gao and Feng 2024). China has kept the top position in the international shipbuilding market since 2010.

4.5. New socioeconomic conditions

Besides commercial operations in Brazil, Chinese oil companies have recently started to support local cultural, social, environmental, and educational activities.

Sinopec is by far the main supporter of social projects among other Chinese oil firms, thanks to its joint venture with Repsol, through it all initiatives are financed. The Spanish firm was already long established in Brazil before the partnership began and it had already a footprint on interactions with local communities.

Repsol-Sinopec has a long list of funded projects in Brazil and they happen in different areas. Among the activities, the firm was involved with the "Orquestra de Camara da Rocinha," focused on forming a new generation of musicians from the *favela* Rocinha; "Academia Perolas Negras," a NGO which in 2024 helped 2,400 children and teenagers of Rio to undergo sports and educational training; and "Plataforma Educativa," which is an itinerant program that offers environmental education and safety lectures to fishing workers. Moreover, during the COVID pandemic, it financed the expansion of vaccine production at local laboratories (Repsol-Sinopec 2024).

CNOOC is the main supporter of the "Orquestra do Forte de Copacabana." The orchestra was created in 2011 as a social project focused on offering musical training for poor youngsters from neighboring shanty towns (*favelas*). It is located inside a former fortress in Copacabana beach, in Rio de Janeiro. Currently, there are 28 players between 13 and 25 years-old enrolled in it (OFC 2024).

In September 2024, the orchestra went to China. It was the first time abroad for most of the members. There were presentations at local schools, such as Peking University, and at a commemorative event for the 50-year anniversary of Brazil-China diplomatic relations, in which the Chinese Vice-President Han Zheng was present.

In conversation with a manager of the project, she highlighted the important and opportune financial contribution of CNOOC. During the initial years of the COVID pandemic, former financiers receded in previous compromises, a situation which posed an existential threat to the orchestra. The timely arrival of CNOOC gave assurances to the continuation of music classes.

CNPC has made a similar approach recently and has been equally involved in local cultural undertakings in Rio de Janeiro. It has sponsored events from the institute "Casa do Choro," which focuses on the preservation and dissemination of popular music from Rio de Janeiro, especially "choro" style. Its activities encompass training professional musicians, producing and broadcasting concerts and events, maintaining and conserving collections, cataloging, recording and preserving musical memory (ICC 2024).

In late October 2024, another social and cultural project sponsored by CNPC began activities. The "Bosque das Artes" ("Arts Forest") was inaugurated on October 31st with the aim to organize Brazilian art exhibitions and to provide art courses and workshops that can benefit up to 11,000 kids per year. The project is located at the iconic tourist attraction "Pao de Acucar" ("Sugar Loaf") and is open daily for visitation (ME 2024).

Discussions with practitioners in the Brazilian oil sector have suggested a trend of behavioral change with Chinese companies, especially CNPC and CNOCC, which are now apparently willing to put down deeper roots in Brazil, after years of continuous investments in the country. Unlike their previous approach of maintaining a low profile and avoiding the spotlight, they are shifting to a strategy that embraces more visibility and greater integration with the local context and elites. Interviewees stressed that this gradual stance adjustment started to be clear during the COVID pandemic, although the reasons are unclear.

5. Conclusions

Oil is an important part of the booming bilateral economic relations. In the process of consolidation of Brazil as a global major oil producer and exporter, China has been having an important role and has become the main destination market of Brazilian petroleum. Reversely, the South American country is Beijing's seventh foreign oil supplier (as of 2024), and thus has become increasingly relevant in PRC's energy security concerns. Additionally, Brazil's huge production prospects became an appealing factor to make Chinese oil firms start/expand operations there.

Despite the existence of growing literature on Brazil-China oil relations, there is a lack of studies on possible regional impacts of Brazilian oil exports to China and of Chinese oil investments in Brazil. This is the main contribution of this paper. Considering all restrictive issues of data quality and quantity raised above, the results obtained so far in this oil-related research are remarkable.

As seen above, at least 44,600 jobs were directedly and undirectedly related to Chinese FDI and infrastructure oil projects in Brazil in the last few years. Given the regional concentration of trade and investment ties, Rio de Janeiro is the state where these occupations were mostly created. Indications of poor working conditions were not found during the research. Interviews have signaled that Chinese oil firms tend to follow local labor rules and there is no evidence of import of Chinese workers in significative quantities. Executive roles are predominantly, though not exclusively, held by PRC nationals, while line positions are primarily occupied by locals. Salaries and benefits are aligned with local standards, and in some cases, even exceed them. Interviewees viewed this as a strategy to attract talented individuals.

No noticeable technology transfer towards Brazilian or Chinese companies was revealed during the research, but there are signs of an upward Chinese learning curve in terms of knowing how to do business in Brazil and how to explore deep-sea oil provinces in general. One indication would be that, after years of investments as minor partners in consortia, some Chinese firms began bidding for and operating certain E&P projects independently, which is the case of CNOOC. Furthermore, the same Chinese corporation has recently made great advancements in terms of profundity in offshore projects back in China.

The emergence of China as the world's largest shipbuilder has impacted Brazil's naval industry. Nowadays, the majority of Petrobras' FPSOs are partially or totally constructed in Chinese waters and less in Brazil. This situation is also related to the crisis that Brazilian shipyards were engulfed in the 2010 decade, when some of them bankrupted and others needed to downsize operations.

Chinese oil firms are getting involved in cultural and educational activities in Brazil, a decision which is interpreted by professionals as an effort to have a bigger exposure and to build closer ties with local communities and elites. CNPC, for instance, has financed the activities of a musical institute and an artistic project in Rio. CNOOC supports an orchestra composed by youngsters from neighboring shanty towns also in Rio. Repsol-Sinopec has a long history of financed events, having been established in Brazil for an extended period.

Not all Chinese investments in Brazil ended up well. Shandong Kerui's first and only deal was not concluded and its contract was terminated after years of construction setbacks and social problems. GASLAB was designed to be the largest gas processing unit in the country and is considered to be a strategic project, as it will increase Brazil's domestic supply of natural gas. Sinopec's plans to build a fertilizer unit in Mato Grosso do Sul stopped before completion. Its Brazilian branch even filed judicial recovery, which ended in mid 2022.

Despite Shandong Kerui's setback, Chinese investments in the Brazilian oil sector tend to be seen through positive lens by local actors.

Firstly, Chinese oil firms' presence in Brazil is welcomed in a segment thirsty for investments. After the discovery of pre-salt provinces, it was clear that, without a financial and logistic expansion of the oil sector, it wouldn't be possible to fully explore the new resources. Foreign hands would be needed, bringing not only new capital, but also managerial and production expertise. It is worth remembering that, in the two landmarks of the pre-salt history–Libra and Buzios auctions–, Chinese companies were present. Buzios showcased the importance of the Chinese presence. In a time when overseas corporations were ambivalent about the exploration prospects of the field and none of them showed willingness to join Petrobras' consortium, CNPC and CNOOC were the only ones that embarked on the partnership.

Secondly, the expansion of the oil industry, fueled by both national and foreign investments –including Chinese– is a key driver of Rio's economic revival. Statistics show that Rio is the Brazilian state whose economy has expanded the least since 1985. Specialists argue that, since Brasilia became the capital in the 1960s, Rio has been caught in a continuous cycle of company and bank exodus (mostly state-owned), infrastructure depreciation and political instability that has been negatively affecting the state's economic performance (Trece 2021). Rio is also currently the subnational unit with the fifth largest unemployment rate (Regueira, 2024). Therefore, the presence of vast oil reserves in the state's coast is thus seen as a tool to keep Rio's economic vitality and industrial power. As of 2021, the state of Rio had the second-largest industrial GDP in Brazil, with 53% of its composition linked to oil and gas activities. In the last ten years, petroleum account for 72% of all values exported by Rio. In 2023, Rio collected no less than R$ 24.8 billion (nearly US$ 4.13 billion as of December 2024) in taxes connected to oil activities (IBP 2024), making it the number one state in the country.

Lastly, no major labor, social, environmental or corruption incidents have erupted so far. Interviews have helped to demystify some of the critics commonly associated with Chinese investments abroad and with exports to the PRC, especially those related to imports of Chinese workers and poor working conditions. As mentioned above, some interviewees even highlighted that Chinese oil corporations sometimes offer more benefits, possibly as a way to attract talents in a place that they are newcomers. Moreover, these talks with local employees have indicated that common criticisms about lack of technology transfer by Chinese companies seems to not apply in the Sino-Brazilian example, because there is a widespread belief that one of the reasons why PRC's oil firms went to Brazil was to obtain some local deep-sea exploration know-how.

Considering the analysis carried out during this and previous research, some policy proposals can be highlighted.

Firstly, the replacement of local shipbuilders by Chinese firms is a concerning issue, yet some observers put it into a broader perspective, in which Brazilian dockyards plunged into crisis while Chinese counterparts emerged as global players with competitive conditions in terms of price, quality and production scale and schedule. The strategic character of the shipbuilding industry requires Brazilian policymakers to adopt a strategic approach. Recent Brazilian governmental initiatives to foster reindustrialization and regain the vigor of local shipyards are welcomed (Araujo 2025). Shipbuilding could be subject to bilateral cooperation under the South-South spirit. Throughout recent Sino-Brazilian political history, petroleum has consistently been a key topic in government discussions and frequently mentioned in high-level documents, such as the Strategic Plan 2022-2031 and the Executive Plan 2022-2026. Considering the Chinese prominence in this industry, Binational schemes could be envisioned to generate employment, establish connections with domestic production chains, and promote technological spillovers. Rio would be one of the most benefited states, as it houses the majority of Brazil's shipyards (25 units) (IBP 2025).

Secondly, financing is currently an important factor in the overall development of the Brazilian oil sector. The industry is increasingly confronting rising production costs, driven not only by the growing logistical challenges of exploring vast resources but also by the heightened demand for operational efficiency and stricter low-carbon requirements. The case of FPSO construction is illustrative. The cost of these huge drilling and storage structures has been growing over the last few years and can reach up to several hundred million dollars. Construction time has also been extended. The existence of long-term funding is now a pre-requisite for the future development of this sector. When visiting Beijing in August 2023, former president of Petrobras, Jean Paul Prates, stressed the relevance of finding innovative financial mechanisms to support the timely construction of FPSOs (Petrobras 2023). At this point, the involvement of Chinese development banks and the recently rehabilitated Brazil-China Cooperation Fund for Capacity Building could be good news (BNDES 2024). In line with Brazilian reindustrialization plans, eventual shipbuilding partnerships in Rio de Janeiro could be included in the negotiations.

Thirdly, binational initiatives on research and development (R&D) could also be fostered. Rio de Janeiro concentrates the most relevant oil-related research institutes. Most of the R&D investments in Brazil's oil sector happens in the city, in research centers such as Cenpes from Petrobras, CoppeComb and CENERGIA COPPE from the Federal University of Rio (UFRJ), FGV Energia, and the Brazilian Petroleum and Gas Institute (IBP), which has a research branch (UniBP). Projects are already starting, such as the recent inauguration of the Brazil-China Institute of Innovation, Science and Technology (BCCSTI), a partnership of Petrobras, UFRJ, CNOOC and China University of Petroleum (CUP) (Ehmann, 2024). Nonetheless, there is potential for more, considering the oil firms' obligation to invest 1 % of their gross production revenue in R&D plans. Investments in R&D can be an inductor of innovation in Rio's economy.

Lastly, the cases of GASLAB and UFN-III were negative experiences that deserve further research in order to understand the reasons behind the failures to complete the projects and thus avoid the repetition of similar situations. This research exercise would not be aimed at singularizing any company or country –those two are not the only cases of foreign firms with setbacks in Brazil–, but at developing better ways to create a sound business environment that maximize potential positive spillovers, mitigate risks and thus attract more foreign investments to the Brazilian oil sector.

References

AEI (American Enterprise Institute). 2024. *China Global Investment Tracker*. AEI: Washington, DC.

AIEN (Association of International Energy Negotiators). 2023. *Joint Operating Agreement (2023)*. AIEN: Houston.

Alves, Ana. 2013. "Chinese Economic Statecraft: A Comparative Study of China's Oil-backed Loans in Angola and Brazil". *Journal of Current Chinese Affairs 42(1)*, pp. 99-130.

ANP (Agencia Nacional do Petróleo). 2024. *Oil, Natural Gas and Biofuels Statistical Yearbook 2024*. ANP: Río de Janeiro.

Araujo, Janaína. 2025. "Ja está em vigor incentivo a producao e geracao de empregos na cadeia do petróleo". *Radio Senado*, January 2.

BACEN (Banco Central do Brasil). 2024. *Relatorio de Investimento Direto 2023*. BACEN: Brasília.

Barbosa, Pedro, 2020. "New Kids on The Block China's Arrival in Brazil's Electric Sector". *Global China Initiative, 12.* Boston University: Boston.

Barbosa, Pedro. 2020. "Petrobras-China Relations: trade, investments, infrastructure projects and loans". *Tempo do Mundo 12 (24)*, pp. 1-30.

Barbosa, Pedro. 2021. "Two Decades of Brazil-China Oil Cooperation: Investments and Infrastructure Projects". *Cuadernos de Trabajo del Cechimex 3*, pp. 1-20.

Barbosa, Pedro. 2024. "No jubileu sino-brasileiro, a confiança mútua é a marca". *Revista Sinóptica (1)*, pp. 34-39.

Barbosa, Pedro. 2024. *China, Brazil and Petroleum – The Role of China in Brazil's Transformation into an Oil Power.* Palgrave Macmillan: Singapore.

Biato, Oswaldo. 2010. *A Parceria Estratégica Sino-Brasileira: origens, evolução e perspectivas (1993-2006).* Funag: Brasília.

Blanchard, Jean Marc. 2024. The Effect of Chinese Outward FDI in the Philippines: Muted Economically and Problematic Politically.

BNDES (Banco Nacional do Desenvolvimiento). 2024. "Reuniao Inaugural do Fundo de Cooperacao Brasil-China". BNDES: Río de Janeiro.

CEBC (Conselho Empresarial Brasil-China). 2024. *Investmentos Chineses no Brasil 2023.* CEBC: Río de Janeiro.

Datagro. 2024. "Petrobras trabalha para a Sinopec reotrnar aos negocios da UFN-3". *Datagro,* March 5.

Dussel Peters, Enrique and Santillán Pérez, Lesbia. 2023. "Empleo generado por China en América Latina y el Caribe (1995-2021)". *Cuadernos de Trabajo del Cechimex 5*, pp. 1-24.

Dussel Peters, Enrique. 2024/a. *Monitor of Chinese Infrastructure in Latin America and the Caribbean 2024.* Red ALC-China: México.

Dussel Peters, Enrique. 2024/a. *Monitor of Chinese OFDI in Latin America and the Caribbean 2024.* Red ALC-China: México.

Ehmann, Marcia. 2024. "UFRJ e governo Chinês criam Instituto China-Brasil de Engenheiros de Destaque, centro de excelência em engenharia". *Centro de Tecnología UFRJ*, November 26.

Energy Institute. 2024. *Statistical Review of World Energy 2024*. Energy Institute: London.

GAC (General Administration of Customs of the People's Republic of China). 2024. *Plataforma de consulta en línea de estadísticas aduaneras*. GAC: China

Gao, Ya and Feng, Difan. 2024. "Chinese Shipyards Are Fully Booked Till 2026, Industry Expert Says". *Yicai Global*, February 28.

Gov.Br (Gobierno de Brasil). 2023. "Presidente Lula realiza tercera visita de Estado a China". *Presidência da Republica*, April 10.

Hiratuka, Célio. 2018. "Impacts of China on the quantity and quality of jobs generated in Brazil between 2000 and 2017". In, Salazar-Xirinachs, José Manuel, Dussel Peters, Enrique and Armony, Ariel. (edit). *Efectos de China en la cantidad y calidad del empleo en América Latina*. ILO: Lima, pp. 153-174.

Howe, Colleen and Aizhu, Chen. 2024. "China's CNOOC posts record interim profit on robust output growth". Reuters, August 28.

Husar, Joerg and Best, Dennis. 2013. *Energy Investments and Technology Transfer Across Emerging Economies. The Case of Brazil and China*. OECD/IEA: Paris.

IBP (Instituto Brasileiro de Petróleo e Gás). 2024. *O setor de oleo e gas e o estado do Rio de Janeiro*. IBP: Rio de Janeiro.

IBP (Instituto Brasileiro de Petróleo e Gás). 2025. *Mapa dos Estaleiros do Brasil*. IBP: Rio de Janeiro.

IBP (Instituto Brasileiro de Petróleo e Gás). n.d. "Todo petroleo e igual? Entenda as principais diferencas". IBP: Rio de Janeiro.

ICC (Instituto Casa do Choro). 2024. *Instituto Casa do Choro*. (at: https://casadochoro.com.br/quem-somos).

ITC (International Trade Center). 2024. *Trade Map*.

Liu, L., 2015. *Zhongguo yu baxi shenhua shiyou maoyi de jiyu yu tiaozhan [Opportunities and challenges of deepening oil trade between China and Brazil]*. Quanguo Shangqing: China, pp. 28-29.

Machado, María. 2024. "Após 16 anos, antigo Comperj é inaugurado, com metade da capacidade em operação". *MegaWhat*, September 13.

MDIC (Ministério do Desenvolvimento, Indústria, Comércio e Serviços). 2025. Comex Stat.

OFC, 2024. Orquestra Forte de Copacabana. (at: https://orquestrafortedecopacabana.com.br/).

People'sDaily. 2024. "China explores the world's first ultra-deepwater, ultra-shallow, 100-billion-square-meter atmospheric field". *Baidu*, August 8.

Petrobras, 2022. "Petrobras informa sobre a venda da UFN-III". *Petrobras*, January 24.

Petrobras. 2018. *Petrobras signs contract for construction of Natural Gas Processing Unit in Itaborai*. Petrobras, March 29.

Petrobras. 2022. *Petrobras on Route 3 Integrated Project*. Petrobras, March 24.

Petrobras. 2022. *Petrobras on Route 3 Integrated Project*. Petrobras, September 23.

Petrobras. 2023. "Petrobras assina acordo com bancos chineses". *Petrobras*, August 8.

Petrobras. 2024. "Petrobras lança Plano de Negócios 2025-2029 com investimentos de US$ 111 bilhões". *Petrobras*, November, 21.

Poder360. 2024. "Xi Jinping confirmou vinda ao Brasil para Cúpula do G20, diz Alckmin". *Poder360*, June 27.

Prazeres, Tatiana. 2024. "Comercio Brasil-China nos ultimos 50 anos e os desafios para as exportacoes brasileiras". In, Nastari, Alfredo (edit). *China e Brasil 50 anos de amizade e parceria*. Nastari Targets: Sao Paulo, pp. 75-78.

PRIO (PetroRio). 2024. "PRIO announces acquisition of 40% of the Peregrino field". PRIO, September 27.

PRIO. 2024. "PRIO conclui aquisicao de 40% do Campo de Peregrino". PRIO, December 5.

Regueira, Chico. 2024. "RJ está entre os 5 estados com mais desempregados do Brasil". *Globo G1*, December 28.

Repsol-Sinopec. 2024. *Repsol-Sinopec: Brazil.*

Ruddy, Gabriela. 2022. "Após dois anos, Sinopec Brasil encerra recuperação judicial". *Valor Globo*, June 24.

Torres, Rafael. 2024. "Bosque das Artes: Projeto Maravilh chega ao Parque Bondinho Pão de Acúcar". *Mercado e Eventos,* October 23.

Trademap. 2024. Trade Map. At: www.trademap.org.

Trece, Juliana. 2022. "Estado do Rio e o que menos cresceu desde 1985". *Blog do IBRE*, September 30.

UNCTAD (United Nations Conference on Trade and Development). 2024. *World Investment Report 2024.* UNCTAD, June 20.

WIPO (World Intellectual Property Organization). 2024. "FAQs: Technology transfer and intellectual property". WIPO.

WIPO (World Intellectual Property Organization). 2024. Intellectual Property and Technology Transfer. WIPO.

World Bank. 2024. *Manufacturing, value added (current US$).* World Bank Open Data.

Xinhua. 2024. "China discovered the first deep-water hundred-million-ton oil field". *Xinhua*, March 8.

5.
Argentine Soybean Exports to China: Myths and Realities in The Pampas Region

Eduardo Daniel Oviedo

Introduction

According to Argentina's National Institute of Statistics and Censuses (2022), the Pampas region encompasses the provinces of Buenos Aires, Córdoba, Entre Ríos, La Pampa, Santa Fe, and the Autonomous City of Buenos Aires (Map 1). Characterized by expansive prairies and a temperate climate, this region is the center of Argentina's political power and economic activity, hosting 65 % of the country's population and 73 % of the Gross Domestic Product, according to the 2022 National Census.

Since the late nineteenth century, the Pampas region has been a prominent global hub for grain and beef production. In recent decades, soybeans have also become a key focus, with the region excelling in their production, processing, and export. Notably, the Pampas accounted for an average of 97.5 % of Argentina's soybean and byproduct exports (Table 10). As the nation's most significant export chain, soybeans contributed 30.6 % of Argentina's total exports in 2021 (see Table 4). This highlights the pivotal role of both the soybean sector and the Pampas region in the country's economy.

Argentina is the world's third-largest soybean producer and the leading exporter of soybean oil and meal. According to the

Map 1. Pampas region, Argentina

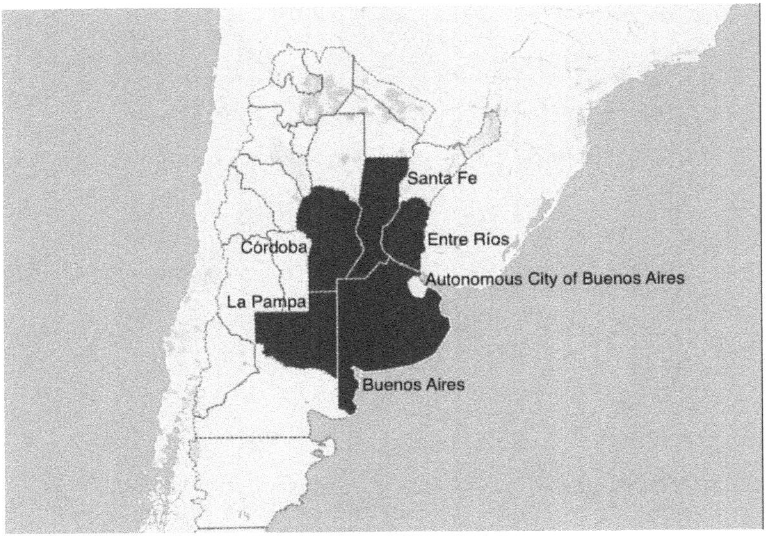

Source: Author' elaboration based on the Argentina's National Geographic Institute (2024).

Food and Agriculture Organization (2024), China is the largest importer of unprocessed soybeans. These factors have contributed to the misconception that China is Argentina's primary partner in the soybean supply chain, significantly influencing the national economy, its value chain, and the Pampas region. However, despite Argentina's highly specialized soybean sector, state interventions in both Argentina and China have caused trade diversions, limiting exports to China. Consequently, these exports have not grown at the same pace as those of Argentina's main competitors, such as Brazil and the United States, according to the United States Department of Agriculture (2024).

Argentina's soybean exports operate within the context of a historical tension between two development models: the spontaneous development model and the state intervention model, as described by Professor Helio Jaguaribe (1968:12). Since the internal political crisis of 2001-2002, state intervention has largely dominated the Argentine economy, except for the period from 2015 to 2018, when

President Mauricio Macri's administration sought to shift toward a spontaneous development approach. This orientation was revived by President Javier Milei in December 2023.

During the period analyzed in this report (2019-2023), soybean exports to China occurred within a framework of state intervention aimed at promoting soybean industrialization to enhance the value of the primary product. Meanwhile, Chinese trade policies have prioritized the import of raw materials over industrialized goods. This has led to trade diversions, establishing the Pampas region as the primary hub for the industrialization and export of soybean by-products, and, to a lesser extent, soybeans themselves, which affect exports to China. As a result, China has remained a marginal trade partner in this sector, primarily purchasing surplus unprocessed soybeans that are not utilized by Argentina's crushing plants.

Building on these starting points, this document aims to challenge prevailing misconceptions and offer a clearer understanding of the actual impact of soybean exports to China on Argentina's soybean value chain and the Pampas region during the period 2019-2023. To achieve this, the document is organized into four sections.

The first section provides a retrospective study of Argentina-China relations, focusing on trade dynamics and the "food paradox." This paradox highlights the contradiction of Argentina –a major agricultural exporter– experiencing chronic trade deficits with China since 2008. This is despite China being recognized by the FAO as the world's largest food importer, particularly of soybeans and beef, two commodities in which Argentina excels.

The second section provides an overview of the importance of the soybean value chain in Argentina, while the third focuses on the Pampas region's contributions to global markets, with a particular emphasis on China. It highlights the significance of the Chinese market and explores how Argentina has underutilized this trade relationship.

The fourth section examines the effects of soybean exports to China on the Pampas region, addressing key aspects such as foreign currency inflows from regional sales to China, impacts on livestock, employment, and the environment, as well as the role of Chinese investments and imports within the production chain. These effects, however, are also influenced by ongoing political tensions between the private sector, Pampas provinces, and the national government regarding the distribution of benefits generated by soybean sales–a dynamic that has historically influenced the volume of exports indirectly.

The final section concludes that the impact of exports to China on the soybean value chain and the Pampas region diverges from the widely held perception of China as a dominant trade partner in Argentine foreign trade and other value chains. It also highlights that this impact is significantly shaped by the prevailing development models in both Argentina and China.

1. Unrealized Potential: Lost Opportunities in the Chinese Market

Historically, the relationship between Argentina and China began relatively late compared to other Latin American countries such as Peru, Brazil, and Mexico (Oviedo 2010). While these countries established diplomatic ties early and hosted large numbers of Chinese workers, Argentina's *Second National Census* of 1895 recorded only 28 Chinese citizens–a figure that rose to 462 in the *Third National Census* of 1914 (Argentina 1898:XLIXV; 1916:206).

The first diplomatic contacts between the two nations date back to the early twentieth century, but formal diplomatic relations were not established until 1945. However, this was short-lived, as the founding of the People's Republic of China in 1949 marked a significant shift.

During the Cold War, Argentine governments chose to continue recognizing the Republic of China (Taiwan) as the legal representative of the Chinese state. Despite the absence of formal diplomatic relations with the People's Republic of China (China), Argentina's annual exports of one million tons of grain between

1964 and 1966 highlighted the growing importance of the Chinese market, particularly in contrast to the limited trade opportunities available with Taiwan.

To counteract the economic attraction of China, Taiwan implemented a "visit diplomacy" campaign, inviting Argentine politicians, military officials, and academics to travel to the island (Oviedo 2010:223-229). Additionally, Taiwan proposed sending agricultural experts to develop a technical cooperation program aimed at improving soybean production, with the goal of enhancing the cultivation of a crop that was somewhat neglected in Argentina at the time and later acquiring it for Taiwan (La Capital Newspaper 1967:7).

Ultimately, in 1972, Argentina decided to interrupt its political ties with Taiwan and "recognize the Government of the People's Republic of China as the sole legal government of China" (Ministry of Foreign Affairs and Worship 1972a).

In the joint communiqué of the establishment of diplomatic relations, both parties agreed "to adopt active measures for the development of trade relations between the two countries" (Ministry of Foreign Affairs and Worship, 1972a). However, the expectations of the Argentine Ministry of Foreign Affairs to expand trade with China were tempered by the *"Opening to the East"* policy promoted by the Peronist governments (1973-1976), which was primarily focused on the Soviet Union and Eurocommunism. The growing importance of the Soviet market for grain sales, amid the Sino-Soviet conflict, hindered Argentina's trade relations with China.

China gained increasing importance during Argentina's military dictatorship (1976-1983). In 1977, both countries signed a trade agreement, and China imported 15,000 tons of soybean oil from Argentina for the first time–a product that, according to the Ministry of Foreign Affairs and Worship (1977:128), showed promising prospects in the Chinese market for exporting grain surpluses. China's economic opening, particularly after the establishment of formal relations with the United States in December 1978, facilitated deeper interactions with Argentina. In 1980, the first visit by an Argentine president to China resulted in a series of cooperation agreements across economic, cultural, and scientific-technical fields, alongside an increase in trade. However, during this visit, President Jorge Videla refused to sign a joint declaration that included an anti-hegemonic clause against the Soviet Union, fearing it would jeopardize grain exports to that country.

Following the restoration of democracy in 1983, Argentine governments continued to strengthen relations with China through official visits, bilateral agreements, and expanding trade, particularly during the economic liberalization of the 1990s. During this period, China began categorizing its international relationships based on their nature and significance. In 2001, Argentina was designated as a "Comprehensive Cooperative Partner," a status that evolved into a "Strategic Partnership" in 2004 and was further elevated to a "Comprehensive Strategic Partnership" in 2014. In February 2022, Argentina officially joined China's Belt and Road Initiative.

The transformation of China into a global power after 1998 (Oviedo 2005) and the subsequent economic decline of Argentina reshaped both countries' positions in the international system, as well as the composition of their trade exchanges. Since 1998, the relationship has shifted from a South-South cooperation model to a North-South model, with China in the North and Argentina in the South (now referred to as the Global South). In terms of trade, a center-periphery pattern emerged, characterized by a predominance of Chinese industrial products and Argentine raw material exports –a phenomenon common throughout South America (Oviedo 2023:331-332). As a result, bilateral trade grew, but at the expense of intraregional trade, as South American economies increasingly replaced regional suppliers with Chinese companies. This shift contributed to regional deindustrialization and a growing specialization in primary goods. This pattern closely resembles that seen in the relation with the United States, the European Union, Japan, and other developed economies.

Looking at the results of the last two decades, we can identify both winners and losers among South American economies in trade with China. While there are various criteria for assessing these outcomes, one of the most important is the transfer of financial resources via trade surpluses. Brazil and Chile stand out as the main winners, while Argentina is clearly positioned among the losers.

Looking back, Argentina maintained positive trade balances with China from 1972 until 1991. However, beginning in 1992, trade liberalization under President Carlos Menem's government led to persistent deficits, which continued until 2000. In 2001, this imbalance was reversed, following a significant devaluation of the Argentine peso by 380 %. Combined with rising global soybean prices, this allowed Argentina to enjoy annual trade surpluses until 2008. Since that year, annual trade balances have been unfavorable, with a cumulative deficit of 93.194 billion USD between 2008 and 2023 (Table 1). During the five-year period from 2019 to 2023, the deficit reached 32.086 billion USD, exceeding the value of Argentina's exports to China during that same period (Table 2).

Table 1. Argentina: General Trends in Trade with China

1972-2023 USD Millions

	Balance
1972-1991	+ 3,345
1992-2000	- 2,827
2001-2007	+ 5,735
2008-2023	- 93,194

Source: Author' elaboration based on the National Institute of Statistics and Censuses of Argentina, INDEC *Informa* (1973-2024).

Argentina's chronic trade deficit stands in stark contrast to the substantial surpluses of Brazil and Chile, which have bolstered the stability of their economies. From 2008 to 2023, Brazil's accumulated surplus reached 283 billion USD, according to data from the Ministry of Development, Industry, Trade, and Services of Brazil (2024), while Chile's surplus totaled 120.326 billion USD, according to the Central Bank of Chile (2024). These figures highlight that, unlike Brazil and Chile, Argentina has been unable to fully capitalize on its trade partnership with China since 2008.

Table 2. Argentina-China Bilateral Trade (2019-2023) USD Millions

	Exports	Imports	Total trade	Balance
2019	6,823	9,258	16,081	-2,435
2020	5,244	8,656	13,900	-3,411
2021	6,156	13,525	19,681	-7,365
2022	7,929	17,501	25,430	-9,573
2023	5,175	14,477	19,652	-9,302
2019-2023	31,327	63,417	94,744	-32,086

Source: National Institute of Statistics and Censuses of Argentina, INDEC *Informa* (2020-2024).

The trade deficit of Argentina can be attributed to two main factors. Firstly, Argentina's escalating export duties favor soybean industrialization, while China primarily seeks raw materials. In 2023, China imported a staggering 111.5 million tons of soybeans, but only 50,000 tons of soybean meal and 400,000 tons of soybean oil, according to the data of United States Department of Agriculture (2024). Argentina's policy of incentivizing soybean crushing reduces the quantity of soybeans available for export to China, contributing to the trade deficit. Since 2008, this deficit reflects the mutual misalignment in trade flows due to what has been termed the "soybean crushing war." Both Brazil and the United States, countries that also prioritize the added value of their production chains (Bergero *et al.* 2018), have better aligned their exports with China's raw material demands, exporting more soybean surpluses than Argentina. In addition, Argentina's high export duties disincentivize soybean production, leading to fewer surpluses available for export to China.

Despite the ongoing trade deficit, China holds a strategic role in Argentina's foreign trade. Between 2019 and 2023, China ranked as Argentina's second-largest export destination and its primary source of imports, during a period affected by weather-related impacts on cereal and oilseed productions in 2020 and 2023 (Table 4). For China, Argentine exports, particularly soybeans and beef, are marginal yet significant in enhancing its food security. Besides these staple exports, barley, fish products, and, from 2022 onward, lithium have also grown in importance.

In 2023, 79 % of Argentina's exports to China were concentrated in four key products: soybeans, beef, barley, and lithium. In contrast, imports from China were highly diversified, including industrial goods such as computers, phones, machinery, industrial inputs, and chemicals like glyphosate. This trade dynamic exemplifies the core-periphery pattern that has defined the bilateral relationship over the past two decades and is likely to continue shaping it in the next years.

Table 3. Main Trade Partnership of Argentina (2019-2023) USD Millions

	Exports				
	2019	2020	2021	2022	2023
1°	Brazil	Brazil	Brazil	Brazil	Brazil
2°	China	China	China	China	US
3°	US	US	US	US	China
4°	Chile	Chile	India	Chile	Chile
5°	Vietnam	Vietnam	Chile	India	Peru
	Imports				
	2019	2020	2021	2022	2023
1°	Brazil	China	China	China	Brasil
2°	China	Brazil	Brazil	Brazil	China
3°	US	US	US	US	US
4°	Germany	Paraguay	Paraguay	Germany	Paraguay
5°	Paraguay	Germany	Germany	Bolivia	Germany

Source: National Institute of Statistics and Censuses of Argentina. *Foreign Trade* (2020-2024).

To promote trade, Argentina and China have signed currency swap agreements, enabling transactions in their respective currencies. Additionally, according to the Ministry of Commerce of the People's Republic of China (2024: 39), ninety major Chinese companies are investing in Argentina. These include COFCO, China Railway, Bank of China, ICBC, Huawei, CCCC, CNOOC,

PowerChina, CITIC, China National Building Materials, Shaanxi Coal and Chemical Industry, COSCO Shipping, Tsingshan Holding Group, China Energy Construction, CRRC, and Zijin Mining. These companies not only drive trade and financial exchanges but also facilitate the temporary and skilled migration of Chinese citizens to Argentina, strengthening the economic and cultural ties between the two countries.

2. Overview of the Soybean Chain in Argentina

Argentina recognizes 63 productive chains (Morra *et al.*, 2022: 3), with the oilseed complex ranking first among export sectors, accounting for 34 % of foreign sales in 2022. In practical terms, one out of every three U.S. dollars generated from exports comes from the sale of soybeans, sunflower seeds, peanuts, and olives. Soybeans and their derivatives make up the bulk of these foreign sales. Excluding drought years like 2023, soybean and derivative exports fluctuated between 27.1 % and 30.6 % of total exports from 2019 to 2023. When oilseeds are combined with cereals –including corn, wheat, barley, and rice– the two sectors together represented half of Argentina's total exports in 2022 (see Table 4)[1].

In any value chain, it is important to distinguish between processes and specific products (Dussel Peters 2018: 52). The process itself involves an industrialization phase, which is part of the scaling-up process (Dussel Peters 2018:5252). This is the case with the soybean value cthain in Argentina, which includes three main stages: the primary sector (comprising production and storage), industrialization (crushing), and export. However, its impact on

1 Following the development of the Vaca Muerta shale oil and gas fields, there are expectations that the energy sector will, in the medium term, equal or surpass the position of the leading value chain currently held by soybeans in Argentine exports. However, the data in Table 4 still shows a significant gap, with soybean exports remaining well ahead.

Table 4. Argentina's Main Export Complexes (2019-2023) USD Millions

Export Complexes	2019	2020	2021	2022	2023
Oilseeds	18,867	16,730	26,389	27,989	16,718
Soybean grain and byproducts	16,943	14,865	23,841	24,868	13,944
Other oilseeds (sunflower, peanut and olive)	1,924	1,865	2,548	3,121	2,774
Cereals (corn, wheat, barley and rice)	10,076	9,539	13,941	16,093	9,382
Automobile	7,126	4,309	7,100	8,678	8,900
Oil, gas and petrochemicals	5,076	3,660	5,208	9,297	8,439
Metalliferous mining and lithium	5,106	3,734	4,942	5,695	5,837
Bovine meat and leather	4,830	4,370	4,772	5,704	4,725
Fruits (grapes, lemon, pears, apples, etc.)	2,304	2,169	2,164	2,041	1,811
Fishing	1,863	1,730	1,990	1,823	1,777
Pharmaceutical	886	864	1,062	1,082	1,091
Other complex					
Total exports	65,115	54,884	77,934	88,446	66,789
Share of soybean complex in total exports	28.9	27.1	30.6	28.1	20.9

Source: Author´s elaboration based on INDEC (2020-2024).

other sectors allows for the identification of five distinct stages, also incorporating suppliers and markets.

Table 5. Argentina Soybean Production Chain

Source: * Ministry of Finance of Argentina, 2019:4.

** Secretariat of Agriculture, Livestock and Fisheries of Argentina, 2023.

In the *primary production stage*, producers (farmers) are responsible for cultivation. Before sowing, they must invest in capital goods (such as tractors and other machinery), agricultural inputs (seeds, agrochemicals, etc.), land leases (if they do not own land), and various services. This stage also requires establishing links with both local and international suppliers.

The Pampas region accounts for 93.4 % of all soybean producers in Argentina. At both the national and regional levels, there is a noticeable decline in the number of producers, particularly in the province of Buenos Aires, where the number dropped by approximately 10 % between the 2018-19 and 2023-24 cropping seasons (Table 6). This decrease in producers is closely linked to a reduction in cultivated area, as shown in Table 17.

Table 6. Soybean Producers in Number: Comparison of the 2018-19 and 2023-24 Seasons

	Producers (2018-2019)	%	Producers (2023-2024)	%	2018-19/2023-24 Variance Percentage
Argentina	62,379	100.0	58,039	100.0	- 6.9
Pampas region	55,897	93.4	54,213	93.4	- 3.0
Buenos Aires	19,802	31.7	17,800	30.7	- 10.1
Córdoba	15,276	22.5	14,732	25.3	- 3.6
Santa Fe	18,116	29.0	16,807	30.0	- 7.2
Entre Ríos	3,871	6.2	3,570	6.1	- 7.7
La Pampa	1,388	2.2	1,304	2.2	- 6.0

Source: Author´s elaboration based on Ministry of Agriculture, Livestock and Fisheries of Argentina (2019, 2024).

After harvest, soybeans are stored in grain elevators or silos before being transported to *industrial processing facilities.* According to the Ministry of Finance of Argentina (2019:4), the country has 49 crushing facilities. At this stage, soybeans can either be sold as raw materials (beans or seeds) or processed into by-products such as meal, pellets, crude oil, and lecithin. After crude soy oil is extracted, it is refined into soy oils, while the transesterification process converts it into biodiesel and glycerin. In Argentina, soybean-derived biodiesel is distributed between the domestic market (45 %) and the global market (55 %), according to data from the Bioeconomy Observatory (2019).

The fifth stage of the soybean production chain involves *final destinations.* Approximately 85 % of soybeans and soybean by-products are exported to international markets, while 15 % are allocated to the domestic market (Table 5). In 2023, the Argentine Customs Office reported exports from 33 soybean exporters, 17 meal and pellet exporters, and 19 oil exporters. Notably, 10 companies accounted for 92.5 % of soybean exports, 98.5 % of meal and pellet exports, and 97.8 % of oil exports.

An official report states that the soybean chain ranks eleventh in its contribution to the national Gross Added Value (GAV), accounting for 2.4 % (Morra *et al.* 2022: 9). Of this, 48 % is generated by the primary sector (production and storage), while 52 % comes from the manufacturing sector (Morra *et al.* 2022: 54).

3. Export Products from the Argentine Soybean Value Chain

In 2023, Argentina's soybean complex exported 13.944 billion USD, representing 20.9 % of the country's total foreign sales (Table 7). Thanks to the productive upgrading process, the 92.6 % of these exports comprised industrialized products, while the remaining 7.4 % were raw materials (soybeans). Argentina also processes soybeans imported from Bolivia, Brazil, Paraguay, and Uruguay.

In 2018 and 2019, restrictions imposed by China on U.S. soybeans led Argentina to import soybeans from the United States for processing and subsequent export, as reported by the National Institute of Statistics and Censuses (2024). Moreover, the U.S. remains a reliable supplier of soybean seeds for planting in Argentina.

The soybean chain is notable for its extensive diversity of export destinations, alongside the legumes, sunflower, medicines, and textile cotton chains (Morra *et al.* 2022:31). Its principal market

Table 7. Argentine Soybean Complex Exports (2019-2023) USD Millions

	2019	2020	2021	2022	2023
Soybean meals and pellets	8,806	7,806	11,796	12,041	8,004
Crude soy oil	3,447	3,894	6,865	6,492	3,530
Refined soy oils	59	121	245	483	638
Soybeans	3,472	2,343	2,814	3,284	1,038
Biodiesel	775	468	1,573	1,851	341
Others (lecithin, glycerol, etc.)	384	353	523	717	393
Total soybean complex	16,943	14,865	23,841	24,868	13,944
Argentina total exports	65,115	54,884	77,934	88,446	66,789
Share of Argentine total exports	26 %	27,1 %	30,6 %	28,1 %	20,9 %

Source: Author´s elaboration based on National Institute of Statistics and Censuses of Argentina (2024).

Table 8. Main Export Destinations of Argentine Soybean Chain Products (2019–2023) USD Millions

	2019	2020	2021	2022	2023
European Union	3,404	2,671	5,045	5,679	2,269
ASEAN members	3,031	2,864	4,014	4,101	2,537
China	3,198	2,173	2,393	3,082	1,253
India	1,659	2,048	3,394	3,184	1,487
Middle East	1,161	1,180	2,112	1,805	1,086
Maghreb and Egypt	1,438	1,066	1,484	1,077	945
Chile	123	198	425	467	431
Rest of ALADI	525	478	1,034	1,029	1,225
Other destinations					
Total	16,943	14,865	23,841	24,868	13,944

Source: National Institute of Statistics and Censuses of Argentina, *Exporting Complexes*, 2020-2024.

is the European Union, followed by member countries of the Association of Southeast Asian Nations (ASEAN), China, and India.

At the country level, India and China are the soybean chain's primary trading partners. In recent years, India has increased its share of Argentine exports, surpassing China as the leading importer (see Table 8).

In 2023, soybean meals and pellets were predominantly exported to ASEAN countries such as Vietnam, Indonesia, and Malaysia, as well as to the European Union and Middle Eastern nations. A substantial 90.3 % of total soybean exports (raw materials) were shipped to China.

Thirty-five percent of crude soy oil was exported to India, with the remainder distributed among China, Bangladesh, Peru, South Korea, and other countries. Refined soy oil was primarily exported to Chile, Spain, and Italy, while lecithin found markets in Chile, the Netherlands, Ecuador, India, and others.

Moreover, 93.5 % of exported biodiesel was destined for the European Union, with the remaining portion sent to Chile. Lastly, soybean seeds for planting were consistently purchased by the United States, Bolivia, and Uruguay.

Table 9. Distribution of the Main Soybean Exports by Countries and Region (2023) USD Millions

	Meals and pellets	Soy oils	Soybeans	Biodiesel	Soy seeds
European Union	1,528			320	
Middle East	1,078				
USMCA		273	55		5
Rest of ALADI	501	603	14		
ASEAN	2,504	14			
India		1,477			
China		310	937		
Uruguay	12				9
Other countries	2,381	1,491	13	21	3
Total	8,004	4168	1,019	341	17

Source: Author´s elaboration based on National Institute of Statistics and Censuses of Argentina (2023).

China plays a dominant role in most of Argentina's export chains. In 2019, two products–soybeans and beef–accounted for 79 % of Argentina's sales to China. However, this percentage dropped to 60 % in 2023 due to the drought. That year, China solidified its position as the leading destination for Argentina's exports of beef, soybeans, barley, and lithium, further strengthening its role in these key sectors of Argentina's foreign trade.

Additionally, China ranked second in the destination of exports of peanuts, tobacco, lead, as well as products from the poultry and fishing sectors.

This outlook highlights China's importance as a trading partner for Argentina, not only in agricultural products like soybeans and barley, but also in emerging sectors such as lithium –a critical resource in the context of the global energy transition (see Table 10).

Table 10. Exports to China by Main Export Complexes (2019-2023) USD Millions

	2019	2020	2021	2022	2023
Soybean	3,198	2,173	2,393	3,082	1,253
Beef	2,368	1,923	1,942	2,469	1,908
Barley	19	82	432	654	631
Lithium				290	364
Fishing complex	431	355	186	228	268
Oil, gas and petrochemicals	227	68	5	182	135
Peanut	103	86	45	76	59
Forest complex	112	103	123	75	59
Pharmaceutical sector	31	30	39	48	28
Dairy	37	38	55	47	29
Grapes	30	27	35	23	20
Total exports to China	7,053	5,397	6,295	8,015	5,270
Argentina total exports	65,115	54,884	77,934	88,446	66,789
% of China in the total exports	10.8	6.9	8	9	7.8

Source: Author´s elaboration based on National Institute of Statistics and Censuses of Argentina (2019-2023).

Since China primarily imports soybeans for its processing facilities, the highest sales peak to China occurred in 2019, when Argentina's industrial complex processed 79.5 % of its soybeans, leaving 20.5 % for raw material. That year, China imported 7.9 million tons of soybeans worth 3.174 billion USD, accounting for 95 % of Argentina's total soybean exports and approximately 8 % of China's total soybean imports.

China has also been a consistent buyer of crude soybean oil, except in 2016 and 2017, according to data from the National Institute of Statistics and Censuses (2024). In 2007, soybean oil sales peaked at 2,208 million tons, but by 2023 they had dropped to 310,000 tons due to the steady development of China's domestic crushing industry following the global economic crisis of 2007-2008 and the 2010 bilateral political crisis (Oviedo 2012). Since then, China has reduced its imports of crude soy oil from Argentina.

China's purchases of soybean meal have been more sporadic. National Institute of Statistics and Censuses data show purchases between 1.3 and 2.3 million tons from 2013 to 2016. In 2019, the National Service of Agri-Food Health and Quality (2019) reported the signing of an agreement for the export of soybean meal to China, although National Institute of Statistics and Censuses data do not record exports to China between 2017 and 2023. However, since 2018, the Simplified Agricultural Information System of the National Institute (2024) has reported sales of meal to a significant confidential destination. In 2023, 626 million USD worth of meal were sent to this destination, representing 7.8 % of total soybean meal and pellet exports. Although the exact destination has not been disclosed, it is presumed to be China, though there is no official confirmation.

Table 11. Argentine Soybean Complex Exports to China (2019-2023) USD Millions

	2019	2020	2021	2022	2023
Soybean meals and pellets	-	-	-	-	-
Soy oils	162	296	418	169	310
Soybeans	3,012	1,867	1,945	2,891	937
Biodiesel	-	-	-	-	-
Others (lecithin, glycerol, etc.)	-	-	-	-	-
Soybean complex exports to China	3,198	2,173	2,393	3,082	1,253
Soybean complex exports	16,943	14,865	23,841	24,868	13,944
Argentina total exports	65,115	54,884	77,934	88,446	66,789

Source: Author's elaboration based on National Institute of Statistics and Censuses of Argentina (2024).

4. Soybean Chain, China, and the Effects on the Pampas Region

The soybean exports from the Pampas region to China have several effects on both the region and the soybean value chain that merit analysis. These effects include:

a) Effects of Exports on Foreign Currency Income

Between 2019 and 2023, the Pampas region contributed an average of 75.4 % of Argentina's total exports. In other words, approximately three out of every four dollars generated from exports came from this region.

Export volumes vary by province. According to the National Institute of Statistics and Censuses of Argentina (2023), in 2023, Buenos Aires accounted for 39.3 % of the country's total exports, followed by Santa Fe with 17.4 %, Córdoba with 12.4 %, Entre Ríos with 1.7 %, La Pampa with 1.2 %, and the Autonomous City of Buenos Aires (CABA) at 0.5 %. Notably, the three leading provincial economies –Buenos Aires, Santa Fe, and Córdoba– represented 69 % of Argentina's total exports, 67.9 % of exports to China, and 82.2 % of soybean complex sales to China.

In 2023, the Pampas region accounted for 97.4 % of soybean complex exports (see Table 12). This significant share highlights the region's alignment with the country's overall commercial destinations (see Table 9). That year, the Pampas region exported 77 % of Argentina's total soybean complex sales to China, amounting to 4.038 billion USD out of 5.270 billion USD in total exports to this market (see Table 13). China only represented 9 % of soybean sector exports, totaling $1.253 billion, of which 89 % originated from the Pampas region. Specifically, Santa Fe contributed 448 million USD (35.7 %), Buenos Aires 322 million USD (25.7 %), Córdoba 285 million USD (22.7 %), Entre Ríos 61 million USD (4.8 %), and La Pampa 26 million USD (2 %), as shown in Table 14.

Since 80 % of oilseed crushing occurs in plants located in the Gran Rosario area along the Paraná River (Calzada and Treboux

Table 12. The Pampas Region in Soybean Complex Exports (2019-2023) USD Millions

	2019	2020	2021	2022	2023
Argentina's total exports	65,115	54,884	77,934	88,446	66,789
Pampas region total exports	48,621	41,271	60,529	68,468	48,427
Share of Pampas region in Argentina exports	74.6	75.1	77.6	77.4	72.5
Total exports of soybean complex	16,943	14,865	23,841	24,868	13,944
Pampas region soybean complex exports	16,377	14,528	23,398	24,236	13,585
Share of the Pampas region on the complex	96.6	97.7	98.1	97.4	97.4

Source: Author´s elaboration based on National Institute of Statistics and Censuses of Argentina (2020-2024).

Table 13. The Pampas Region in Soybean Complex Exports to China (2019-2023) USD Millions

	2019	2020	2021	2022	2023
Total exports to China	7,053	5,397	6,295	8,015	5,270
Share of total exports of Argentina	11 %	10 %	8 %	9 %	8 %
Pampas región exports to China	5,506	4,304	5,171	6,546	4,038
Share of total exports of Argentina to China	78 %	80 %	82 %	82 %	77 %
Soybean complex exports to China	3,198	2,173	2,393	3,082	1,253
Share of total exports to China	45 %	40 %	38 %	38 %	24 %
Share of soybean complex exports	18.8	14.6 %	10 %	12.4 %	9 %

Source: Author´s elaboration based on National Institute of Statistics and Censuses of Argentina (2020-2024).

2021), the soybean chain holds a significant share of total exports from Santa Fe province. In 2022, this chain accounted for 65.3 % of provincial exports, with China representing only 7.4 %. However, 3.3 % of these were soybean complex exports to China, which accounted for 45.2 % of the province's total sales to China.

In Córdoba, the soybean complex accounted for 36.9 % of total exports and China's imports for 8.6 %. Of the total exports from the soybean complex, 6.5 % were directed to China, representing 63.6 % of the province's sales to that market. In Buenos Aires, the complex contributed 20 % to provincial exports, with China accounting for 9.7 %. However, sales from the complex to China represented only 2.7 % of the province's total exports. In Entre Ríos and La Pampa, the soybean complex represented 10 % and 7.2 % of total exports, respectively, while sales to China reached 27.5 % and 20.6 % of total exports from those provinces.

Table 14- The Soybean Chain and China in the Pampas Provinces (2022-2023)

FOB Value in USD Millions

Province	2022	% region	2023	% region
Buenos Aires				
Total exports	33,972	49.6	26,298	54.3
Soybean chain exports	6,602	9.9	4,156	8.5
Exports to China	3,101	4.5	2,150	4.4
Soybean chain exports to China	914	1.3	323	0.6
Share of soybean chain export to China in Buenos Aires total exports	2.7 %		1.2 %	
Share of exports to China in Buenos Aires total exports	9.1 %		8.2 %	
Share of soybean chain in the Buenos Aires total exports to China	29.4 %		15.0 %	
Córdoba				
Total exports	12,845	18.7	8,308	17.1
Soybean chain exports	4,748	6.9	2,207	4.5
Exports to China	1,117	1.6	448	0.9
Soybean chain exports to China	836	1.2	285	0.6
Share of soybean chain export to China in Córdoba total exports	6.5 %		3.4 %	
Share of exports to China in Córdoba total exports	8.6 %		5.4 %	
Share of soybean chain in the Córdoba total exports to China	75 %		63.6 %	

Entre Ríos				
Total exports	1,910	2.7	1,114	2.3
Soybean chain exports	192	0.2	61	0.1
Exports to China	525	0.7	229	0.5
Soybean chain exports to China	191	2.7	61	0.1
Share of soybean chain export to China in Entre Ríos total exports	10 %		100 %	
Share of exports to China in Entre Ríos total exports	27.5 %		20.6 %	
Share of soybean chain in the Entre Ríos total exports to China	36.3 %		nr	
La Pampa				
Total exports	1,182	1.7	777	1.5
Soybean chain exports	85	0.1	26	0.05
Exports to China	241	0.3	144	0.3
Soybean chain exports to China	85	0.1	26	0.05
Share of soybean chain export to China in La Pampa total exports	7.2 %		3.3 %	
Share of exports to China in La Pampa total exports	20.4 %		18.6 %	
Share of soybean chain in the La Pampa total exports to China	35.2 %		18 %	
Santa Fe				
Total exports	19,160	27.9	11,612	23.9
Soybean chain exports	12,520	18.3	7,101	14.6
Exports to China	1,417	2.1	985	2.0
Soybean chain exports to China	641	0.9	424	0.9
Share of soybean chain export to China in Santa Fe total exports	3.3 %		3.6 %	
Share of exports to China in Santa Fe total exports	7.4 %		8.5 %	
Share of soybean chain in the Santa Fe total exports to China	45.2 %		43 %	
Total of Pampas region exports	68,468		48,427	

Source: Own elaboration based on Ministerio de Economía (2023-2024).

NR: no record.

The soybean value chain is the most significant in the Pampas region, with a crucial role across all provinces, particularly in Santa Fe, Córdoba, and Buenos Aires. China's role as an importer of raw materials is relatively diminished in the context of soybeans, as the region exported 89 % of the 9 % of total soybean chain exports to China. This suggests that China's importance decreases at the local level, especially in Buenos Aires province, where soybean sales to China accounted for 9.1 % of total exports in 2022. In contrast, China's significance grows in Córdoba and is particularly critical for the economies of Entre Ríos and La Pampa, where China is their primary trading partner. While soybean exports to China are not as significant for Santa Fe, the province remains important due to its dominance, accounting for 80 % of Argentina's industry facilities and export ports. Notably, China's relevance increases in these provinces when considering exports from other value chains, such as beef and cereals.

b) Export Duties, Trade Diversions, and Pampas-National Tensions

The foreign exchange income generated by exports to China should benefit producers and stimulate economic development in the region. However, the national government's imposition of high export duties on soybeans and their by-products siphons off approximately one-third of these resources. This reduction impacts profit margins and reinvestment capacity, discourages production, and weakens the "spillover effect" on provincial economies. Notably, in 2023, the Pampas region accounted for 97.5 % of soybean value chain sales and 77 % of soybean exports to China. As a result, export duties have become a major point of contention between provincial governments, producers, and the national government.

According to The World Bank (2024), Argentina imposes the highest percentage of export duties globally, followed by Kazakhstan, Russia, Tajikistan, Guinea-Bissau, the Solomon Islands, and 51 other countries that apply such taxes. Between 2002 and 2022, these duties accounted for approximately 5.5 % of total revenue

(Allan *et al.* 2024). The Argentina National Budget Office (2024) reports that export duties represented 8.9 % of national budget revenues in 2024. This underscores the significance of this revenue source for the national-state and complicates any potential replacement, as noted by Allan *et al.* (2024).

Export duties and other fiscal measures have reignited the long-standing debate about development in Argentina. Since the struggles for national consolidation in the nineteenth century, two development models have been in conflict: spontaneous development and state intervention (Jaguaribe 1968: 12), creating tensions between the central government and the provinces. Historical records indicate that Argentina has imposed export duties since 1850 (Allan *et al.* 2024). By the late nineteenth century, under the spontaneous development model, Argentina specialized in exporting meat and grains from the Pampas region to Europe, primarily to the United Kingdom. However, the 1929 Economic Crisis, the Great Depression, the rise of protectionism, and the loss of the "British partner" (Lanús 2001:299-427) led to the collapse of the agri-export model.

Since then, state intervention has fostered Import Substitution Industrialization (ISI) and the welfare state, partially financed by revenues from grain exports. Institutions such as the Grain Regulatory Board (established in 1933) evolved into the Argentine Institute for Exchange Promotion (1946) and later into the National Grain Board (1963). These state entities facilitated connections between producers and international markets, set prices, and guided exports. Although this model of direct intervention was abolished in 1991, it was indirectly reintroduced in 2002 with the imposition of export duties, generating ongoing conflicts between producers and provinces against the national government –a tension that persists to this day.

Export duties place a heavy burden on the soybean sector. Decree 790 of 2020 establishes tariffs of 33 % for soybeans, 31 % for crude soy oil and its by-products (meals, pellets, and expellers), 30 % for bulk refined oil, and 25 % for refined oil in containers of up to 5 liters (Argentine Oilseed Industry Chamber 2024). Practically one out of every three ships of soybeans destined for China generates revenue solely for the state in export duties. In contrast, the United States and Brazil –Argentina's main competitors– do not impose such taxes; instead, they promote agricultural stimulus policies.

These tariffs adversely affect producers, reduce landowners' income, and decrease provincial revenues, as export duties are not shared with subnational units. They also hinder local development by limiting reinvestment and the expansion of agricultural activities in the region, thereby obstructing increases in yield per hectare. For instance, a comparative study by the Rosario Board of Trade shows that Argentina maintained an average soybean yield of 2.7 tons per hectare, while Brazil's yield increased from 2.77 tons at the beginning of the century to 3.43 tons per hectare (D'Angelo *et al.* 2024). This duty has fueled ongoing tensions between the national government, producers, and the producing provinces, particularly Buenos Aires, Santa Fe, and Córdoba, a conflict that has been evident since the Argentina' agrarian crisis of 2008.

Export duties transfer foreign currency to the national government, which uses these funds to subsidize the industrial sector, implement redistributive policies, lower domestic food prices, or finance social assistance programs as part of the welfare state. Some argue that this duty aims to reduce the profitability of large landowning families in the Humid Pampas or to compensate for the environmental impact of agricultural production. However, the burden of the duty primarily falls on the producer, who has no influence over the final price of soybeans, which is set on the Chicago Board of Trade. Consequently, the benefits of high soybean prices do not automatically reach producers and provinces, as the national government collects at least a quarter of the value of soybeans in taxes.

Export duties significantly impact trade with China. Both Argentina and China employ state intervention development models that affect bilateral trade dynamics: Argentina imposes taxes on soybean and its byproducts, while China, according to Bergero *et al.* (2018), levies import tariffs of 9 % on oil, 5 % on meals, and

3 % on soybeans. Additionally, China imports only small quantities of industrialized byproducts, aside from a minimal amount of crude soy oil. In 2023, China consumed 18.1 million metric tons of soy oil but imported only 400,000 tons, of which 310,000 tons originated from Argentina (Table 11).

These trade policies have created a "war" for soybean crushing, as both countries possess substantial processing facilities. According to Li Feng, Assistant Director of Yihai Kerry Company, China's soybean crushing industry has an annual capacity ranging from 190 million to 200 million metric tons (Li, 2023). In Argentina, the national crushing capacity is approximately 68.6 million tons annually, with 80 % concentrated in the Gran Rosario area along the Paraná River (Calzada and Treboux 2021).

Although the differential in export duties between soybeans and by-products is only 2 % (except for refined oils), it incentivizes the export of by-products, diverting these sales to other markets. In 2023, out of the 13,944 billion USD exported by the soybean sector, 57.4 % corresponded to soy meals and pellets, 25.3 % to crude soy oil, 7.4 % to soybeans, 4.5 % to refined soy oil, 2.4 % to biodiesel, and 2.8 % to other products. The main destinations for meals and pellets included ASEAN countries, the European Union, and the Middle East. Crude soy oil was primarily exported to India, with smaller amounts going to China, South Korea, Bangladesh, and Morocco. Refined soy oil's main destination was Chile, while 90.2 % of soybeans were exported to China. Without these differential duties, Argentina would likely export more soybeans to China, following the practices of the United States and Brazil, but would shift to a primary export goods model.

Export duties enable value addition, generate employment, and shift trade toward industrialized products. However, they also distort Argentina's trade balance, potentially showing a surplus with China while creating deficits with other trading partners, such as the European Union, with whom Argentina currently maintains surpluses or balanced trade. Thus, while export duties promote industrialization and employment, they do so at the expense of trade liberalization, creating tensions and lowering profitability for producers and provincial governments. Furthermore, state intervention through exchange rate control further facilitates the transfer of resources from producers to the state.

c) Chinese Investments in the Soybean Chain

Historically, Argentina lacked Chinese oilseed processing and export facilities. In 2014, COFCO (China's National Cereals, Oils, and Foodstuffs Corporation) acquired 51% of Noble Agri, a Singapore-based company with a processing plant at the port of Timbúes in Santa Fe province. A month later, COFCO expanded its presence in the cereal and oilseed trade by purchasing a 51% stake in Nidera, a Dutch agribusiness company with operations in Argentina.

By 2016, COFCO had acquired the remaining 49% of Noble Agri, and in 2017, it secured the final 49% stake in Nidera (COFCO International 2024). In just three years, COFCO achieved full ownership of both companies operating in Argentina. While these acquisitions did not create new jobs, they did help preserve existing employment.

These acquisitions positioned COFCO prominently in the processing and export of oilseeds and cereals in Argentina and globally. The grain trade in Argentina is fragmented among various companies, but COFCO consistently ranked among the leading exporters of beans, flours, pellets, and soybean oil. In 2023, the company was the eighth-largest exporter of soybean beans, the seventh-largest exporter of pellets, and the sixth-largest exporter of oil, according to Argentine Customs data (see Table 13).

In 2017, the China National Chemical Corp (ChemChina), a company that also operates in Argentina, acquired 97% of Syngenta's shares for 43 billion USD. Following an agreement between COFCO and Syngenta, ChemChina gained control of Nidera Seeds in November of that year. Syngenta specializes in the development, production, and marketing of seeds for planting, agrochemicals, and biodiesel, and acts as an exporter through Syngenta Agro. Although Syngenta's share of soybean chain exports is smaller

Table 15. Ranking of Exports by Exporter of Soybeans and By-Products (2023) Metric tons

Companies	Soybeans	%	Meals and Pellets	%	Soy oils	%
CHS de Argentina	502,543	26.7				
Amaggi Argentina	278,044	14.7				
Cargill	234,734	12.8	2,260,326	13.8	605,507	18.0
ADM Agro	202,240	10.7				
LDC Argentina	143,570	7.6	1,974,209	12.1	446,934	13.3
ACA	137,570	7.3	153,170	0.9	44,900	1.3
COFCO International	70,577	3.7	1,573,846	9.6	314,220	9.3
Oleaginosa Moreno - Viterra	70,057	3.7	4,465,533	27.3	1,019,235	30.4
Syngenta Agro	69,526	3.6	117,155	0.7	33,196	0.9
Bunge Argentina	35,000	1.8	1,783,408	10.9	255,837	7.6
Aceitera General Deheza			1,885,857	11.5	176,330	5.2
Molinos Agro			1,711,537	10.5	374,285	11.1
Others						
Total	1,881,179	100	16,351,394	100	3,357,120	100

Source: Author´s elaboration based on Argentina Customs (2023).

compared to COFCO's (see Table 15), its strategic importance in the seed market is significant.

Syngenta leads in the research, development, production, and marketing of sunflower seeds, while Nidera ranks second. This merger resulted in the companies controlling 60 % of the market (CNDC, 2021). Consequently, the National Commission for the Defense of Competition (CNDC) raised objections to the acquisition. However, in 2023, following a divestment proposal to sell various assets to Nuseed company in the sunflower seed sector, the CNDC and the Secretary of Commerce approved Syngenta's acquisition of Nidera (CNDC 2023: 2-3).

These Chinese companies have invested in a country specialized in agricultural production and export, navigating a fragmented market characterized by competitiveness and the presence of major transnational companies in grain trading. In doing so, they have assimilated top-tier practices and knowledge in a peripheral country.

A cost study by the Rosario Board of Trade indicates that for soybeans, truck transport over distances exceeding 710 kilometers accounts for 12.3 % of the total sale price, while for distances of 1,150 kilometers, the cost rises to 15.6 %. In contrast, rail transport reduces these costs to 6.9 % and 9.5 %, respectively, representing savings of 44 % and 39 % (Sesé, Treboux, and Ybañez 2021). However, due to Argentina's outdated railway system, 85 % of grain production is still transported by truck, in stark contrast to practices in the United States and the European Union (Alvarado Ledesma 2024). Given this scenario, developing the railway network is a strategic factor in the transportation of soybeans and other commodities from crop areas to ports. Under the state intervention model, Belgrano Cargas y Logística, a state-owned company responsible for freight railway transport in Argentina, has received substantial investments from China Machinery Engineering Corporation (CMEC) through intergovernmental loans granted by Chinese banks and international agencies. These funds have been used to acquire rolling stock and rehabilitate 1,500 kilometers of cargo rail lines. However, in January 2025, President Javier Milei decreed the privatization of Belgrano Cargas y Logística, creating new challenges for CMEC, which had been investing in the company for the past decade.

d) The Role of Chinese Suppliers

Another way in which Chinese companies are integrated into the soybean chain is through the sale of agricultural inputs. Argentina imports various raw materials for agricultural production from China, primarily glyphosate. Additionally, due to a deficit in domestic fertilizer production, Argentina imports phosphate and urea for planting cereals and oilseeds, which are essential inputs in the primary stage of the production chain. According to the Ministry of Economy of Argentina (2023:26), in 2022, Argentina imported 12 % of its total fertilizers from China (see Table

16). Furthermore, Argentina also imports other capital goods that indirectly impact the soybean sector, such as tractors, machinery, engines, tools, and generators.

Table 16. Argentine Soybean Complex Main Imports from China (2020-2023) USD Millions

	2020	2021	2022	2023
Glyphosate	167	334	552	168
Monoammonium phosphate	83	229	194	113
Urea	3	9	0,8	8

Source: Author´s elaboration based on National Institute of Statistics and Censuses of Argentina (2024).

It is important to note that Argentina operates under capital controls and multiple exchange rates. Producers sell their soybean production at the official exchange rate, minus export duties, but purchase imported agricultural inputs at either the real dollar rate or the official rate –both of which are consistently higher than the price at which they sell their exports. This disparity generates significant additional costs for producers, further constraining their profits.

e) Expansion of the Crop Area and Displacement of Livestock

Growing international demand, along with biogenetic and other technological advancements, has expanded Argentina's agricultural frontier. The area planted with soybeans increased from 12.5 million hectares during the 2002/03 campaign to a peak of 20.5 million hectares in 2015/16 (see Table 17). Corn followed a similar trend, with its cultivated area rising from 3 million hectares in 2002 to 10.5 million hectares by 2023, according to the Secretariat of Agriculture, Livestock, and Fisheries of Argentina (2024). Barley and cotton also saw comparable growth over this period.

The expansion of crop areas has transformed production in the Pampas region, where soybeans and corn have become increasingly dominant. This shift has pushed a portion of the livestock industry to peripheral areas with less fertile land. A 2019 study by Argentina's Secretariat of Agriculture, Livestock, and Fisheries revealed a 19.3 % decline in the number of livestock establishments in the Pampas region between 2011 and 2019. In contrast, the northeastern region of Argentina saw a 49.4 % increase in the number of establishments during the same period. The report also indicates that 43 % of livestock establishments with fewer than 50 animals in the Pampas region closed during this timeframe.

Map 2. Geographical Distribution of the Surface Area Reported by Departments Soybean Campaign (2021-2022) (by Department in has.)

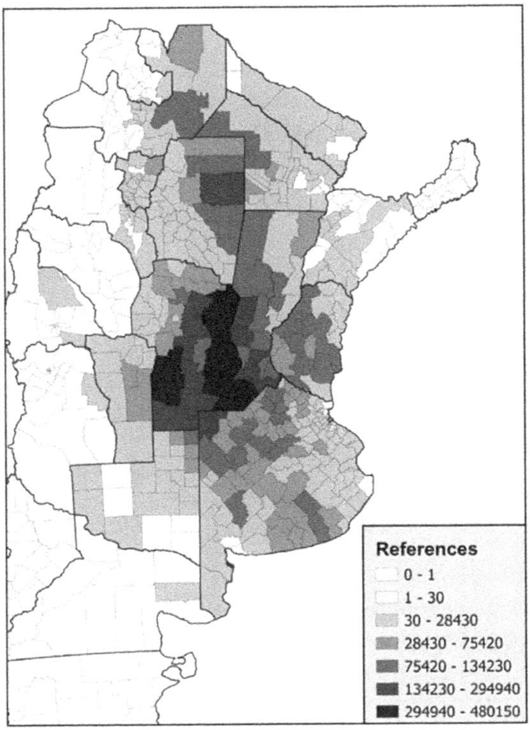

Source: Ministry of Agriculture, Livestock and Fisheries of Argentina (2022).

The displacement of livestock to peripheral agricultural areas resulted in a notable loss of added value and employment in the Pampas region. However, despite the relocation of some livestock activities, the sector increased exports due to rising demand from China and, to a lesser extent, from the European Union, the United States, Chile, Israel, and other markets.

Table 17. Estimated Area Planted with Soybeans in Argentina (2002-2023) Metric hectares

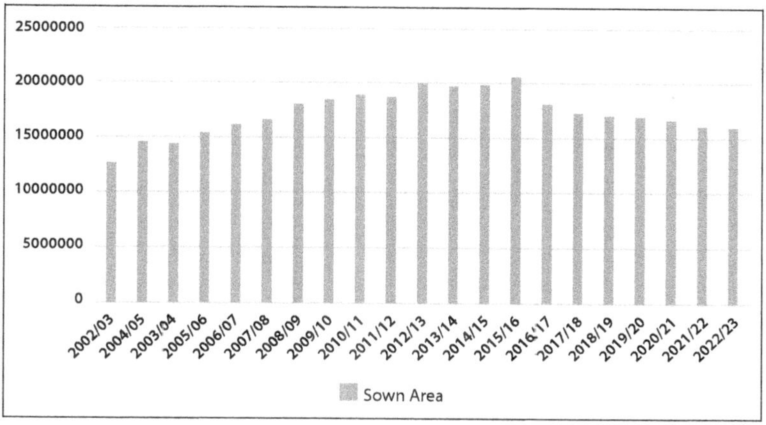

Source: Author's elaboration based on Secretariat of Agriculture (2024).

The term "agriculturalization"[2] –a more precise descriptor than the simplistic "soyization"– was not the only factor contributing to the decrease in the number of livestock establishments in the Pampas region. The higher profitability and ease of cultivating soybeans, corn, or barley led many producers to shift from livestock to crop production. Additionally, advances in biotechnology and agricultural modernization increased yields per hectare while reducing employment in the sector, prompting many rural workers to migrate to large cities, primarily to the suburbs of Buenos Aires, Rosario, and Córdoba.

2 "The process of 'agriculturization' is defined as the increasing and continuous use of land for agricultural crops instead of livestock or mixed uses." (Manuel-Navarrete 2005:7).

Other factors, such as high internal transportation costs to the ports, elevated export duties, the greater profitability of alternative crops, and the impacts of drought, have contributed to a declining trend in the area planted with soybeans. This area decreased from 20.5 million hectares in the 2015/16 season to 15.9 million hectares in the 2022/23 season (Table 17). Unlike the expansion trends seen in the United States and Brazil, Argentina recorded a slight contraction in soybean cultivation, resulting in idle capacity in the crushing industry and forcing companies to import soybeans from other countries. This trend is particularly evident in the province of Buenos Aires, where the planted area dropped from 6.8 million hectares in 2015/16 to 5 million hectares in 2023, according to the Secretariat of Agriculture, Livestock and Fisheries of Argentina (2024). Only the province of Misiones in the north of the country has increased its soybean planting area since 2016.

f) Labor Impact

The soybean sector employs 386,495 people, including registered employees, informal workers, and the self-employed (Morra *et al.* 2022: 64). Characterized by high labor informality, the sector ranks seventh in the country, with 59.2 % of its workforce in informal employment. It is also the eighth-largest provider of employment in Argentina, accounting for 2 % of total employment (Morra *et al.*, 2022: 19). An approximate figure provided by the Rosario Board of Trade indicates that the soybean sector generated 404,183 jobs in the third quarter of 2021, accounting for 2.5 % of total employment in Argentina (Table 18).

To estimate employment in the soybean sector, the Mediterranean Foundation (2011) established a multiplier of 0.015 per hectare planted. This means that for every 1,000 hectares of soybeans planted, approximately 15 jobs are created across various sectors of the chain. Based on this indicator, Sorrentino and Thomasz (2014:26) estimate that "for every job created in the oilseed processing industry (which is 90 % soy), 18 jobs are generated in the

Table 18. Employment in the Soybean Chain by Stage of Economic Activity

Stage	Employees	Share in the Total Soybean Chain	Share in the Total of the AAC*
Inputs and machinery	35,733	9 %	36,8 %
Primary sector	246,847	61 %	17,1 %
Industrialization	36,731	9 %	4,7 %
Trade	46,938	12 %	5,0 %
Transport and storage	33,439	8 %	18,6 %
Related services	4,495	1 %	39,8 %
TOTAL	404,183	100 %	11,7 %

Source: Author´s elaboration based on Tomás Rodríguez Zurro – Emilce Terré, Rosario Board of Trade (2022).

* Argentine Agri-Food Chain.

rest of the economy." Given that soybeans account for 90 % of oilseeds, each job in the soybean manufacturing industry generates around 16.2 jobs in the broader economy.

Using both multipliers, it is possible to estimate the employment generated by soybean and crude soy oil exports to China.

Table 19. Employment Estimates from Soybean Chain Exports to China (2019–2023)

	Product export to China	Export tons	Extruded Oil	Yield*	Has.	Index**	Total Employment	Pampas region Employment
2019	Soybeans Crude soy-oil	8,962,120,000 252,029,000	 70 %	3,333	2,688,904 108,023	0.015 0.0162	40,333 1,749	38,961 1,734
2020	Soybeans Crude soy-oil	5,475,487,309 415,426,666	 70 %	2,919	1,875,809 203,311	0.015 0.0162	28,137 3,293	27,489 3,217
2021	Soybeans Crude soy-oil	3,745,285,116 372,735,000	 70 %	2,806	1,334,666 189,764	0.015 0.0162	20,021 3,074	19,640 3,015
2022	Soybeans Crude soy-oil	4,924,688,387 130,700,000	 70 %	2,763	1,782,370 107,060	0.015 0.0162	26,735 1,734	26,039 1,688
2023	Soybeans Crude soy-oil	1,736,405,971 310,422,214	 70 %	1,744	995,645 254,277	0.015 0.0162	14,934 4,119	14,545 4,011

* Secretariat of Agriculture, Livestock and Fisheries of Argentina. *Estimaciones agrícolas* (2024). ** Sorrentino y Thomasz (2014:25).

For soybeans, the amount exported to China is divided by the national average yield per hectare, as provided by the Secretariat of Agriculture, Livestock, and Fisheries of Argentina (2024), and then multiplied by the employment multiplier of 0.015. In the case of crude soy oil, it is important to note that the yield of extruded oil from soybeans is estimated at 70 % for Argentina (Maciel, Wagner, and Bartosik, 2022:1). Therefore, the quantity of soybeans required to produce the amount of soy oil exported to China must first be calculated. Once this amount is determined, it is divided by the yield and multiplied by 0.0162, the employment multiplier for soybean manufacturing.

As a result, exports from the soybean complex to China employed 19,053 people in 2023: 14,934 in the production of soybean beans and 4,119 in oil processing. Employment peaked in 2019, with a total of 42,082 workers: 40,333 in soybean production and 1,749 in soy oil processing. This estimate refers to total exports from the complex to China, which, in addition to the Pampas region, includes soybeans produced in other provinces. Since the Pampas region accounted for approximately 97.4 % of complex sales in 2023 and 96.6 % in 2019 (according to Table 12), the total employment generated by exports to China in the Pampas region would amount to 18,556 workers in 2023 and 40,695 in 2019.

According to the 2018 National Agricultural Census, the Pampas region was home to 210,670 farm residents, representing 30 % of Argentina's agricultural population (Table 20). This figure includes producers, partners, family and non-family members of producers, workers, and unemployed residents. Excluding the unemployed, the soybean sector accounted for 40,695 jobs in 2019 (28.8 %) and 18,556 jobs in 2023 (13.1 %) of the region's 141,027 employed residents.

Mechanization and intensive farming practices have significantly reduced job opportunities in the Pampas region, where agricultural employment accounts for only 28.2 % of the 500,004 agricultural jobs nationwide. This contrasts with other provinces, such as Misiones and Santiago del Estero, where a larger share of the workforce remains engaged in agricultural activities (Argentina, 2021).

Table 20. Resident persons by legal type, relationship with the producer and work in the farming unit, by province (as of June 30, 2018)

Province	Total	Producers, partners and producers' relatives						Employed	Non-employed residents
		Total	Producers or partners	Working relatives	Non-working relatives	Working non-relatives	Non-working non-relatives		
Buenos Aires	87,977	52,173	8,241	16,314	8,306	10,927	8,385	21,091	14,713
Córdoba	45,744	35,014	5,305	12,272	5,808	6,984	4,645	7,204	3,526
Entre Ríos	33,299	27,869	5,510	10,858	6,341	3,020	2,140	3,248	2,182
La Pampa	9,726	8,109	1,687	3,387	1,406	1,405	224	1,336	281
Santa Fe	33,924	23,664	3,128	6,601	2,950	6,144	4,841	6,365	3,895
Pampas region	210,670	146,829	23,871	49,432	24,811	28,480	20,235	39,244	24,597
Country total	700,670	595,505	106,074	271,745	106,720	58,952	52,014	63,233	42,012

Source: Author´s elaboration based on *Argentina 2018 National Agricultural Census. Final Results* (2021:704).

g) Environmental Liability

Soybean exports generate significant environmental impacts in productive areas that must be carefully evaluated. These effects, generally detrimental to the environment, are borne entirely by society or, when a direct causal relationship can be established, by the responsible companies. Various authors have estimated the environmental liability associated with soybean cultivation in Argentina (Merenson n.d.; Moreno Halberstadt 2016; Carlosiano and Morey 2022). This liability includes aspects such as soil erosion, nutrient export, deforestation, loss of the environmental service of carbon sequestration and storage, as well as the valuation of 'virtual water' (Merenson n.d.:2).

Crop rotation and other Good Agricultural Practices, promoted by non-profit organizations and state entities such as the National Institute of Agricultural Technology (INTA) and the National Service of Agri-Food Health and Quality (SENASA) in Argentina, help mitigate the soil erosion caused by soybean cultivation. These practices include rotating soybeans with crops like corn, wheat, or peas, depending on the region. However, according to Professor Sergio Montico, water erosion in the Pampas region continues to degrade soils, diminishing both their productive capacity and their ability to provide essential ecosystem services (Hiba 2024).

Although a strong association has been found between the deforestation of native forests and the area planted with soybean (Pincén *et al.* 2010). Deforestation is not a pressing problem in the Pampas region, except in the province of Córdoba. There, deforestation affected 20,571 hectares, accounting for 9.7 % of the national total in 2022, according to the Ministry of Environment and Sustainable Development of Argentina (2022:9). In total, the deforested area in the Pampas region reached 28,392 hectares, equivalent to 13.7 % of the national total. However, 80 % of deforestation in Argentina is concentrated in the northern provinces, such as Santiago del Estero, Salta, Formosa, and Chaco (Greenpeace, 2023), because of the expansion of the agricultural frontier. In those provinces, the area planted with soy has remained stable, except in Misiones, where it has continuously grown since 2011, although with a slight decline in 2021, according to data from the Secretariat of Agriculture, Livestock, and Fisheries of Argentina (2024).

In recent years, the EU Deforestation Regulation (EUDR) prohibits the entry into the European Union of soybean and other products from areas deforested after December 31, 2020. This regulation will come into effect on December 31, 2025. "China has recently voiced opposition to the EUDR, primarily due to concerns about sharing geolocation data. This data is seen as a security risk, complicating compliance for Chinese exporters" (Steward 2024). In contrast, local and transnational companies based in Argentina are already adapting to this new regulation. For example, in May 2024, COFCO announced the export of "18,000 metric tons of certified Argentine deforestation-free soy meal at its Timbúes port terminal on the Paraná River near Rosario. This is the first fully traceable and segregated shipment of deforestation-free soy products for COFCO International" (COFCO 2024). This action was carried out in collaboration with the Sectoral Vision Platform of the Gran Chaco Argentino (VISEC), a non-profit organization led by the Argentine Oilseed Industry Chamber, the Center for Cereal Exporters, and the Rosario Board of Trade, which operates in Argentina with a monitoring, reporting, and verification system to ensure the traceability of soy and meats (VISEC 2024).

The use of glyphosate presents a different case, as its application has been regulated locally following the detection of a strong correlation between glyphosate contamination and increased

Map 3. The Territorial Expansion of Soybean Production in Argentina

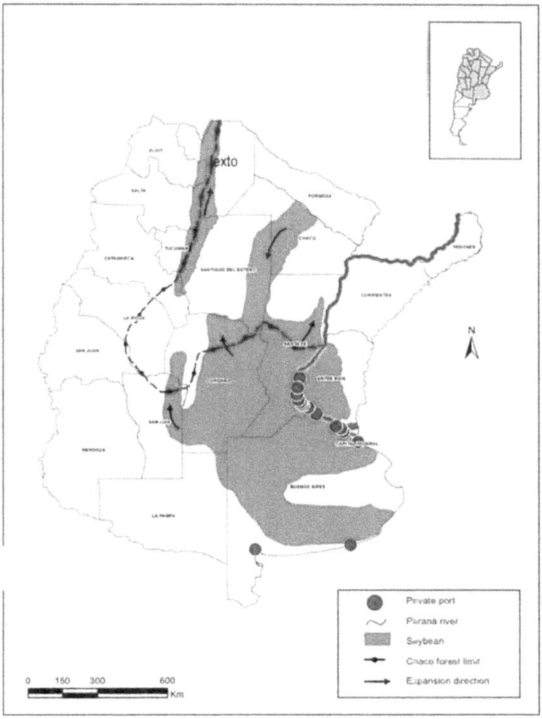

Source: Author´s elaboration based on Reboratti (2010).

cancer cases in agricultural areas (Lajmanovich 2020:67). The health impact on populations near cultivation areas has prompted legislation on the application distance of agrochemicals in several provinces of the Pampas region. Additionally, a deterioration in water quality has been reported in the Paraná and Gualeguay rivers, as well as the presence of glyphosate in rainwater samples in the provinces of Buenos Aires, Entre Ríos, Santa Fe, and Córdoba. Pollution of groundwater has also been documented, affecting terrestrial and amphibious fauna (Lajmanovich 2020:67). Besides glyphosate pollution, the environmental liability includes the export of water, a resource that has been traded on the Wall Street Stock Exchange since 2020.

5. Conclusions

The widespread perception of the significant benefits that soybean exports to China bring to Argentina stands in stark contrast to the multifaceted impact this activity generates at the state, regional, provincial, and productive levels.

At the national level, soybean exports have not been sufficient to generate a surplus in bilateral trade, as has been the case in Brazil and even Paraguay, a country that does not maintain diplomatic relations with the People's Republic of China. Despite China being the world's largest importer of soybeans and the continued growth of bilateral trade, Argentina has accumulated a trade deficit of 93.194 billion USD from 2008 to 2023. This disconnection between Argentina's soybean sector and China's growth has persisted even amid cordial political relations. However, the trade deficit with China does not fully reflect the real potential of Argentina's soybean complex exports. Export duties and differential tax rates on soybeans, designed to encourage the export of soybean by-products (such as oils, biofuels, pellets, and soybean meals), have significantly distorted trade flows while simultaneously promoting the scaling-up of industrial processing. From this dynamic, several key conclusions can be drawn:

1. Exports of the soybean complex to China accounted for between 9 % (2023) and 18.8 % (2019) of Argentina's total soybean exports, with approximately 80 % of these exports originating in the Pampas region. However, the situation varies across provinces: Santa Fe, home to 80 % of the crushing industry, is highly dependent on the soybean complex, while Buenos Aires is less reliant.
2. Nearly all excess unprocessed soybeans exported by Argentina are primarily destined for China. There is significant potential for increased demand from China if Argentina expands its supply of unprocessed soybeans for export.
3. Given Argentina's advancements in agricultural technology, soybean exports to China have a limited impact on employment in the Pampas region, with most jobs concentrated in the primary sector and only a small share in the industrial sector.
4. Companies such as COFCO and Syngenta play a pivotal role in Argentina's crushing and export sectors, with Syngenta also actively engaged in seed production, particularly in Santa Fe province. These firms compete with both multinational and local companies in a highly competitive market, leveraging valuable information and acquiring knowledge and expertise. Additionally, other Chinese firms contribute as suppliers of essential agricultural inputs, including urea, glyphosate, and other critical products for primary production.
5. The Pampas provinces lead in soybean cultivation in Argentina. Driven by international prices and demand from emerging economies like China and India, the cultivated area has expanded to other provinces. However, fiscal disincentives, internal freight costs, and climatic factors have led to a contraction in the planted area, marking a shift from expansive to more restrictive trends since 2016.
6. Agricultural intensification has also displaced livestock farming in the Pampas to less fertile lands, leading to the closure of establishments and a decline in both added value and

employment in the region. Nevertheless, meat exports to China and other countries have helped sustain the dynamism of the livestock sector.

7. It is also essential to consider the unintended consequences of soybean production. The environmental impact of soybean and other crop production is a major concern in the Pampas region, with soil degradation, water erosion, and contamination of rivers and groundwater from agrochemical use being the most significant issues. These environmental liabilities are not reflected in export values.
8. Regarding deforestation, the Pampas region meets the European Union's Deforestation Regulation (EUDR) requirements, although full implementation will require stronger product traceability and adjustments within the value chain. COFCO and other companies' deforestation-free exports support this claim. However, the regulation functions as a non-tariff barrier and reflects the European Union's protectionist policies, causing some companies to hesitate in exporting to Europe. This, in turn, creates an opportunity to increase exports to China.

In the context of trade imbalances, the central government benefits from the flow of exports and the tax revenue generated by the agricultural sector. Export duties on soybeans and other agricultural products have been justified, in part, by the need to promote industrial development and strengthen social welfare. However, this policy has resulted in reduced profitability for producers, limiting their capacity for reinvestment and diminishing the economic multiplier effect for subnational actors, which has led to a decline in fiscal revenues in the Pampas provinces. While the national-level benefits in terms of tax revenue are clear, these do not translate similarly at the provincial level. The transfer of resources from producers and provinces to the central government has reduced the positive economic impact in the Pampas region.

The main losers in this scenario are soybean producers. The heavy fiscal burden placed on them has led to a deterioration in productive specialization and a decline in sector competitiveness, as reflected in decreasing yields per hectare and a reduction in the cultivated area, further exacerbated by adverse weather conditions. In contrast, the primary beneficiaries are the industrial sector and exporters, including companies such as COFCO and Syngenta. These actors pay export duties at the time of shipment but recover these costs upfront by purchasing soybeans from producers, effectively acting as intermediaries between producers and the state in collecting duties. In recent years, manufacturing companies have faced increased idle capacity. To address this, they have partially offset the shortfall by temporarily importing soybeans from Bolivia, Brazil, Paraguay, Uruguay, and even the United States.

Argentina's tax policy, in conjunction with China's raw material purchasing strategy, creates distortions in soybean exports. These taxes disincentivize local production and undermine sector competitiveness, generating tensions between the private sector, the Pampas provinces –which in part rely on soybean production– and the central government, which aims to balance fiscal revenues while promoting industrialization and a welfare state. Meanwhile, the Pampas provinces face challenges in retaining the economic benefits of soybean production. The central government's export duty regulations and exchange rate controls result in a significant transfer of financial resources to the national treasury.

Argentina's chosen development model will shape the extent of its soybean exports to China. If spontaneous development is prioritized, productive specialization and free market, along with the complete elimination of export duties and differentials, could exponentially increase soybean exports to China, albeit at the expense of industrialization. In contrast, if state intervention is pursued, the persistence of high export duties and differentials would limit the sale of unprocessed surpluses to China, and trade tensions are likely to continue. This model would largely depend on expanding production in a context of declining cultivated areas since 2016, which discourages productive specialization and leads to a relative decrease in sector competitiveness, as reflected in lower yields per hectare. The absence of a clear dominant development model has resulted in a pendulum-like policy, where both approaches frequently challenge each other, shifting the agricultural policy orientation of Argentina's governments.

Therefore, it is suggested to reduce the export duty rate to the minimum necessary, with differentials, to facilitate value-added sales from the industry while encouraging increased production. In this case, exports to China could grow in terms of the sale of unprocessed surplus soybeans –as is already happening– but in greater quantities due to the incentive created by lowering export duties.

This controversy has intensified since the inauguration of President Javier Milei. The shift in the economic orientation of the new government, which began in December 2023, has reignited the debate between spontaneous development and state intervention. However, despite the government's advocacy for spontaneous order, free trade and the temporary reduction of export duties[3], as of the time of writing, soybean exports remain regulated by the model of state intervention, characterized by the imposition of export duties, differentials on processed products, and exchange rate controls. Resolving this contradiction will undoubtedly alter the current impact of soybean exports on the Pampas region.

In summary, soybean complex exports generate foreign currency, create jobs, and simultaneously and simultaneously pose environmental challenges that must be considered when evaluating their broader impact. Chinese companies invest in a highly specialized, globally competitive sector, while also supplying inputs for the primary stage of the production chain. However, state trade policies introduce significant distortions in exports, and Argentina's tax policies disincentivize production, creating tensions between the private sector, the Pampas provinces, and the national government. A shift from the current state intervention

3 Through Decree 38 of January 25, 2025, President Javier Milei officially announced the temporary reduction of export duties. As a result, the tariff on soybean beans was reduced from 33 % to 26 %, while the tariff on soybean oils and meals dropped from 31 % to 24.5 %, for a period of six months (Boletín Oficial de la República Argentina 2025).

model to a spontaneous approach -or an increase in productivity combined with a reduction in export duties and taxes within the framework of the interventionist model- could expand soybean exports to China and amplify their effects on the Pampas region and the soybean value chain.

References

Allan, Tomás, Corfield, Kevin, O'Farrell, Juan and Freytes, Carlos. 2024. *Discutir los derechos de exportación:hacia un nuevo marco fiscal para el agro.* Fundar: Buenos Aires.

Alvarado Ledesma, Manuel. 2024. "La producción enfrenta un costo elevado por el atraso del ferrocarril". *Diario La Nación*: Buenos Aires, March 23.

Argentina's National Geographic Institute. 2024. (at: https://www.ign.gob.ar)

Argentina' National Budget Office. 2024. "El presupuesto en cifras". Buenos Aires.

Argentine Oilseed Industry Chamber. 2024. "Aranceles y Reintegros del Complejo Soja". CIARA: Buenos Aires.

Argentina. 1898. "Second National Census". Buenos Aires, May 10.

Argentina. 1916. "Third National Census". Buenos Aires, June 1.

Argentina, 2021. "2018 National Agricultural Census. Final results". Buenos Aires.

Argentina. 2024. "Law 27.742: Law of Bases and Starting Points for the Liberty of Argentines". Buenos Aires, June 27.

Bergero, Patricia, Calzada, Julio, Di Yenno, Federico, and Terré, Emilce. 2018. "La remoción del escalonamiento arancelario desincentiva el agregado de valor de las exportaciones del complejo soja". *Rosario Board of Trade*, November 16.

Boletín Oficial de la República Argentina, Decree 38, Buenos Aires, January 25, 2025.

Central Bank of Chile. 2024. *Statistics and data.* Santiago de Chile.

Calzada, Julio and Rossi, Guillermo. 2016. "84 % de la soja argentina se exporta como grano, harina, aceite y biodiesel". *Rosario Board of Trade*, March 18.

Calzada, Julio and Treboux, Jaiver. 2021. "El Gran Rosario concentra el 80 % de la capacidad de industrialización de semillas oleaginosas del país". *Rosario Board of Trade*, October 29.

COFCO International (China National Cereals, Oil & Foodstuffs International.) 2024. "Nuestra historia". COFCO: Buenos Aires.

COFCO (China National Cereals, Oil & Foodstuffs International). 2024. "First COFCO soymeal shipment aligned with upcoming EU Deforestation Regulation (EUDR) requirements loads in Argentina". COFCO: Buenos Aires.

Comisión Nacional de Defensa de la Competencia. 2021. "Informe de objeción - fusión Syngenta / Nidera". CNDC: Buenos Aires.

Comisión Nacional de Defensa de la Competencia. 2023. "Aprobación de la operación SYNGENTA/NIDERA y del compromiso de desconcentración en el mercado de semillas de girasol a favor de la empresa NUSEEDS". CNDC: Buenos Aires.

D'Ángelo, Guido, Ferrari, Bruno and Calzada, Julio. 2024. "Brecha de rendimiento, semilla y tecnología en Argentina y Brasil". *Rosario Board of Trade*, August 2.

Diario La Nación. 2024. "Son 18.000 toneladas a Europa: una empresa china exportó desde la Argentina harina de soja certificada libre de deforestación". *Diario la Nación,* May 16.

Dussel Peters, Enrique. 2018. *Cadenas Globales de Valor. Metodología, teorías y debates.* National Autonomous University of Mexico: Mexico.

Fundación Mediterránea. 2011. "Cadena de la Soja y sus Productos Derivados". *IERAL*, August 26.

Food and Agriculture Organization of the United Nations. 2022. "FAOSTAT, Major Commodities Importers", *FAO*: Rome.

Maciel, Gisela, Wagner, Jorge, and Bartosik, Ricardo. 2022. "Recomendaciones para ganar eficiencia en el procesamiento de soja por extrusado-prensado". *Visión rural.*

Contardi, Matías, Marín, Natalia, and Terré, Emilce. 2024. "Argentina recupera el primer puesto en el mercado internacional de harina de soja". *Rosario Board of Trade*, August 23.

Greenpeace. 2024. *Deforestación en el Norte de Argentina.* Informe Anual 2023.

Hiba, Jorgelina. 2024. "Creímos que el suelo era indestructible: advierten sobre una 'grave' degradación de las tierras en la Argentina". *La Nación:* Buenos Aires, December 2.

Instituto Nacional de Semillas. 2023. *Sistema de Información Simplificado Agrícola (SISA).* Buenos Aires, May 4.

Jaguaribe, Helio. 1968. *Economic and Political Development.* Harvard University Press: Cambridge.

La Capital. 1967. "Fomentaríase el comercio con China nacionalista". March 30.

Lajmanovich, Rafael Carlos. 2020. "Consecuencias del modelo transgénico de cultivos resistente a herbicidas en Argentina: ¿es solo un problema de distancias?" *Ciencia digna* 1(1). Pp. 64-69.

Lanús, Archibaldo, Juan. 2001. *Aquel apogeo. Política internacional argentina (1910-1939).* Emecé: Buenos Aires.

Li, Jane. 2023. "Leading Chinese crushers warn about fierce competition hurting profits". *Agricensus*, November 2.

Navarrete, Manuel, David and Gallopin, Gilberto. 2005. *Análisis sistemático de la agriculturización en la pampa húmeda argentina y sus consecuencias en regiones extra-pampeanas: sostenibilidad, brechas de conocimiento e integración de políticas.* CEPAL: Santiago de Chile.

Merenson, Carlos. 2011. "Estimación del Pasivo Ambiental del Cultivo de la soja en Argentina". *Centro de Estudios e Investigación Social "Nelson Mandela DD. HH".*

Ministerio de Ambiente y Desarrollo Sostenible de Argentina. 2022. *Monitoreo de la superficie de bosque nativo de la República Argentina.* Buenos Aires.

Ministry of Agriculture, Livestock and Fisheries of Argentina. 2019. "Simplified Agricultural Information System". *INASE-MAGyP:* Buenos Aires.

Ministry of Agriculture, Livestock and Fisheries of Argentina. 2022. "*Simplified Agricultural Information System*". INASE-MAGyP: Buenos Aires.

Ministry of Agriculture, Livestock and Fisheries of Argentina. 2024. "*Simplified Agricultural Information System*". INASE-MAGyP: Buenos Aires.

Ministry of Development, Industry, Trade and Services of Brazil. 2024. *Comex Stat.* (at: https://comexstat.mdic.gov.br/es/home)

Ministry of Economy of Argentina. 2023. "Informes de cadena de valor: Agroquímicos y Bioinsumos", *Ministry of Economy of Argentina.*

Ministerio de Economía, Dirección Nacional de Estudios Regionales y de Cadenas de Valor. 2024. *Exportaciones regionales y provinciales, 2023-2024.*

Ministry of Finance of Argentina. 2019. "Informe de Cadena de Valor. Oleaginosas: Soja"

Ministry of Foreign Affairs and Worship of Argentina. 1972. *Comunicado Conjunto sobre el Establecimiento de Relaciones Diplomáticas entre la República Argentina y la República Popular China*. Bucharest, February 16.

Ministry of Foreign Affairs and Worship of Argentina. 1972. *Memoria.* Buenos Aires.

Ministry of Foreign Affairs and Worship of Argentina. 1977. *Memoria.* Buenos Aires.

Ministry of Commerce of the People's Republic of China. 2024. *Guía de país (región) para la inversión y la cooperación extranjeras. Argentina.* MOFCOM: Beijing

Morra, Fernando, Guzmán Martin, Lódola, Agustín, Kohon Florencia and Storti, Luciana. 2022. *Cadenas Productivas Argentinas.* Buenos Aires.

National Institute of Statistics and Censuses of Argentina. 2024. *Foreign Trade.* INDEC 8(4). Buenos Aires

National Institute of Statistics and Censuses of Argentina. 2023. *Foreign Trade.* INDEC 7(4). Buenos Aires.

National Institute of Statistics and Censuses of Argentina. 2022. *Foreign Trade.* INDEC 6(4). Buenos Aires

National Institute of Statistics and Censuses of Argentina, 2022. *National Census of Population, Households and Housing.* INDEC: Buenos Aires.

National Institute of Statistics and Censuses of Argentina, 2024. *Foreign trade consultation system.* INDEC: Buenos Aires.

National Institute of Statistics and Censuses of Argentina. 2024. *Exporting Complexes.* 2020-2024. INDEC: Buenos Aires.

National Institute of Statistics and Censuses of Argentina. 2024. *Origin of the Provincial Export.* 2020-2024. INDEC: Buenos Aires.

National Service of Agri-Food Health and Quality of Argentina. 2019. "Acuerdo histórico: La Argentina logra exportar harina de soja a China". *SENASA*: Buenos Aires.

Oil Guide Network. 2022. "The seven major international grain traders at the center of the world grain stage". *ABCD+*, August 8.

Oviedo, Eduardo, Daniel. 2005. *China en expansión.* EDUCC: Córdoba.

Oviedo, Eduardo, Daniel. 2012. "Argentina y China: causas de la disputa en torno al aceite de soja". *Estudios de Asia y África*, pp. 337-376.

Oviedo, Eduardo Daniel. 2023. *Relaciones internacionales en tiempos de auge chino y declive argentino.* Areté: Buenos Aires.

Observatorio Bioeconomía de la Secretaría de Agricultura, Ganadería y Pesca de la República Argentina. 2019. *Biodiesel.* Magyp: Buenos Aires.

Pincén, Daniel, Viglizzo, Ernesto, Carreño, Lorena and Frank, Federico. 2010. "La relación soja-ecología-ambiente: entre el mito y la realidad". In, Viglizzo, Ernesto y Jobbágy, Esteban (eds.). *Expansión de la Frontera agropecuaria en Argentina y su impacto ecológico-ambiental.* INTA-IAI: Buenos Aires.

Reboratti, Carlos. 2010. "Un mar de soja. La nueva agricultura en Argentina y sus consecuencias". *Revista de Geografía Norte Grande*, pp.63-76.

Rodríguez Zurro, Tomás and Terré, Emilce. "Empleo, exportaciones y actividad: ¿qué aporta la cadena soja a la Argentina?". *Rosario Board of Trade*, April 1.

Rositano, Florencia, Pessah, Sebastián, Durand, Patricia, and Laterra, Pedro. *Coupled socio-ecological changes in response to soybean expansion along the 2001–2010 decade in Argentina.* Anthropocene.

Secretariat of Agriculture, Livestock and Fisheries of Argentina. 2019. "Evolución del Sector Ganadero (Comparación 2019 vs 2011)". *Sagyp*: Buenos Aires

Secretariat of Agriculture, Livestock and Fisheries of Argentina. 2024. *Estimaciones Agrícolas (at:* https://datosestimaciones.magyp.gob.ar)

Secretariat of Agriculture, Livestock and Fisheries of Argentina. 2023. "Ranking Exportaciones por Exportador de Granos y Subproductos 2023" *Ministry of Economy.*

Sesé, Alfredo, Treboux, Javier and Ybañez, Pablo. 2021. "Se inauguró un nuevo acceso ferroviario en Timbúes: enviar mercadería al Gran Rosario desde el norte del país puede resultar un 40 % más barato". *Rosario Board of Trade*, November 19.

Steward, Pete. 2024. "China's Response to EUDR's Changes in Global Trade". *ResourceWise*, August 14.

The World Bank. 2024. *Indicator: Taxes on exports (% of tax revenue).* World Bank: Washington.

United States Department of Agriculture. 2024. *Market and Trade Data.*

VISEC (Sectoral Vision Platform of the Gran Chaco Argentino). 2024. *Somos VISEC* (at: https://www.visec.com.ar).

6.
The Territorial Impacts of Exporting Copper from Peru to China

Kehan Wang and Marco Curi

Introduction

The global value chain (GVC) of copper is a cornerstone of the modern economy, serving as a fundamental resource for industries such as construction, electronics, manufacturing, and renewable energy. Copper's unique properties, including its high conductivity and durability, make it indispensable for producing technologies essential to the global energy transition, such as solar panels, wind turbines, and electric vehicles. The GVC of copper is characterized by a division of roles: resource-rich nations like Peru dominate the extraction and export of raw materials, while industrialized economies such as China specialize in refining, manufacturing, and consumption. This division underscores the strategic importance of Peru as a critical upstream supplier of copper in the GVC. Between 2008 and 2023, copper accounted for 66 % of Peru's mining exports to China, highlighting the extent to which this resource defines Peru's role in global trade and its economic ties with the world's largest consumer of copper. At the subheading level, in 2023, 92 % of Peruvian copper exports to China fell under subheading 260300, copper ores and concentrates. This overwhelming reliance on the export of unprocessed materials underscores the persistent lack of value-added activities within Peru's copper industry, a limitation driven by significant technical, political, and economic barriers to domestic refining. Such a dynamic reflects and reinforces the discussions about the structural asymmetries inherent in the center-periphery framework, particularly in the context of Peru's trade relations with China.

The relationship between Peru and China has evolved over time, shaped by historical ties and deepening economic integration. While their economic interactions date back to the arrival of Chinese laborers in the mid-nineteenth century, the foundations for modern bilateral relations were laid during the 1990s. This period was marked by neoliberal reforms in Peru, which opened its economy to foreign investment, and by China's rapid industrialization under Deng Xiaoping's economic policies. In the early 2000s, as China's economic growth accelerated, its demand for raw materials –including copper– surged, transforming the bilateral relationship. The 2009 Free Trade Agreement (FTA) between Peru and China was a milestone, fostering a boom in trade that positioned China as Peru's largest trading partner by 2011. The FTA facilitated the export of Peruvian copper and other raw materials, while also increasing the import of Chinese technology, manufactured goods, and infrastructure services. By the 2010s, this relationship further expanded under China's Belt and Road Initiative, which integrated Peru into a broader framework of global connectivity and investment, particularly in infrastructure and energy.

China's investments in Peru's mining sector exemplify this deepening economic partnership. Major projects, such as the Las Bambas mine, operated by MMG, and the Toromocho mine by Chinalco, have been impactful for the sector, injecting significant foreign direct investment and boosting copper production capacity. Additionally, other key investments, including Shougang's acquisition of Empresa Minera de Hierro del Perú in the 1990s and more recent ventures in infrastructure like the Chancay Port, have reinforced China's role as a significant actor in Peru's economic landscape (Dussel Peters 2024/a). These investments are not without challenges, as they have reshaped territorial dynamics and sparked debates over their environmental, social, and governance implications.

This paper investigates the territorial impacts of Peru's copper exports to China, focusing on the interplay of economic benefits, environmental consequences, and social challenges. Section 2 examines the historical evolution of economic relations between Peru and China, emphasizing the integration of Peru into the global copper value chain and its implications for bilateral trade. Section 3 analyzes the dynamics of Peru's copper exports, highlighting their dominance in trade relations and their critical role in meeting China's industrial and energy needs. Section 4 explores the impacts, environmental consequences, and social conflicts arising from the copper trade, discussing both the opportunities it creates and the vulnerabilities it exposes. Also, this section provides an analysis of the local impacts of the Las Bambas project in the Apurímac region, where the project is situated. This comprehensive analysis aims to deepen understanding of the complex interplay between global resource governance and local development, situating Peru's copper trade within broader debates on sustainability and territorial transformation. Finally, Section 6 provides a conclusion and policy suggestions.

1. Economic Relationship Between Peru and China

The economic relationship between Peru and China dates back to 1849 when the first Chinese indentured laborers arrived in Peru, primarily to replace enslaved labors. The formal diplomatic relationship was established in 1874 with the signing of the Treaty of Friendship, Commerce, and Navigation in Tianjin (Lausent-Herrera 2011). After the establishment of the People's Republic of China, there had not been a diplomatic relationship between the two countries for decades during the Cold War. In 1971, Peru followed the United States' lead in recognizing China, marking the beginning of slow but steady economic ties.

By the 1990s, the bilateral relationship gained momentum. In Peru, Alberto Fujimori's neoliberal reforms, beginning in 1990, stabilized the economy, while in China, Deng Xiaoping's reforms since 1978 laid the groundwork for the country's rapid industrialization. In 1992, Shougang Group, one of China's largest metallurgical companies, made its first direct investment in Peru by acquiring the debt-ridden Empresa Minera de Hierro del Peru. This was the beginning of China's growing involvement in Peru's mining sector. In 1994, Peru and China signed an agreement on the Encouragement and Mutual Protection of Investments (Ministry of Foreign Affairs 2024), signaling the start of stronger economic relations.

The bilateral relationship accelerated during the 2000s, as China embarked on a breakneck economic boom after entering the World Trade Organization (WTO), and demands for raw materials skyrocketed. In 2001, China became a formal member of the WTO. Peru granted China market economy status in 2004. The take-off of the Chinese economy ignited a boom cycle in the global commodity market around 2007 (Kaplan 2014; Gallagher 2016). In 1999, China also encouraged companies to "go out" and compete globally. During the *China boom*, trade and foreign direct investment from China expanded rapidly, especially in the mining sector.

In 2007, two Chinese companies made historic investments in Peru. Xiamen Zijin acquired the Rio Blanco copper project from a British junior mining company for over 2,500 million USD. The project had been fiercely resisted by the local communities even before the acquisition (Sanborn, 2009; Bebbington *et al.*, 2007), and, to this day, the future of this project is still uncertain (Sanborn *et al.*, 2024). The other investment was the acquisition of the Toromocho copper project by the Aluminum Corporation of China (Chinalco) (Fairlie 2014). The project finished construction in 2013 and has been one of the largest copper mines in Peru.

In 2009, Peru and China signed a Free Trade Agreement (FTA), making Peru the second country in the region, only after Chile, to have an FTA with China. By 2011, China had overtaken the United States as Peru's largest trading partner, a position it still holds. The

FTA opened up markets for copper and other Peruvian exports, while also facilitating the import of Chinese manufactured goods, technology, and infrastructure. By the 2010s, the relationship between the two countries evolved further with China's Belt and Road Initiative (BRI). The Belt and Road aimed to expand China's global influence through infrastructure development, positioning Latin America as a critical extension of the initiative.

The economic relationship between Peru and China reached another milestone during the 2016 APEC Forum, where the two countries upgraded their relationship to a "comprehensive strategic partnership." By 2019, Peru formally joined the BRI, deepening economic cooperation in infrastructure, energy, and mining. One evidence of the diversification of Chinese investments in Peru was the rise of Chinese construction companies in winning contracts for public projects (Cynthia *et al.*, 2024). Even though Chinese companies have not bid for new mega-mining projects in the recent decade, foreign direct investment from China has stayed strong. In 2019, China Ocean Shipping Company (COSCO) acquired 60 % of the Chancay port from the Peruvian mining company Volcán and has reportedly invested 3,000 million USD for constructing the largest port in Pacific South America (Narrea 2022, 2024). The same year, a subsidiary of China Three Gorges acquired the largest electricity distribution company in Peru, Luz del Sur, for 3,590 million USD. In 2023, another state-owned giant from China, China Southern Power Grid, acquired the distribution company Enel Peru for 2,900 million USD (Dussel Peters 2024/b).

In 2024, Peru hosted another APEC Forum, marking yet another milestone in Sino-Peruvian relations. Peruvian President Dina Boluarte visited China early that year, and Chinese President Xi Jinping visited Peru in November during the Forum, indicating the ongoing strengthening of economic and political ties. These visits resulted in further agreements, particularly in the digital economy, science, and technology, signaling a further diversification of the bilateral relationship beyond traditional sectors like mining.

However, despite the robust economic relationship between Peru and China, significant challenges persist, particularly regarding Peru's role in the global copper value chain. While mineral trade –especially copper– has improved, Peru's position remains constrained by systemic and technical barriers, highlighting its dependence on raw material exports and its limited capacity to refine copper domestically. This dynamic underscores deeper structural issues that hinder Peru's ability to capitalize on its resource wealth fully.

The global trend of vertical disintegration in the copper industry has reinforced Peru's role as an exporter of raw copper concentrates, avoiding the substantial costs and technological demands of local refining (Lagos *et al.*, 2021). Among the principal barriers are the lack of advanced infrastructure to process concentrates containing impurities such as arsenic, the significant environmental costs associated with stringent regulations, and the competitive pressures exerted by global leaders like China (Ministerio de Minería de Chile 2023). China's dominance in the refining sector, underpinned by economies of scale, technological advancements, and lower labor costs, has rendered local refining in Peru economically unfeasible (Zhang and Santa Gadea 2023).

Even other South American countries, such as Chile, with its comparatively advanced industrial capacity, grapple with similar challenges. Over 50 % of Chilean copper concentrates are currently exported unprocessed, a figure projected to rise to 70 % by 2030 due to the increasing costs and declining competitiveness of domestic refining (Ministerio de Minería de Chile 2023). For Peru, which faces even greater technological and infrastructural deficits, overcoming these hurdles would require extraordinary investments and comprehensive policy interventions.

As articulated by Dussel Peters (2016), this dynamic aligns with the theoretical construct of a center-periphery framework within the global copper trade, wherein Peru predominantly supplies raw materials, while China specializes in the export of manufactured goods characterized by medium- and high-level technological sophistication. Beyond the economic implications, the local impacts of mining operations reveal a complex interplay of benefits and challenges. On the one hand, mining has facilitated regional development through employment generation, infrastructure improvements, and enhanced public services, particularly in rural areas (Lagos *et al.* 2021). On the other hand, these gains are often offset by severe externalities, including environmental degradation, water contamination, and the displacement of indigenous communities. Such issues are further exacerbated by inadequate governance, leading to social tensions and prolonged conflicts (Sanborn and Chong 2017).

2. Exports to China: Dominance of the Mining Sector

In 2023, China solidified its position as the foremost destination for Peru's exports, accounting for 36 % of the total–a share that significantly surpassed exports to other major partners like the United States (14 %), Canada (4 %), India (4 %), and South Korea (4 %) (see Table 1 for details). This marks a dramatic shift from 2008, when the United States was Peru's leading trading partner, receiving 19 % of its exports. At that time, Peru had already signed a Free Trade Agreement (FTA) with the United States, which came into effect in 2009. By contrast, exports to China in 2008 accounted for only 12 %, approximately one-third of the share in 2023.

On the import side, Peru's imports from China grew substantially between 2008 and 2023, with China's share in total imports rising from 14 % to 26 %. This shift placed China as Peru's largest source of imports, surpassing the United States, whose share grew slightly from 19 % to 21 %. By 2023, Peru's primary import sources included Brazil (7 %), Argentina (5 %), Mexico (3 %), Chile (3 %), Colombia (2 %), Canada (2 %), Ecuador (2 %), and Germany (2 %) (see Table 2 for details). Mobile phones became the leading import from China in 2023, reflecting a shift from 2008, when portable data processing machines, such as computers, laptops, and notebooks, dominated the import landscape.

Table 1. Top Peruvian export markets in 2008 and 2023 ($US Billion and Percentage)

Nº	Country	2008		2023	
		FOB Value	%	FOB Value	%
	Total	30.6	100 %	64.6	100 %
1	China	3.6	12 %	23.1	36 %
2	USA	5.8	19 %	9.2	14 %
3	Canada	1.9	6 %	3.0	5 %
4	India	0.3	1 %	2.5	4 %
5	South Korea	0.5	2 %	2.4	4 %
6	Japan	1.8	6 %	2.3	4 %
7	Chile	1.7	6 %	1.9	3 %
8	Spain	1.0	3 %	1.9	3 %
9	Netherlands	0.8	3 %	1.8	3 %
10	Brazil	0.9	3 %	1.7	3 %
	Others	12.4	40 %	14.8	23 %

Source: Own elaboration based on Adex Data Trade (2024).

Table 2. Top Peruvian import markets in 2008 and 2023 ($US Billion and Percentage)

Nº	Country	2008		2023	
		CIB Value	%	CIB Value	%
	Total	**29.9**	**100 %**	**52.1**	**100 %**
1	China	4.1	14 %	13.5	26 %
2	USA	5.6	19 %	11.0	21 %
3	Brazil	2.4	8 %	3.7	7 %
4	Argentina	1.6	5 %	2.7	5 %
5	Mexico	1.2	4 %	1.8	3 %
6	Chile	1.2	4 %	1.3	3 %
7	Colombia	1.3	4 %	1.2	2 %
8	Canada	0.4	1 %	1.2	2 %
9	Ecuador	1.8	6 %	1.2	2 %
10	Germany	0.9	3 %	1.1	2 %
	Others	*9.6*	32 %	*13.4*	26 %

Source: Own elaboration based on Adex Data Trade (2024).

Between 2008 and 2023, an overwhelming 86 % of Peru's exports to China were driven by the mining sector, significantly surpassing other sectors such as fishing (11 %), agriculture (1 %), and oil and gas (1 %) (see Figure 01 for more detail). Within Peru's mining exports to China during this period, copper was the dominant commodity. Copper concentrates alone constituted 66 % of Peru's mining exports to China, far exceeding refined copper, which represented only 9 %. This underscores Peru's critical role in the global copper value chain as a supplier of raw materials essential for China, which serves as the most significant downstream actor in the copper GVC (Bamber and Fernandez 2021).

Figure 1. Leading Peruvian export sectors to China, accumulated from 2008 to 2023

Source: Own elaboration based on Adex Data Trade (2024).

The evolution of Peru's export structure highlights the increasing dominance of copper within total exports. Copper's concentrate share in Peru's exports to China rose from 41 % in 2008 to 67 % in 2023, reflecting both the growing global demand for copper and Peru's strategic position as a key supplier to China's manufacturing, electronics, and energy sectors (see Figure 2 for details). In 2023, 77 % of the copper exported from Peru went to China, while the figure was only 31 % in 2008 (Figures 3 and 4). While other commodities such as fishing products, oil, and gas also contributed to Peru's exports, copper remains the most significant driver of Peru's trade with China.

Figure 2. Peru's exports to China between 2008 and 2023, by sector

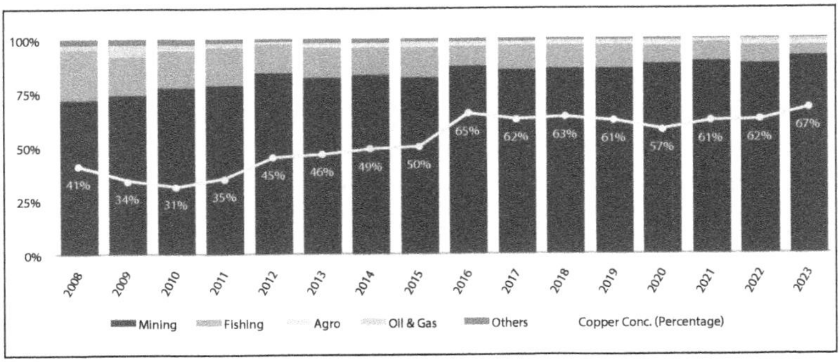

(*) Copper concentrate as a percentage of total Peruvian exports to China

Source: Own elaboration based on Adex Data Trade (2024).

Figure 3. Top export destinations of Peruvian copper conc. in 2008 (%)

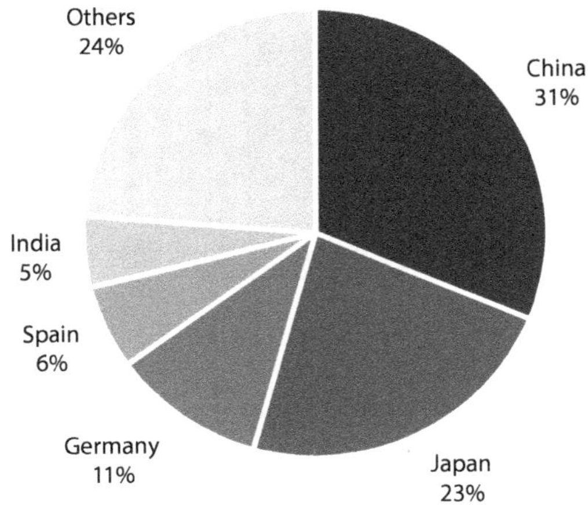

Source: Own elaboration based on Adex Data Trade (2024).

Figure 4. Top export destinations of Peruvian copper conc. in 2023 (%)

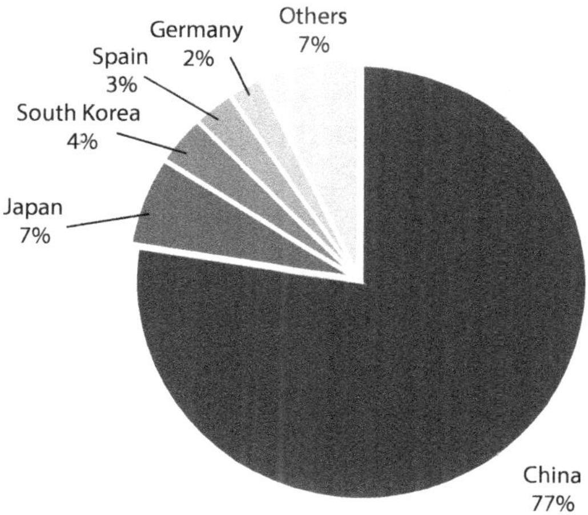

Source: Own elaboration based on Adex Data Trade (2024).

Copper's dominant position in Peru's exporting portfolio has been driven by global demand patterns, with China at the center of these trends. Peru's copper exports primarily represent the upstream stages of the copper GVC, where raw material extraction in Peru is followed by refining, manufacturing, and consumption in China. With 45 % of the world's refinery capacities (USGS 2024), 56 % of the world's imports of copper ores and concentrates go to China (OEC 2024) (see Figure 5). Chile and Peru collectively lead as China's largest raw copper suppliers, with Peru supplying 20 % of Chinese demands (OEC 2024) (see Figure 6).

The copper export GVC is concentrated in the hands of a few major mining firms. In 2023, the top five companies controlled 70 % of Peru's copper concentrate exports, collectively generating 10.9 billion USD in revenue. Minera Las Bambas led the export sector, accounting for 19.2 % of Peru's copper concentrate exports to China. It was followed by Compañía Minera Antamina (18.2 %), Minera Cerro Verde (13 %), Anglo American Quellaveco (11 %), and Compañía Minera Antapaccay (9 %) (see Table 3). These companies play a significant role in shaping the local and global

Figure 5. World Importers of Copper Ores and Concentrates (2022)

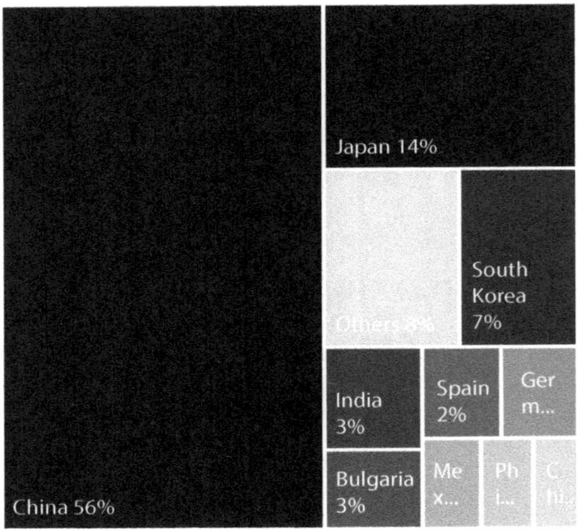

Source: Own elaboration based on OEC (2024).

Figure 6. World Exporters of Copper Ores and Concentrates to China (2022)

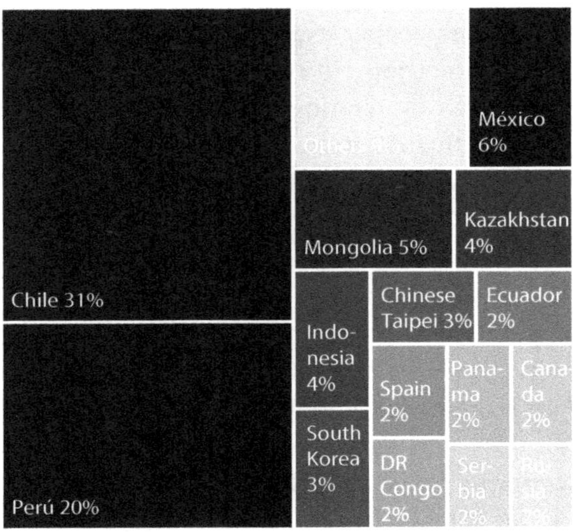

Source: Own elaboration based on OEC (2024).

dynamics of the copper GVC. Their operations influence local economies and reflect major policies of resource governance in Peru's mining sector.

Table 3. Ranking of Peruvian copper conc. exporters to China in 2023 (in US Billion and Percentage)

Nº	Exporter	2023	
		FOB Value	%
	Total	15.6	100 %
1	Mineria Las Bambas S.A	3.0	19 %
2	Compañía Minera Antamina S.A	2.8	18 %
3	Sociedad Minera Cerro Verde S.A.A.	2.1	13 %
4	Anglo American Quellaveco S.A.	1.7	11 %
5	Compañia Minera Antapaccay S.A.	1.3	8 %
6	Trafigura Peru S.A.C.	1.3	8 %
7	Hudbay Peru S.A.C.	0.9	6 %
8	Minera Chinalco Perú S.A.	0.7	5 %
9	Glencore Peru S.A.C.	0.4	3 %
10	Ixm Tracing Peru S.A.C.	0.3	2 %
	Others	1.1	7 %

Source: Own elaboration based on Adex Data Trade (2024).

In addition to copper exports, Peru's imports from China have grown substantially, totaling over 144 billion USD between 2008 and 2023. These imports have a more diversified sectoral composition compared to exports, for example, 50 % of Peru's imports from China are concentrated in the metal and mechanical sector, which includes machinery, electrical equipment, and vehicles. Other key imports include chemicals (14 %), steel and metallurgy (10 %), textiles (6 %), and clothing (5 %) (see Figure 7 for more details). This diverse import portfolio underscores the growing complexity of Peru's trade relationship with China, which now extends beyond raw material exports to include a broad range of industrial and consumer goods.

Figure 7. Leading sectors of Peruvian imports from China, accumulated from 2008 to 2023

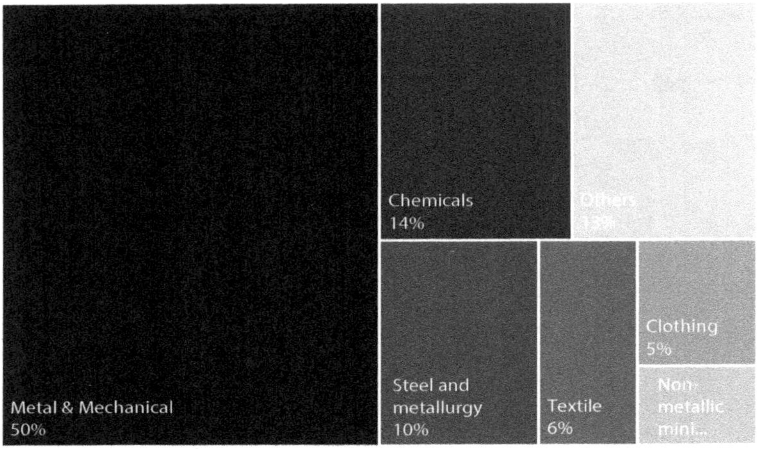

Source: Own elaboration based on Adex Data Trade (2024).

Copper's importance in trade between Peru and China is further amplified by its role in the global energy transition. As China accelerates its shift toward cleaner energy sources, copper is essential in the production of renewable energy technologies, such as solar panels, wind turbines, and electric vehicles (EVs). In response to this growing demand, Peru's mining companies have expanded their production capacities. The copper GVC, therefore, not only involves the flow of materials but also reflects broader global shifts in energy and manufacturing trends, positioning Peru as an integral part of China and even the world's clean energy transition.

3. Impact of Exporting Copper to China in Peru

The copper trade with China, as part of a broader global copper GVC, has substantial impacts on Peru's local communities and national economy. Mining regions, particularly those in southern

Peru, where copper extraction is concentrated, experience both economic benefits–such as job creation and infrastructure development–and challenges related to environmental degradation and social conflict. Chinese investments have played a pivotal role in shaping these territorial dynamics, with Chinese firms often involved in the largest mining projects.

3.1 Macroeconomic Impact of the Peruvian Copper Industry

The mining industry is integral to Peru's economy, with copper at the forefront. According to the annual report of the Peruvian Ministry of Mining and Energy (MINEM, 2024), in 2023, the mining sector contributed 9.1 % to Peru's national GDP and 65.1 % of Peru's total exports, reinforcing its importance as a driving force for the country's economic growth. Copper is central to Peru's mining industry. In 2023, Copper alone accounted for 59.7 % of the mining sector's GDP. Peru produced 2.7 million metric tons of copper in 2023, securing its place as the second-largest copper producer in the world. The copper sector is also the largest contributor to Peru's exports, accounting for 34.7 % of the total value of exports.

The mining industry also plays a significant role in employment. In 2023, direct employment in Peru's mining sector reached 225,681 jobs (MINEM 2024), making it one of the largest sources of direct employment, particularly in regions like Arequipa, La Libertad, and Moquegua, where mining activities dominate. Furthermore, for every direct mining job, an estimated eight indirect jobs are created (MINEM 2024) in sectors such as transportation, services, and retail, illustrating the mining sector's broad economic impact across the country.

With mining being an influential sector of the economy, it is no surprise that it has contributed significantly to national and local economic development. For example, the study of Aragón and Rud (2013) found that large mining projects like the Yanacocha mine in Cajamarca not only contribute to the local economy and reduce the poverty rate through tax revenues but, more importantly, through backward linkages and integration with the local suppliers. In a similar vein, Loayza and Rigolini (2016) found that mining has a positive effect on per capita consumption and brings down extreme poverty in the adjacent areas.

The positive effects of mining on economic development in Peru are largely attributed to *Canon Minero*, a revenue-sharing regime between the central government and the subnational governments. Through this institution, contingent sums of mining revenues are transferred to the regions and localities where the resources were produced. While some studies have shown that *Canon Minero* has a significant impact on boosting the local economy and reducing poverty (Casas and Málaga 2013; Del Pozo *et al.* 2013), others also revealed that the institution's inefficiency has diminished the positive effects (Herrera 2008; Arellano-Yanguas 2013; Manrique *et al.* 2016). The local government often receives more resources than warranted by its fiscal capacity and needs. Since the revenue cannot be saved locally, it leads to inefficient spending and corruption. The variation in the local government's capacity to use *Canon Minero* across different regions also created different results in economic development (Crabtree 2013; Velarde 2017).

Despite its significant contributions to the economic development of the country, the copper industry poses a major challenge to Peru's macroeconomic stability due to its susceptibility to global price fluctuations. The phenomenon of the "resource curse" –also known as the paradox of plenty– illustrates how countries rich in natural resources, like copper, can face economic instability, social inequality, and corruption despite their wealth (Englebert and Ron 2004; Humphreys *et al.* 2007). Peru is not immune to this curse. While copper mining generates substantial revenues, it also makes Peru highly dependent on copper exports, leaving the economy vulnerable to the cyclical nature of copper prices.

This cyclical vulnerability is further shaped by China's dominant role in the global copper market. The relationship between China's copper demand and its global price is defined by a complex and structural interdependence, driven by the convergence of macroeconomic, industrial, and trade-related factors. As the world's largest consumer, China accounts for over 35 % of global refined copper imports, positioning itself as a pivotal force in price determination. The literature highlights that key variables such as GDP growth, industrial production, and urbanization in China serve as critical indicators of demand, exerting a direct influence on international price fluctuations (Becerra *et al.* 2022).

This influence is magnified by the dynamics of global trade relations. Shifts in trade structures, particularly those triggered by geopolitical tensions with strategic partners, have led to significant disruptions in copper flows. Such changes not only reshape supply chains but also affect the stability and competitiveness of the global market. Thus, the interplay between China's copper demand and global prices reflects a highly sensitive system, influenced by both external shocks and structural complexities (Muñoz 2014).

In the past twenty years, Peruvian macroeconomic performance was tightly related to global copper prices and the demand from China (See Figure 8). When China's demand for copper rises, driven by industrial growth, infrastructure development, and the energy transition, copper prices increase, leading to higher export revenues and boosting Peru's GDP growth. For example, during the 2011-2013 period, when copper prices reached record highs, export revenues soared, and Peru's economy grew significantly. However, during downturns in Chinese demand, such as the slowdown in 2014-2016, copper prices fell sharply, dropping from around 6,000 USD per metric ton to approximately 4,500 USD (IMF 2024). This decline led to reduced export revenues and a slowdown in Peru's GDP growth, as copper accounts for a substantial share of the country's total exports and fiscal revenues. The cyclical nature of copper prices, influenced by China's economic cycles, creates volatility, leaving Peru's economy vulnerable to global price fluctuations. With copper making up 65.1 % of Peru's total exports in 2023 (MINEM 2023), this dependence on copper exposes the economy to significant risks during price downturns.

Figure 8. Copper prices, Chinese demand of copper & Peruvian GDP from 2001 to 2023

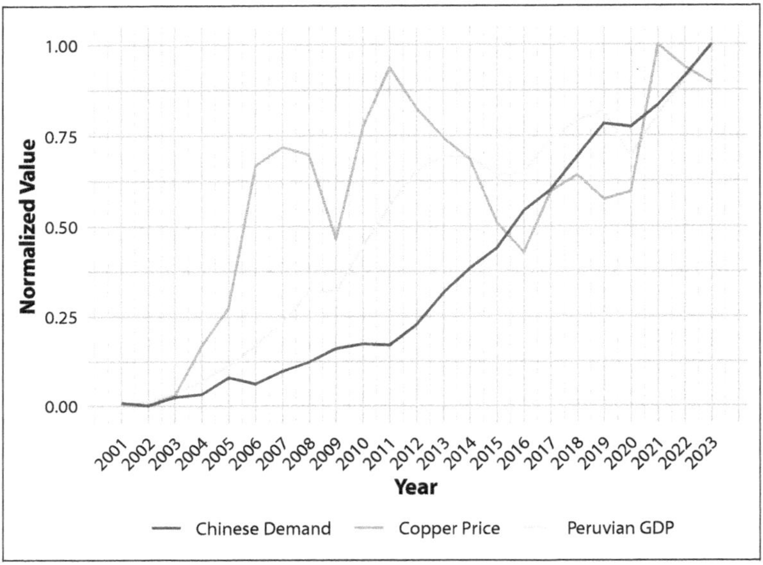

Source: Own elaboration based on World Bank (2024/a/b) and IMF (2024).

3.2 Environmental Challenges of Mining in Peru

The environmental impacts of mining in Peru are a significant concern, especially for the approximately 1.6 million Peruvians living within five kilometers of active or decommissioned mines, with two-thirds of these individuals residing near 29 mining clusters (Van Geen *et al.* 2012). Studies in historical mining regions such as Cerro de Pasco and the Mantaro River Basin reveal high levels of lead contamination and waste accumulation (Van Geen *et al.* 2012; Cayetano 2013). The environmental impact of newer mining projects, such as the Las Bambas copper project, owned by a Chinese company, has also drawn attention (Astete, Gastañaga, and Pérez 2014). There is a high risk of exposure to mercury around mining areas, both for the people engaged in mining and for groups engaged in other activities, especially for children (Wyatt *et al.* 2017; Weinhouse *et al.* 2017).

The Peruvian government has implemented several reforms in response to these environmental risks. The creation of the Ministry of Environment (MINAM) and the Environmental Evaluation and Oversight Agency (OEFA) marked significant steps in strengthening environmental governance. The OEFA is critical in auditing and enforcing regulations for the mining, energy, and industrial sectors. The Servicio Nacional de Certificación Ambiental para las Inversiones Sostenibles (SENACE) was also established to review and approve Environmental Impact Assessments (EIAs) for high-risk projects, providing an independent certification system for mining and hydrocarbon operations.

EIAs became mandatory in Peru's mining sector in the early 1990s, with MINEM responsible for reviewing and approving these assessments until the establishment of MINAM in 2008 (De Echave *et al.* 2009). This change aimed to improve transparency and environmental oversight. However, the EIA process has been criticized for being largely informative, with limited participation from local communities. Studies on the Conga copper project highlight that the EIA process is often used to create an appearance of consensus without genuinely addressing local concerns about environmental impacts (Zavaleta 2013; Pinto Herrera 2014). Similarly, Yrivarren (2017) argues that the EIA's technical discussions are often skewed by the interests of mining companies, undermining the neutrality of the process.

Additionally, the EIA process is criticized for using overly simplistic methodologies that fail to fully capture the potential environmental risks (Uscuchagua 2016). The technical reports and supporting documents are frequently withheld from the public, reducing community involvement in decision-making (Wiener 2017). This has led to conflicts over mining projects, as discrepancies in EIA assessments contribute to local opposition and social unrest (Jaskoski 2014; Sosa and Zwarteveen 2014).

Despite institutional reforms, environmental governance in Peru's mining sector continues to face challenges. The power of extractive interests continues to influence the sector, weakening the enforcement of environmental regulations and hindering the development of more sustainable practices (Leyva 2013). International pressures and policy entrepreneurs will be key in pushing for stronger environmental protections and more effective governance in Peru's mining sector.

3.3 Social Conflicts and Challenges to Social Governance

Social conflicts in the mining sector, often involving local communities, mining companies, and the State, have accounted for approximately 60 % of all social unrest in Peru (Defensoría del Pueblo 2020). While the environmental impacts of mining are often at the forefront of these disputes, the causes of social unrest in the mining sector are deeply rooted in various socio-political and economic factors. Over the past two decades, scholarly literature has highlighted several fundamental causes, including water resource competition (Bebbington *et al.* 2008; Arotoma 2017; Li 2016; Yacoub 2015; Sosa and Zwarteveen 2016), the lack of state action in managing these conflicts (Orihuela and Paredes 2017; Gustafsson 2019), and the misconduct and mistrust towards mining companies (Fraser 2018; Irwin and Gallagher 2013; Zhang 2023). These tensions, compounded by differing value systems and tensions between indigenous and Western worldviews (Merino 2015; Salas 2017), have shaped the complex landscape of social conflict in Peru's mining regions.

Water grabbing has been an increasingly important cause of social conflicts around mining. In many mining regions, especially in the Andean and coastal regions, local communities rely on water for agriculture, livestock, and daily consumption. Even the prospect of depletion and contamination of water sources by large-scale copper mines –often involving toxic substances such as cyanide and mercury– have provoked fierce resistance from local communities, particularly Indigenous groups (Bebbington *et al.* 2013; Boelens *et al.* 2015). As the protests against the Tambo Grande copper project in the Andean highlands (Arce 2014) and the Tía María copper projects in the coastal south (Arce 2022) show, conflicts between the local communities and the mining companies often center around land usage and water rights.

Moreover, there is a pervasive mistrust towards mining companies that has deepened over time. Many mining companies, particularly those owned by foreign investors, are seen as prioritizing profit over social and environmental responsibility, leading to widespread perceptions of corporate negligence (Perla 2012; Gustafsson 2018; Zhang 2023). Local populations with little to no direct benefit from mining operations may feel alienated by the development processes and skeptical of companies' commitments to sustainable practices and social responsibility.

Equally important is the role of the Peruvian State in exacerbating social conflicts. Despite the recognition of indigenous peoples' rights to consultation and participation in development projects under ILO Convention 169, the State's enforcement of these rights has been weak (Dargent *et al.* 2017). The Prior Consultation Law, enacted in 2011 after years of conflict related to extractive industries in indigenous territories, aims to ensure free, prior, and informed consultation for communities impacted by mining. However, the implementation of the law has been criticized for being slow and largely symbolic, often failing to incorporate indigenous peoples' worldviews and values into decision-making processes (Jaskoski 2014; Leyva 2018). These shortcomings have contributed to the ongoing perception of exclusion among local communities, who often see the State as complicit in the corporate exploitation of their land and resources.

In response to these rising social conflicts, the Peruvian government has implemented several reforms aimed at improving dialogue and conflict resolution. One of the central mechanisms is the *Mesa de Diálogo* (Dialogue Roundtable), a platform designed to facilitate negotiation and mediation between mining companies, local communities, and government representatives. The goal of the dialogue roundtables is to provide a forum where all stakeholders can voice their concerns and work toward peaceful resolutions to conflicts (De la Puente 2017). These platforms have been integral in allowing affected communities to engage with the government and corporations in an attempt to find mutually agreeable solutions to environmental, economic, and social issues.

However, in practice, the *Mesa de Diálogo* has shown significant limitations. Studies have shown that while these platforms often legitimize the conflict resolution process, they rarely lead to substantive changes in governance or the resolution of underlying issues (Flores 2016; De la Puente 2017, 2019). Dialogue tables are often used as delaying tactics rather than genuine conflict resolution mechanisms. When there is little political will from the State to address the core grievances of local communities, these dialogues become an empty process, perpetuating the status quo without yielding meaningful outcomes. The power imbalances at the table, with mining companies often holding more influence than local communities, undermine the effectiveness of these platforms. The lack of active governmental participation also means that dialogue tables often fail to generate binding agreements or tangible solutions. Local communities, in turn, feel frustrated by the lack of concrete results and the disconnection between the dialogue process and actual policy or operational changes on the ground.

Another aspect of the mishandling of mining conflicts by the state is the criminalization of protests and the subsequent radicalization of conflicts. When communities take to the streets to voice their grievances over environmental degradation or violations of their rights, they are often met with state repression rather than dialogue. As Vásquez (2013) and the Oxfam report (2015) indicate, the criminalization of protests not only undermines the possibility of peaceful negotiations but also escalates tensions, pushing communities to adopt more confrontational tactics. The criminalization of protest –which labels local resistance as "illegal" or "violent"– further alienates communities from the State, solidifying their belief that dialogue and peaceful negotiation will not lead to substantive change (Arellano-Yanguas 2011). These dynamics, combined with weak state institutions and the lack of coordination between government bodies, fuel the escalation of conflicts and often result in prolonged confrontations between local communities, mining companies, and the government.

3.4. Chinese Companies' Learning Process: Las Bambas

Bambas mine, located in the Apurímac Region of southern Peru, is one of the largest copper mining projects in the country and a significant player in the global copper supply chain. Initially developed by the Swiss company Xstrata since 2004, it was acquired by a Chinese consortium led by the state-owned MMG Limited. in 2014, marking it one of the largest Chinese investments in Peru's mining sector, valued at 7 billion USD (Sanborn *et al.* 2024). Since the commercial production initiated in 2016, the mine has contributed significantly to Peru's copper exports, solidifying its role as a vital source of copper for global markets. As a key resource, it is integral to the country's economy, supporting local employment and infrastructure projects while enhancing Peru's position as a major exporter of copper globally.

Las Bambas was ranked as the fifth-largest copper producer in Peru in 2023, generating over 302,033 tons of copper concentrate, equivalent to 11 % of the national production (MINEM 2024; Las Bambas 2024). At the local level, Las Bambas is a cornerstone project as it remains the sole copper operation in the Apurímac region. But what does this project truly represent for the region?

In Peru, mining contributes to local well-being primarily through economic transfers to regional governments and job creation. Resource transfers are distributed in the form of *canon minero*, mining royalties, as well as concession fees and penalties. These funds are channeled into public infrastructure and development projects in mining regions. In 2023, Apurimac was the sixth region in Peru to receive the highest resource transfers, largely due to Las Bambas, which accounted for over 90 % of the value of minerals extracted in the region in 2022 (EITI 2023).

Canon minero, royalties, and concession fees serve as mechanisms through which mining contributes to regional economic development. The *Canon minero* comprises 50 % of the corporate income tax paid by mining companies to the State, allocated to subnational governments to finance public investment projects. Mining royalties, on the other hand, are payments made by companies based on the gross value or operating margin of extracted minerals and are primarily used for local infrastructure and services. Finally, concession fees are annual payments made by companies to maintain active mining rights, with penalties imposed if minimum commitments are not met, ensuring efficient resource utilization (MINEM 2024).

Las Bambas has been a key economic driver for the Apurímac region since commencing operations in 2016. Initially, the company's contributions were centered on contractual royalties, established in its concession agreement at 3 % of monthly sales. By June 2023, these contributions had totaled approximately 480 million USD, peaking in 2021 with a record payment of around 92 million USD (Yauri 2023; EITI 2023). Furthermore, in 2021, Las Bambas began declaring and paying corporate income tax, which enabled the generation of canon for the first time in 2022. That year, Apurimac received 120 million soles from this source (Yauri 2023). It is important to note that the delay in income tax payments reflects the recovery of substantial investments made during the construction and implementation phase of the project, a common scenario in large-scale mining endeavors where initial costs result in losses or low operational margins during the early years. The province of Cotabambas, where the mine is located, was the primary recipient of these funds, receiving 56 % of the total transfers.

In terms of employment, Las Bambas has created over 8,000 direct and indirect jobs, with 44 % of the workforce sourced from nearby communities (Las Bambas 2024). However, these figures must be contextualized against the region's high dependency on mining activity, leaving limited room for the development of diversified, long-term economic structures. While women's participation in operational roles stands at 14 %, exceeding the national average, this underscores the ongoing need for stronger policies to ensure gender equity in a historically male-dominated sector.

Nonetheless, despite the potential positive contributions of the Las Bambas company to the Apurímac region, it has faced and continues to face notable challenges. One of the most contentious issues surrounding the Las Bambas project is land acquisition. The need to resettle Fuerabamba, a community located on the mine's property, led to significant tension with the local population. Fuerabamba, along with other nearby communities such as Huancuire and Pumamarca, sold land to the mining company to allow for the development of the mine. The land acquisition process was mired in controversy, particularly over the price paid for the land. Fuerabamba was compensated at just 20 cents of nuevo sol per square meter, a price considered far too low compared to other neighboring communities. For example, Huancuire sold their land at 2.49 USD per square meter, and Pumamarca received 0.46 USD per square meter (CooperAcción 2015). These discrepancies fueled a sense of injustice and inequality, leading to protests and public outcry. Although initial negotiations were based on national land laws, the compensation rates caused resentment, as local communities felt exploited.

The disagreement over land prices was compounded by the relocation process. Fuerabamba, which had to relocate due to the proximity of the mine, was promised improved living conditions in the newly constructed settlement, but many residents felt the compensation and resettlement conditions were inadequate. Although agreements were reached between MMG and the community, tensions remained over the promises made, particularly regarding the conditions of the new housing, the relocation of agricultural land, and the provision of public services. Despite efforts to renegotiate, the initial land acquisition deals continue to be a point of contention, and the community remains deeply divided over the fairness of the compensation.

Employment and local development also became central issues in the social conflicts surrounding the mine. The district of Challhuahuacho, where the mine is located, became the focal point of these disputes. Although MMG made promises to hire local laborers and support regional development, many residents felt excluded from the economic opportunities generated by the mine. In February 2015, a strike erupted in Challhuahuacho, with about 1,000 community members demanding the fulfillment of previous promises, including job creation and financial support for the community. The protestors also called for the company to cease the contamination of the Challhuahuacho River, a result of the lack of a proper water and sanitation system in the town. They further demanded the establishment of a social fund, asking for 10 % of the profits to be allocated to community development (Ramos 2018).

To address the rising tensions, the government initiated the Challhuahuacho District Development Roundtable (MDCH) in February 2015 (*Defensoría del Pueblo* 2015). This was a forum designed to facilitate dialogue between the government, MMG, and local community representatives. The establishment of the roundtable was a positive step, as it created a space for dialogue on critical issues such as employment, environmental concerns, and social infrastructure. Sub-roundtables were set up to focus on specific areas, including social and productive infrastructure, mining and environmental issues, agricultural development, and social responsibility. However, despite the formal creation of the roundtable and agreements made within the sub-roundtables, little meaningful progress was made. Although MMG promised to hire local workers, particularly for forest nurseries, and to support infrastructure projects like water and sanitation systems, these commitments were not fulfilled in a timely manner.

As the months passed, frustrations grew as the promised projects failed to materialize. The lack of tangible results led to renewed protests in early 2017, with the community once again blocking access roads and demanding the company meet its obligations (Defensoría del Pueblo 2017). The government, in turn, declared a state of emergency in February 2017 (RPP 2017) and called for new rounds of dialogue under the framework of MDCH. MMG's promises of employment were questioned, with demands for increased labor in forest nurseries and a wage increase for existing workers. To this day, this has been the pattern of interaction between the rural communities of Challhuahuacho, headed by the Federation of Peasants, the state, and the company. Despite the formation of the MDCH almost ten years ago, the dialogue process has remained stalled as the government and MMG continued to offer explanations rather than concrete solutions. The roundtable became increasingly ineffective, with community representatives threatening to abandon the discussions and continue with the protests.

Another big challenge faced by Las Bambas has been the protests surrounding the use of local roads for mineral transportation. These disputes began with the Environmental Impact Assessment (EIA) process. The mining company Xstrata presented its initial EIA in 2010, which was later approved by MINEM (Ministry of Energy and Mines) in 2011. According to the original EIA, the project was designed to include three primary areas: the Las Bambas mining site, a pipeline, and the Tintaya copper project (which was also owned by Xstrata). The pipeline was intended to stretch 206 kilometers, transporting minerals from the Las Bambas plant to the molybdenum plants in Tintaya, located in Espinar, Cusco (Defensoría del Pueblo 2016/a).

However, in 2013, Xstrata merged with Glencore International PLC, forming the Glencore Xstrata PLC conglomerate. Following the merger in December 2013, the Peruvian Ministry of Energy and Mines (MINEM) approved the first of several amendments to the EIA through a Sustainable Technical Report (ITS). This tool allows for changes to be made to a project's components with minimal environmental impact. While it is understandable from a business perspective that MMG, the new owner of the Las Bambas project, shifted from the pipeline to trucks to transport the copper concentrates, as Las Bambas and Tintaya now belonged to two separate companies, this decision drastically changed the environmental and social dynamics of the project.

The shift to trucking was implemented without adequate consultation with local communities, leaving local residents frustrated and marginalized. As a result, a series of social conflicts began to emerge, driven by environmental concerns, road conditions, and the strain of increased truck traffic. These protests culminated in September 2015, when a provincial strike was called by community leaders demanding more transparency and accountability from MMG and the government regarding the transportation route and its environmental and social implications. The situation escalated after September 28, 2015, when a group of protestors tried to enter the mine's facilities, resulting in a deadly clash with the National Police. This violence led to the deaths of three protestors and dozens of injuries and arrests (CooperAccion 2015).

In response to the escalating tensions, the government declared a state of emergency on September 29, lasting for 30 days in the provinces of Cotabambas, Espinar, and Chumbivilcas (CooperAccion 2015). As part of the government's effort to defuse the crisis, a dialogue roundtable was established in the province, intended to address the modifications to the EIA and facilitate communication between the community, MMG, and the government. The government called for information workshops to explain the changes made to the EIA, but tensions persisted, particularly since the leaders of the defense fronts and protest committees, who had promoted the mobilizations, were initially excluded from the negotiations. This exclusion exacerbated existing grievances and contributed to a sense of disenfranchisement among the community leaders.

Despite these tensions, the government pushed forward with the creation of the "Working Roundtable for the Development of the Province of Cotabambas" (MTDC) in November 2015. The roundtable was formed with various ministries, local authorities, and civil society representatives from the province. The first meeting of the MTDC took place in February 2016. Although the formation of the MTDC was a step towards reconciliation, the implementation of its agreements faced significant delays; for this reason, the Provincial community leaders withdrew from the roundtable in March amid mounting tensions along the road (Red Muqui 2016).

By early 2016, as the mine began commercial operations, between 200 and 300 trucks transported copper and molybdenum concentrates daily from the Las Bambas mine to the port of Matarani. The heavy traffic from the trucks contributed to increased dust, noise, and vibrations, significantly affecting communities along the transportation routes. In August 2016, communities along these routes organized road blockages to protest against the environmental and social impact caused by the trucks (*La Republica*, 2016). This protest led to further clashes with the police, resulting in one death and 17 injuries during an incident in October (Defensoría del Pueblo 2016/b).

In December 2016, a high-level government commission led by Vice President Vizcarra arrived in Cotabambas to present a Development Plan for the Province. In front of the local mayors, community organization leaders, and regular villagers, Vizcarra announced that MMG would need to modify its EIA within three months and that the government would compensate the communities for the lands used by the company to move minerals. However, the compensation amount was disputed: the government offered 17 million soles, while the communities valued the land at 50 million soles. The announcement also proposed an investment of 2 billion soles over five years, which MMG, the State, and the Regional Government would jointly fund (El Peruano 2016). In February 2017, the local officials led by the Provincial Mayor accepted the government's offer. The final validation of the plan excluded some sectors of the population, particularly those who had driven the agenda at the Cotabambas Roundtable and promoted the September 2015 strike. For this reason, the disagreements over the Development Plan ultimately led to further protests (La Republica 2016).

The MTDC process struggled to address the pressing concerns of the local communities. In March 2017, the Judiciary ordered eighteen months of preventive detention for the Mayor of the Cotabambas Province, Odilón Huanaco, for alleged acts of corruption during his term as Mayor of the Challhuahuacho District (La Republica 2017). The political instability and the loss of credibility in local officials make it harder to enforce the agreements made with the company and the central government during the dialogue roundtables. While new roundtables were established to address the new protests and demands to fulfill the old agreements, they, too, failed to yield significant progress, leaving local communities frustrated and skeptical about the government's willingness to resolve their concerns.

Despite the economic benefits the mine brings to Peru, including job creation, infrastructure development, and a substantial boost to Peru's copper exports, the Las Bambas mine exemplifies the complex challenges that Chinese foreign investments can face in regions with deep-seated social dynamics and environmental concerns. The dialogue roundtable process, while established as a platform for negotiation and conflict resolution, has shown limitations in addressing the root causes of unrest and dissatisfaction. The case highlights the importance of genuine engagement with local communities, transparent communication, and accountability in future foreign investments to ensure that projects are both economically viable and socially responsible.

4. Conclusions and Policy Suggestions

The trade relationship between Peru and China in the copper sector highlights the complexities inherent in global value chains (GVCs), where economic flows are structured in ways that often reinforce asymmetries in power, technological innovation, and territorial development (Dussel Peters 2018). Peru's role in the global copper value chain remains predominantly upstream, centered on the extraction and export of raw materials. In 2023, 92 % of its copper exports to China were conducted under subheading 260300 (copper ores and concentrates), reflecting the continued absence of value-added processes domestically. This reliance on raw material exports underscores the structural challenges facing Peru's copper industry and reinforces the asymmetries characteristic of center-periphery dynamics in its trade relationship with China.

The asymmetries in the Peru-China trade relationship exacerbate structural inequalities. Investments in large-scale mining projects, such as Las Bambas, have transformed territorial dynamics by generating local economic opportunities. The case of the Las Bambas mining project exemplifies the duality of most large-scale mining projects in Peru, acting as both a driver of regional development and a source of structural challenges. As the fifth-largest copper producer in the country, Las Bambas significantly contributes to Peru's copper exports, accounting for 11 % of national production in 2023. In the Apurímac region, it serves as the sole copper operation, delivering substantial economic benefits through *canon minero*, royalties, and concession fees that finance public investment and infrastructure projects. Yet this dependency on mining underscores vulnerabilities such as limited economic diversification, environmental degradation, and social tensions. While Las Bambas has generated over 8,000 jobs and fostered a workforce with notable local representation, challenges remain in ensuring long-term sustainability and promoting gender equity in a male-dominated industry.

However, these benefits are unevenly distributed and often overshadowed by environmental degradation and inadequate social inclusion. Social tensions remain acute, as evidenced by the fact that 60 % of social conflicts in Peru are related to mining activities. These conflicts stem from a lack of meaningful consultation mechanisms, environmental mismanagement, and insufficient alignment between corporate practices and community needs. Environmental challenges are another critical concern. Despite the establishment of governance frameworks –such as SENACE and OEFA–, Peru continues to face challenges in ensuring compliance with environmental standards. Current practices often fail to adequately mitigate long-term ecological impacts or involve communities in decision-making processes. Global Value Chains (GVCs) must be understood not only as economic mechanisms but also as instruments that shape territorial governance and sustainability.

Addressing these structural issues will be essential to maximizing mining's benefits while mitigating its adverse impacts on social and economic resilience.

Policy Recommendations

Economic diversification is a critical strategy for reducing Peru's dependence on copper and mitigating the risks associated with commodity price fluctuations. Proactive investment in alternative sectors such as agroindustry, renewable energy, and technology can provide new avenues for sustainable growth. For example, Peru's agricultural sector offers significant potential for high-value exports, particularly in organic and specialty markets. Meanwhile, the country's abundant natural resources make it well-suited for future renewable energy projects, which could position it as a leader in clean energy within the region. Moreover, fostering research and innovation through dedicated funding and the establishment of technological hubs could unlock opportunities in emerging industries, integrating Peru into other GVCs beyond copper.

Environmental governance must be strengthened to address the ecological challenges associated with mining activities. Institutions like SENACE and OEFA require greater financial and technical capacity to ensure effective oversight and enforcement of environmental regulations. Improving the transparency and rigor of Environmental Impact Assessments (EIAs) is a priority, with an emphasis on methodologies that account for long-term ecological risks. Local communities should be actively involved in the EIA process to ensure that their concerns are addressed. Additionally, aligning Peru's environmental standards with international benchmarks would enhance the sustainability of the mining sector and improve its global competitiveness.

Resolving the persistent social conflicts surrounding mining activities requires institutional reforms. Dialogue Tables should be restructured to ensure that the agreements reached are binding and enforceable. Independent monitoring mechanisms should be introduced to oversee the implementation of these agreements, ensuring accountability. Empowering local communities through training programs focused on negotiation, governance, and resource management can enhance their capacity to participate effectively in decision-making processes. Establishing a dedicated Ombudsman's Office for extractive industries would provide an impartial platform for mediating disputes and addressing grievances, fostering trust among stakeholders.

Efficient management of mining revenues is vital to translating the economic benefits of the sector into sustainable development outcomes. The creation of a sovereign wealth fund could stabilize revenues over time, enabling investments in critical areas such as education, healthcare, and infrastructure. This fund would also serve as a buffer against the volatility of copper prices, ensuring fiscal stability during downturns. Transparency mechanisms, such as public reporting of revenue allocation, are essential for reducing corruption and inefficiency. Reforming the canon minero to ensure that resources are distributed equitably and used effectively would further maximize its impact on local development.

Promoting sustainability in mining practices is crucial for balancing economic growth with environmental stewardship. Companies should be incentivized to adopt green technologies, including renewable energy sources, water-efficient extraction methods, and waste recycling systems. Robust land rehabilitation plans should be mandatory to restore ecosystems impacted by mining operations. Aligning these efforts with international sustainability frameworks, such as the UN Sustainable Development Goals, would ensure that Peru's mining sector contributes positively to global environmental objectives.

Building local capacities is a foundational step toward enhancing Peru's integration into the copper GVC. Expanding vocational training programs tailored to the needs of the mining and manufacturing sectors would equip workers with the skills required for higher-value roles. Increased investment in science, technology, engineering, and mathematics (STEM) education would foster innovation and prepare a workforce capable of driving industrial growth. Encouraging multinational corporations to share knowledge and technology with local firms would further accelerate this process. Additionally, Peru should engage actively in international trade and environmental forums to advocate for fairer terms of participation in GVCs, ensuring that its contributions as a resource-rich nation are adequately recognized and rewarded.

By implementing these policies, Peru can transform its current reliance on raw material exports into a foundation for sustainable, inclusive, and resilient development. This approach not only addresses existing vulnerabilities but also helps the country to take full advantage of its strategic role in the global economy.

References

ADEX (Asociación de Exportadores). 2024. *Balanza Comercial China-Perú y ranking aduanero*. Perú.

Aragón, Fernando, Rud, Juan. 2013. "Natural resources and local communities: Evidence from a Peruvian gold mine". *American Economic Journal: Economic Policy*, 5(2), pp. 1–25.

Arce, Moisés, Hendricks, Michael, and Polizzi, Marc. 2022. *The Roots of Engagement: Understanding Opposition and Support for Resource Extraction*. Oxford University Press.

Arce, Moisés. 2014. *Resource extraction and protest in Peru*. University of Pittsburgh Press: United States of America.

Arellano-Yanguas, Juan. 2011. "Mining and conflict in Peru. Sowing the minerals, reaping a hail of stones". In, Bebbington, Anthony (Ed.), *Social Conflict, Economic Development and the Extractive Industry: Evidence from South America*. Routledge, pp. 89-111.

Arellano-Yanguas, Juan. 2013. "Minería y desarrollo: ideas para repensar el canon". In, De Echave, Jose, Hoetmer, Daza, Mar, Raphael, Castro (eds.). *Minería y movimientos sociales en el Perú: instrumentos y propuestas para la defensa de la vida, el agua y los territorios*. Programa Democracia y Transformación Global, CooperAcción, AcSur Las Segovias y Entrepueblos, pp. 535-550.

Arotoma, Ingrid. 2017. "La negociación por el proyecto minero Quellaveco en la Región Moquegua: 2000-2012: élites regionales, participación local y conciencia hídrica.". Tesis de licenciatura. *Repositorio de Tesis PUCP*.

Astete, John, Gastañaga, María, and Pérez, Doris. 2014. "Niveles de metales pesados en el ambiente y su exposición en la población luego de cinco años de exploración minera en Las Bambas, Perú 2010". *Revista Peruana de Medicina Experimental y Salud Pública*, 31(4), pp 695-701.

Bamber, Penny and Fernandez, Karina. 2021. "Innovation and Competitiveness in the Copper Mining Global Value Chain Developing Local Suppliers in Peru." *Interamerican Development Bank.*

Bebbington, Anthony and Williams, Mark. 2008. "Water and mining conflicts in Peru". *Mountain Research and Development, 28*(3), pp. 190-195.

Bebbington, Anthony, Connarty, Michael, Coxshall, Wendy, O'Shaughnessy, Hugh, and Williams, Mark. 2007. *Minería y desarrollo en el Perú, con especial referencia al Proyecto Rio Blanco, Piura*. Instituto de Estudios Peruanos, Oxfam Internacional, Centro de Investigación y Promoción del Campesinado, Peru Support Group.

Bebbington, Paul, McBride, Orla, Steel, Craig, Kuipers, Elizabeth, Radovanoviĉ, Mirjana, Brugha, Troalach, Jenkins, Rachel, Meltzer, Howard, and Freeman, Daniel. 2013. "The structure of paranoia in the general population". *The British Journal Of Psychiatry*, *202*(6), pp. 419-427.

Becerra, Miguel, Jerez, Alejandro, Garcés, Hugo, and Demarco, Rodrigo. 2022. "Copper price: A brief analysis of China's impact over its short-term forecasting". *Resources Policy*.

Boelens, Rutgerd, Damonte, Gerardo, Seemann, Miriam, Duarte, Bibiana, and Yacoub, Cristina. 2015. "Despojo del agua en Latinoamérica: introducción a la ecología política del agua en los agronegocios, la minería y las hidroeléctricas". In, Yacoub, Cristina, Duarte, Bibiana and Boelens, Rutgerd (Eds.). *Agua y ecología política: el extractivismo en la agroexportación, la minería y las hidroeléctricas en Latinoamérica*. Justicia Hídrica y Ediciones Abya Yala, pp. 11-32.

Casas, Carlos and Málaga, Alexandra. 2013. *La importancia de los recursos naturales en la generación de recursos para el Estado y el Sistema de transferencias intergubernamental peruano*. Universidad del Pacifico: Perú.

Cayetano, Jose. 2013. "Cumplimiento de la normatividad ambiental por el sector minero-metalúrgico y su impacto ambiental en el río Mantaro, Región Junín". Tesis de maestría. *Repositorio UNCP*.

Chávez, Yeiddy. 2021. "El reasentamiento de la ciudad de Morococha: Las relaciones de poder en la vieja y nueva Morococha". Tesis de maestría. *Repositorio institucional FLACSO*: Andes.

CA (CooperAcción). 2015. "Informe Especial 2015: Caso Las Bambas". CA

Crabtree, John. 2013. *Uso y abuso del sistema de canon: la distribución de los beneficios de las industrias extractivas en la Región Cusco*. Centro Bartolomé de las Casas: Cusco.

Dargent, Eduardo and Urteaga, Madai. 2016. "Respuesta estatal por presiones externas: los determinantes del fortalecimiento estatal frente al *boom* del oro en el Perú (2004-2015)." *Revista de Ciencia Política, 36*(3), pp. 655-677.

De Echave, José and Yauri, Josselin. 2023. *La creciente presencia china en la economía peruana*. Cooperacción: Lima.

De la Puente, Lorena. 2017. "Cuando el diálogo es parte del problema. La institucionalización de las mesas de diálogo en el Perú: el caso del conflicto en Espinar". *Cuaderno de trabajo. PUCP*: Lima.

De la Puente, Lorena. 2019. "´No estuvimos a la altura de la situación´: límites de la participación ciudadana en la mesa de diálogo de Espinar (2012-2013)." *Debates en Sociología,* (45), pp. 33-57.

DP (Defensoría del Pueblo). 2015. *Reporte de Conflictos Sociales N°136*. Defensoría del Pueblo: Lima.

DP (Defensoría del Pueblo). 2016. "El Camino Hacia Proyectos de Inversión Sostenibles: Balance de la Evaluación de Impacto Ambiental en el Perú.". *Defensoría del Pueblo*: Lima.

DP (Defensoría del Pueblo). 2016. *Reporte de Conflictos Sociales N°152*. Defensoría del Pueblo: Lima.

DP (Defensoría del Pueblo). 2017. *Reporte de Conflictos Sociales N°157*. Defensoría del Pueblo: Lima.

DP (Defensoría del Pueblo). 2020. *Vigésimo cuarto informe anual 2020*. Defensoría del Pueblo: Lima.

Del Pozo, Cesar, Guzmán, Esteban, and Paucarmayta, Valerio. 2013. ¿Minería y bienestar en el Perú? Evaluación de impacto del esquema actual y esquemas alternativos de redistribución del canon minero. Elementos de discusión para el debate. CIES and CBC: Cusco.

Dussel Peters, Enrique. 2016. *La Nueva Relación Comercial de América Latina y el Caribe con China ¿Integración o desintegración regional?*. Universidad Nacional Autónoma de México: Mexico.

Dussel Peters, Enrique. 2018. *Cadenas Globales de Valor: Metodologías, teoría y debates*. Universidad Nacional Autónoma de México: Mexico.

Dussel Peters, Enrique. 2024/a. "Chinese Infrastructure Projects in Latin America and The Caribbean". In, Dussel Peters, Enrique, Cook, James A, and Alter, Joseph A (Eds.). *Connecting China, Latin America, and the Caribbean*. University of Pittsburgh Press: United States of America, pp.131-159.

Dussel Peters, Enrique. 2024/b. *Monitor of Chinese* OFDI *in Latin America and the Caribbean 2023*. Red ALC-China: Mexico.

EITI (Iniciativa para la Transparencia de las Industrias Extractivas). 2023. *Cuarto Estudio de Transparencia Regional* EITI *Apurímac Periodo 2022*. Apurímac: Perú.

EP (El Peruano). 2016. "Provincia apurimeña tendrá crecimiento cualitativo. Gobierno busca definir ruta del desarrollo de Cotabambas. Comunidades campesinas revisarán la propuesta del Ejecutivo el sábado 17 en asamblea". *El Peruano*. December 9.

Englebert, Pierre and Ron, James. 2004. "Primary commodities and war: Congo-Brazzaville's ambivalent resource curse". *Comparative Politics*, pp. 61-81.

Fairlie, Alan. 2014. "La Inversión Extranjera Directa de China en Perú. Los Casos de China Fishery Group y Chinalco". In, Dussel Peters, Enrique (edit.). *La Inversión Extranjera Directa de China en América Latina: 10 casos de Estudio.* Red ALC-China: Mexico, pp. 133-226.

Flores, César. 2016. *Conviviendo con la minería en el sur andino. Experiencias de las mesas de diálogo y desarrollo de Espinar, Cotabambas y Chamaca*. Cooperacción y Oxfam: Lima.

Fraser, Jocelyn and Kunz, Nadja. 2018. "Water stewardship: Attributes of collaborative partnerships between mining companies and communities". *Water, 10*(8).

Gallagher, Kevin. 2016. *The China triangle: Latin America's China boom and the fate of the Washington Consensus.* Oxford University Press: United Kingdom.

Gustafsson, Maria - Therese. 2018. *Private politics and peasant mobilization Mining in Peru*. Palgrave Macmillan.

Gustafsson, Maria Therese, and Scurrah, Martin. 2019. "Unpacking the extractivist state: The role of weak state agencies in promoting institutional change in Peru". *Extractive Industries and Society, 6(*1), pp. 206-214.

Herrera, Pedro. 2008. ¿Quitarle a los ricos para darle a los pobres? Una propuesta de redistribución de los recursos del canon y regalías mineras a nivel municipal. PUCP, (268).

Humphreys, Macartan, Sachs, Jeffrey, and Stiglitz, Joseph Eugene. (Eds). 2007. *Escaping the Resource Curse*. Colombia University Press: New York.

IMF (International Monetary Fund). 2024. "Primary commodity prices". *Commodity Data Portal.* All commodities and Energy. Non-Fuel Commodities. Industrial Inputs. Metals: Copper.

Irwin, Amos and Gallagher, Kevin. 2013. "Chinese mining in Latin America: A comparative perspective". *The Journal of Environment & Development, 22*(2), pp. 207-234.

Jaskoski, Maiah. 2014. "Environmental licensing and conflict in Peru's mining sector: A path-dependent analysis". *World Development*, (64), pp. 873-883.

Kaplan, Stephen. 2014. *The China boom in Latin America: An end to austerity*. Working Papers 2014-19. The George Washington University, Institute for International Economic Policy: United States of America.

LR (La República). 2016. "Cotabambas reinicia huelga para pedir a Estado y Las Bambas que cumplan los compromisos asumidos". *La república*. April 7.

LR (La República). 2017. "Apurímac: Alcalde Odilón Huanaco desapareció S/ 10 millones". *La República*. March 3.

Lagos, Gustavo, Parra, Roberto, Pérez, Victor, Peters, David, and Salas, Juan Carlos. 2021. *Análisis económico de las cadenas globales de valor y suministro del cobre refinado en países de América Latina*. ECLAC: Santiago de Chile.

Las Bambas. 2024. *Informe de Sostenibilidad 2023*. MMG Las Bambas: Lima.

Lausent-Herrera, Isabelle. 2011. "The Chinatown in Peru and the Changing Peruvian Chinese Community". *Journal of Chinese Overseas*, 7, pp. 69-113.

Leyva, Ana. 2013. "El sistema de gestión ambiental bajo la lupa de los conflictos sociales". In, Hoetmer, Raphael, Castro, Miguel, Daza, Mar, De Echave, José and Ruiz, Clara (eds.). *Minería y movimientos sociales en el Perú. Instrumentos y propuestas para la defensa de la vida, el agua y los territorios*. Programa Democracia y Transformación Global, CooperAcción, AcSur Las Segovias y Entrepueblos, pp. 511-526.

Leyva, Ana. 2018. *Consúltame de verdad: aproximación a un balance sobre consulta previa en el Perú en los sectores minero e hidrocarburífero*. CooperAcción.

Li, Fabiana. 2016. "In defense of water: Modern mining, grassroots movements, and corporate strategies in Peru". *Journal of Latin American and Caribbean Anthropology*. *21*(1), pp. 109-129.

Loayza, Norman and Rigolini, Jamele. 2016. "The Local Impact of Mining on Poverty and Inequality: Evidence from the Commodity Boom in Peru". *World Development*, 84, pp. 219–34.

Manrique, Gonzalo, Contreras, Álvaro and Guerrero, Natalia. 2016. "Evaluación del efecto de transferencias de canon minero en los resultados educativos: análisis a nivel de instituciones educativas de las regiones de Arequipa, Moquegua y Tacna". Informe final. *CIES y Apoyo Consultoría.*

Merino, Roger. 2015. *Coloniality and indigenous territorial rights in the Peruvian Amazon: A critique of the prior consultation law.* University of Bath: United Kingdom.

MINEM (Ministerio de Energía y Minas). 2023. *Anuario Minero 2022*. MINEM: Lima.

MINEM (Ministerio de Energía y Minas). 2024. *Anuario Minero 2023*. MINEM: Lima.

MN (Ministerio de Minería. 2023). *Estrategia Nacional para el Fortalecimiento de la Capacidad de Fundición de Refinaría.* Ministerio de Minería: Santiago de Chile.

Muñoz, Ercio. 2014. "El efecto de sorpresas en el crecimiento de China sobre el precio del cobre". [Nota de Investigación]. *Repositorio del Banco Central de Chile.*

Narrea, Omar. 2022. "Sharing Chinese and Peruvian Visions about the Future Chancay Port: Exploring Opportunities under the Belt and Road". *Centro de Estudios sobre China y Asia-Pacífico.*

Narrea, Omar. 2024. "Sailing The Pacific Ocean with Chinese Infrastructure: The Case of Chancay Port". In, Dussel Peters, Enrique, Cook, James A, and Alter, Joseph A (Eds.). *Connecting China, Latin America, and the Caribbean.* University of Pittsburgh Press, pp. 261-283.

OEC (Observatory of Economic Complexity). 2024. *Copper and ores concentrates: Historical Data.* At: https://oec.world/en.

Orihuela, Jose Carlos and Paredes, Martiza. 2017. "Fragmented Layering: Building a Green State for Mining in Peru". In, Orihuela, Jose Carlos, Paredes, Maritza and Ulfe, Maria Eugenia (Eds.), *Resource Booms and Institutional Pathways: The Case of the Extractive Industry in Peru.* Springer International Publishing, pp. 97-117.

Velazco, Rondon David and Quedena, Zambrano, Rosa Maria. 2015. "La criminalización de la protesta social y el caso Majaz". *Oxfam*: Lima.

Perla, Cecilia. 2012. "Extracting from the extractors: The politics of private welfare in the Peruvian mining industry". Tesis de doctorado. *Brown University Repository*: United States of America.

Pinto Herrera, Honorio. 2014. "Estudio de impacto ambiental del Proyecto Minero Conga". *Revista de Investigaciones Sociales, 18*(32), pp. 185-200.

Ramos, Leonidas. 2018. *Gobernanza y gobernabilidad: el caso Las Bambas*. CooperAcción.

R M (Red Muqui). 2016. "Dirigentes sociales de Cotabambas se retiraron de mesa de trabajo con el Ejecutivo". *Boletín Informativo de Red Muqui.*

R P P (Radio Programas del Perú). 2017. "Buscan Diálogo tras Estado de Emergencia por Paro en Challhuahacho". February 11.

Salas, Guillermo. 2017. "Mining and the living materiality of mountains in Andean societies". *Journal of Material Culture, 22*(2), pp. 133-150.

Sanborn, Cynthia and Chonn, Victoria. 2017. "La inversión china en la industria minera peruana: ¿Bendición o maldición?". In, Ray, Rebecca, Gallagher, Kevin P, López, Andrés and Sanborn, Cynthia (eds.). *China en América Latina: Lecciones para la cooperación Sur-Sur y el desarrollo sostenible*. Universidad del Pacífico: Lima, pp. 217-269.

Sanborn, Cynthia, Pareja, Amanda, and Quispe, Diego. 2024. *De Marcona a Chancay: la presencia económica y empresarial china en el Perú, 1992 – 2023*. Universidad del Pacífico: Perú.

Sanborn, Cynthia. 2009. "China INC., las industrias extractivas y el Perú: un estudio exploratorio". In, Sanborn, Cynthia and Torres, Victor (eds.), *La economía china y las industrias extractivas: desafíos para el Perú*. Fondo Editorial de la Universidad del Pacífico: Lima, pp. 225-379.

Sosa, Milagros and Zwarteveen, Margreet. 2016. "Questioning the effectiveness of planned conflict resolution strategies in water disputes between rural communities and mining companies in Peru". *Water International, 41*(3), pp. 483-500.

Uscuchagua, Mayvi. 2016. "Optimización de metodologías de evaluación de impacto ambiental del sector minero en las regiones Junín, Pasco y Huánuco". Tesis de maestría. *Repositorio* UNCP.

USGS (United States Geological Survey). 2024. *Mineral Commodity Summaries 2024.*

Van Geen, Alexandra, Bravo, Carolina, Gil, Vladimir, Sherpa, Shaky and Darby, Jack. 2012. "Lead exposure from soil in Peruvian mining towns: A national assessment supported by two contrasting examples". *Bulletin of the World Health Organization*, 90(12), pp. 878-886.

Vásquez, Mirtha. 2013. "La criminalización de la protesta social como estrategia de desarticulación del movimiento social en el Perú". In, De Echave, Jose, Hoetmer, Daza, Mar, Raphael, Castro (Eds.). *Minería y movimientos sociales en el Perú: instrumentos y propuestas para la defensa de la vida, el agua y los territorios.* Programa Democracia y Transformación Global, CooperAcción, AcSur Las Segovias y Entrepueblos: Lima, pp. 415-434.

Velarde, Lourdes. 2017. "El impacto del canon minero en el índice de desarrollo humano a través de los gastos públicos en saneamiento, educación y transporte, 2010-2012: caso Áncash y Cajamarca". Tesis de licenciatura. *Repositorio Universidad de Lima*

Weinhouse, Caren, Ortiz, Ernesto, Berky, Axel, Bullins, John Hare-Grogg, Rogers Laura, Morales, Ana-Maria, Hsu-Kim, Heileen and Pan, William. 2017. "Hair mercury level is associated with anemia and micronutrient status in children living near artisanal and small-scale gold mining in the Peruvian Amazon". *The American Journal of Tropical Medicine and Hygiene*, 97(6), pp. 1886-1897.

Wiener, Leonidas. 2017. "Problemas de gobernanza en una actividad extractiva: el caso Las Bambas". Tesis de maestría. *Repositorio de Tesis* PUCP

World Bank. 2024/a. *Copper ores and concentrates imports by country.* World Bank: Washington D.C.

World Bank. 2024/b. *World Development Indicators. Perú.* GDP *(current US$)*. World Bank: Washington D.C.

Wyatt, Lauren, Ortiz, Ernesto, Feingold, Beth, Berky, Axel, Diringer, Sarah, Morales, Ana Maria and Pan, William. 2017. "Spatial, temporal, and dietary variables associated with elevated mercury exposure in Peruvian riverine communities upstream and downstream of artisanal and small-scale gold mining". *International Journal of Environmental Research and Public Health*, 14(12), 1582.

Yacoub, Cristina. 2015. "Los guardianes del agua frente a las lógicas mineras en el Perú: el caso Conga". In, Boelens, Rutgerd, Duarte, Bibiana and Yacuob, Cristina (Eds.). *Agua y ecología política: el extractivismo en la agroexportación, la minería y las hidroeléctricas en Latinoamérica*. Justicia Hídrica y Abya Yala Quito, pp. 157-174.

Yauri, Josselin. 2023. *Las Bambas y los aportes mineros a la región Apurimac*. (CooperAccion, Documento de trabajo).

Zavaleta, Mauricio. 2013. *La política de lo técnico: una aproximación al desarrollo del conflicto Conga. En Asociación Servicios Educativos Rurales. Los límites de la expansión minera en el Perú*. SER: Lima, pp. 109-152

Zhang, Adela. 2023. "Trust as affective infrastructure: Constructing the firm/community boundary in resource extraction". *The Cambridge Journal of Anthropology*, *41*(2), pp. 71-86.

Zhang, Yuyan and Santa Gadea, Rosario. 2023. *En búsqueda de un camino para evitar la trampa del ingreso medio: Los casos de China y Perú*. Universidad del Pacífico: Perú.

7. The Territorial Impacts of Ecuadorian Shrimp Exports to China

Carolina Viola-Reyes and Giuliana Vera-Díaz

Introduction

This chapter aims to discuss the territorial impact of the Ecuadorian shrimp value chain aimed at the Chinese market. To achieve this, we introduce a multiscale approach, with a particular emphasis on the impacts that materialize at the territory-body scale. From this perspective, we propose discussing the relevance of place and locality as privileged sites for empirically visualizing the impacts of the global geoeconomy. At the same time, it suggests observing territories as socio-political constructs and bodies as the ultimate space of state sovereignty (Agamben 1998). It is here, in these extraction territories, that one can see, in their raw form, the impacts of the global geoeconomy characterized by relations of ecological imperialism (Foster and Clark 2020).

In Ecuador, the shrimp industry finds its origins in the 70s. In moments of weak state regulation, shrimp farming for export expanded through the illegal occupation of extensive areas of mangrove swamps. It is estimated that 70 % of the ecosystem was devastated by the installation of shrimp ponds (C-Condem 2007), causing irreversible damage to nature and the mangrove communities. Like any commodity, it has exhibited volatile behavior determined by international demand, in addition to frequent plagues and disease outbreaks that affect the industrial shrimp farming. The development of new genetically plague-resistant variants has enabled the industry's continuous growth until the 2000s (Piedrahita 2018).

In the 21st century, the shrimp industry has been one of the sectors that has benefited the most from closer ties to China. In 2000, shrimp exports generated an income of USD 754 million, growing exponentially to USD 6.1 billion in 2024. By 2023, exports to China accounted for 54 % of the total shrimp and prawn exports, followed by the United States with 20 % (CFN 2024).

In order to understand the complexity of the territorial effects of the shrimp value chain and the Sino-Ecuadorian relationship, this chapter is organized in four sections. The first presents a review of the literature on the Sino-Ecuadorian relationship. The second section focuses on a description of the trade relationship between China and Ecuador. The third section characterizes the value chain of shrimp exported to China. The fourth section examines the territorial impacts of the shrimp export industry, and we conclude by proposing some conclusions that address the research objectives.

1. Studies on the Sino-Ecuadorian Relationship

Despite the moderate economic and political relevance of this small Andean country within the Latin American context, since 2025 Ecuador has established itself as one of the hotspots for Chinese investments in the region, emerging as an interesting case study for the analysis of the dynamics of territorialization and deterritorialization by the Asian giant in Latin America (Sacher 2017; Viola 2016, 2021). As a result, in the last decade, academic production on Sino-Ecuadorian relations has increased, encouraging studies and research on Chinese presence in Ecuador. These deliberations tend to focus on three main approaches: the potential of the economic and trade relationship, the asymmetry within the relationship and its consequences, and lastly, the socio-environmental dimension, with an emphasis on threats and impacts on local communities and nature.

Regarding the first approach, Salinas-de Dosh (2012) stands out for analyzing the growth of Chinese investments, particularly in infrastructure since 2010, examining their effects on Ecuador's economy. The article provides evidence of the growth of Chinese investments in mining and oil operations since 2005, in a context of China's increasing interest in natural resources and, in turn, Ecuador's search for new strategic alliances. In this regard, Reyes and Lee (2017) discuss the political economy of the relationship between China and Ecuador from the pragmatism of an international relations realist lens. These authors emphasize the potential of the relationship and the challenges it presents for the Ecuadorian state; the weakness of state capacities debilitates, in most cases, the pursuit of better conditions in negotiations.

From this critical analysis on the opportunities derived from the Chinese presence in the region, Jenkins, Dussel Peters, and Mezquita Moreira (2008) describe both the opportunities and threats of the relationship in *The Impact of China on Latin America and the Caribbean*. In this regard, it is noteworthy to mention the compilation by Adrian Hearn and León-Maríquez (2011). Similarly, it is essential to mention the *Monitor of Chinese* OFDI *in Latin America and the Caribbean* coordinated by Dussel Peters at Red ALC-China, published annually since 2015, as well as the periodic reports titled *Economic Relations between China and Ecuador: Trade, Investment, and Cooperation*. These periodic reports systematically describe the evolution of trade, investment, and cooperation relations over the past decade, highlighting the progressive strengthening of the relationship between China and Ecuador from an economic, political, and cultural perspective.

Another topic of interest in Chinese relations concerns cooperation, specifically South-South cooperation. In this regard, although China is a rising power, its discourse positions it as a country from the Global South that has emerged successfully (Viola-Reyes and Mora-Vera 2025). In this regard, Vadell, Brutto, Leite, and Crivelli (2020) highlight the emergence of a new paradigm for cooperation, an alternative and superior model to traditional Official Development Assistance (ODA), which could translate into benefits for the Latin American region. In response, from a critical geopolitical approach to international cooperation relations with the Asian giant, Viola-Reyes and Mora-Vera (2025) discuss the contradictions between the principles of South-South cooperation and the so-called Beijing Consensus in contrast to the Washington Consensus, revealing, on one hand, the continuities and patterns in the traditional relations with the West that maintain the dependent model of natural resource extraction, as well as differences in strategies and tools for influence and intervention (Viola-Reyes and Mora-Vera 2025).

The issue of asymmetries and the deepening of exchange relationships dependent on natural resources in Latin America had already been addressed by Gallagher and Porzecanski (2010); the authors emphasize that the relationship with China represents a threat to the industrialization of Latin American countries. This concern is also shared by Jenkins (2009, 2010, 2015), who warns on the de-industrialization effects of China's growing presence in Brazil and alerts to the deepening of the dependent primary-export model in other countries such as Ecuador or Peru. Another concern is the growing indebtedness and its effects on dependency. In this context, Ray and Myers (2024) note that between 2004 and 2023, Ecuador received approximately USD 11.8 billion from the "Chinese policy banks," ranking third, behind only Venezuela and Brazil. Ecuador is the third destiny, in terms of relevance, for Chinese loans in Latin America.

Regarding the environmental dimension, there are several studies that showcase Ecuador as a critical example of the problems that stem from oil, mining, and infrastructure investments in ecologically sensitive and culturally diverse territories, especially in areas where Indigenous communities and Native peoples are present (Ray and Chimienti 2017; Sacher 2017; Viola-Reyes 2016, 2021). Socio-environmental concerns also frame the research conducted by Diana Castro and Paulina Garzón (2018) on hydroelectric infrastructure in Ecuador, financed with Chinese capital, emphasizing the negative impacts generated at the territorial, social, and economic levels as a result of implementing these projects.

From the case study viewpoint, the research on the territorialization process of the Coca Codo Sinclair hydroelectric project conducted by Viola-Reyes (2016) and the warnings about the socio-environmental and cultural impacts of the neo-extractivist policy financed with Chinese capital (Viola-Reyes 2021) are examples of concrete evidence of the environmental injustices that this asymmetrical relationship can entail. Similarly, in the mining sector, the research carried out in Zamora and Morona Santiago by William Sacher (2017) describes the dispossession processes inherent in mega-industrial mining and the characteristics that the dispossession process takes on when led by China. These contributions see the relationship with China as a new form of ecological imperialism (Foster and Clark 2020), driven this time by the metabolic gap created by the predatory development model established decades ago by the Asian giant.

In conclusion, research developed in Latin America on the case of Ecuador shows that China established itself, in the first two decades of the 21st century, as a strategic ally in public infrastructure for the Ecuadorian government, providing resources and technology for the development of projects primarily aimed at enhancing the extraction capacity of commodities for the international market. China's focus on this small Andean country must be analyzed within its regional context, where the Asian giant seeks to expand its presence to secure access to essential resources, such as minerals, oil, and food, through financing and investments in strategic sectors.

In this regard, most studies focus on analyzing mining and oil operations, as well as large infrastructure projects. In this chapter, we aim to contribute new evidence regarding shrimp value chains from a territorial perspective. This sector of the Sino-Ecuadorian relationship has been seldom explored, despite its exponential growth; therefore, this research aims to fill a gap in the existing literature on shrimp value chains targeting the Chinese market.

2. Commercial Relationship Between China and Ecuador

On May 10th, 2023, Ecuador signed a Free Trade Agreement (FTA) with the government of Beijing, focusing on the progressive liberalization of trade in goods between the two countries (Ministerio de Producción, Comercio Exterior, Inversiones y Pesca 2022). The FTA comprises 16 chapters, including one on e-commerce; however, at the request of the Ecuadorian government, no chapters on labor rights or environmental standards were included. This decision is explained by the urgency in which the Ecuadorian government negotiated the agreement: a record time of eight months, between April and December of 2022. Beyond the specific content of the FTA, the agreement establishes a

Figure 1. Ecuador: Oil and Non-oil Exports to China of (2014–2024) ($US million)

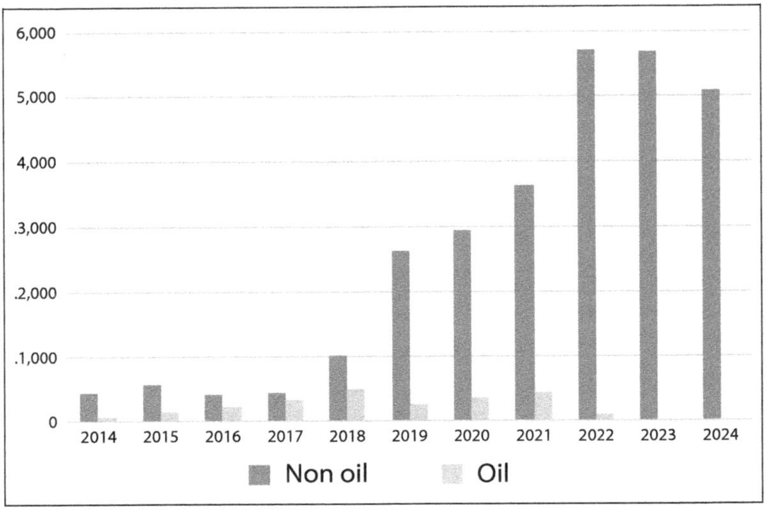

Source: Own elaboration based on data from the Central Bank of Ecuador (2024).

commercial relationship that has been growing qualitatively and quantitatively over the past decade.

Since 2021, total exports have exceeded USD 5 billion annually, with non-oil exports showing the most significant growth since 2018 (Figure 1). By 2024, non-oil exports reached a total of USD 5.085 billion, compared to USD 4.6 billion in oil exports. Regarding the composition of non-oil exports to China, it is concentrated in shrimp, prawns, and other crustaceans, as well as in lead and copper concentrates, cocoa, bananas, balsa wood, timber, and wood products (Figure 2).

Figure 2. Ecuador: Exports to China by Main Products ($US million) (2014-2024)

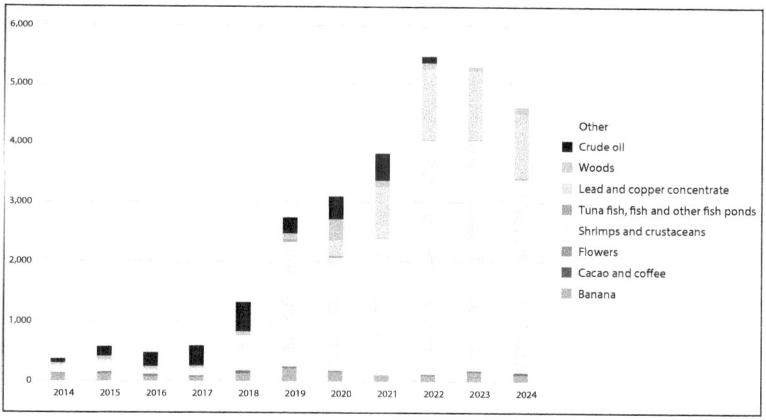

Source: Own elaboration based on data from the Central Bank of Ecuador (2024).

On the import side, Ecuador imported approximately USD 6.4 billion-dollar worth of products from China in 2022, including metal manufactures, automobiles, mobile phones, computers, machinery, and parts. Throughout the period analyzed, Ecuador's trade balance with China has been negative (Figure 3). In 2022 and 2023, there was a significant improvement in the trade balance, with a considerable decrease in the deficit, which was reduced to USD 484 million and USD 244 million, respectively. This signifies a substantial improvement compared to the USD 1.1 billion-dollar deficit recorded in 2021.

Figure 3. Ecuador: Trade Balance with China (2016–2023) (million USD)

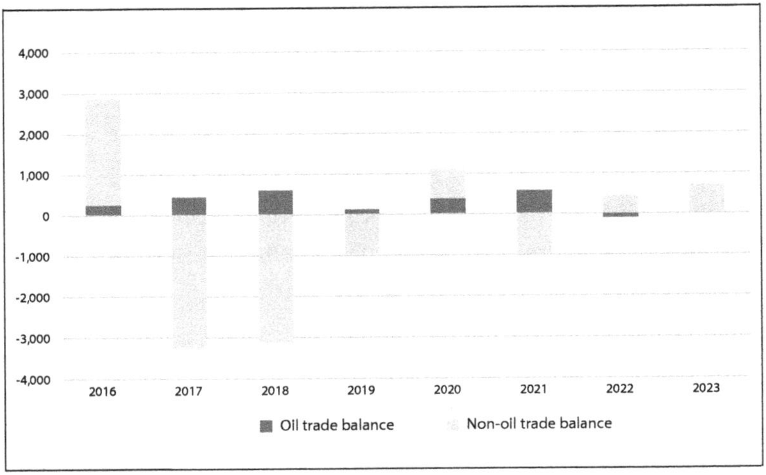

Source: Own elaboration with data from the Central Bank of Ecuador (2024).

Figure 4. Ecuador: Shrimp Exports ($million dollar and million pounds) (1994-2024)

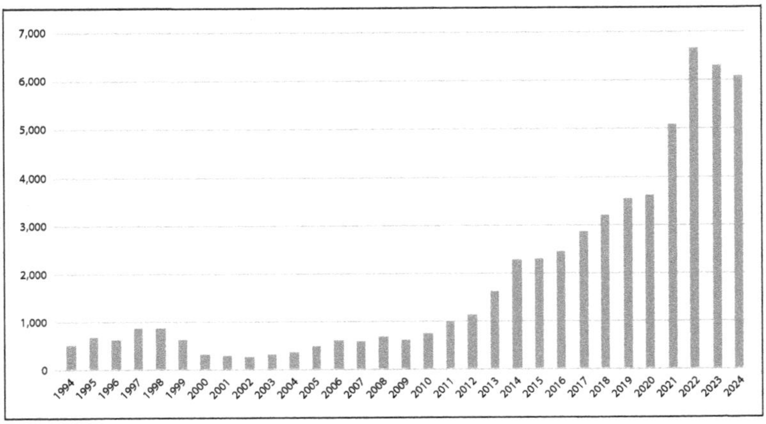

Source: Own elaboration based on National Chamber of Aquaculture (2024).

Ecuador's exports to China are led by shrimp and prawns, accounting for 63.6 % of total exports in 2024, while other sectors, such as minerals, oil, and agricultural products, have adopted a complementary role in the export matrix (Figure 2). From the beginning of the century, the specialization and economic upgrading of the shrimp sector have allowed it to consolidate as a star product in Ecuador's export repertoire. The following graph illustrates shrimp exports over the last four decades, showcasing that after the White Spot Syndrome crisis, which led to a reduction in shrimp exports between 2000 and 2004, the sector's relevance has not dwindled and has shown an increase of 2480 % between 2014 and 2024 (Figure 4).

This exponential growth has, as one of its primary drivers, the increased demand for Ecuadorian shrimp from China, where Ecuador has established a significant market niche. Table 1 shows the importance of the Chinese market for Ecuadorian shrimp. In 2024, shrimp exports to China represented 50.62 %, with Europe as the second destination, accounting for less than half of what was exported to China at 21.77 %, and the United States as the third destination, representing 18.15 % of total exports for that year (Table 1). This data places China as the primary destination for Ecuador's shrimp value chains.

Table 1. Ecuador: Shrimp Exports by Country (share over total) (2019-2024)

	2019	2020	2021	2022	2023	2024
China	38.94	54.32	52.02	58.74	57.98	52.62
United States	19.55	14.91	20.21	19.57	18.14	18.15
European Union	22.64	18.92	19.14	14.67	16.05	21.77
Rest of Asia	13.03	8.13	5.20	4.47	5.24	4.63
America	5.33	2.83	2.93	2.04	1.90	1.87
África	0.01	0.01	0.04	0.05	0.58	0.45
Oceania	0.00	0.00	0.00	0.00	0.12	0.08

Fuente. Own elaboration based on data from the National Chamber of Aquaculture (2024).

Hence, in 2019, shrimp exports to China already contributed USD 1.4 billion annually; however, by 2024, shrimp exports represented an annual income of USD 3.2 billion. This trajectory is characterized by a compound annual growth rate of over 50 % between 2007 and 2024, showcasing the industry's productive capacity and the role Chinese demand plays in transforming privileged sectors of Ecuador's export matrix (CNA 2024).

3. The Shrimp Global Value Chain

The methodological discussion on Global Value Chain (GVC's) analysis has led to the intersection of various approaches in understanding their composition and impacts (Dussel Peters 2018). Such convergence is significant for analyzing Ecuador's positioning. Traditional analysis methodologies enable a closer examination of the shrimp sector in Ecuador, including its productive structure, local and global geographical scope, industry organization, economic scaling tools, the economic and social conditions of its environment, institutional conditions, and the mapping of stakeholders and interest groups (Gereffi *et al.* 2016). However, given Ecuador's condition as a developing country and considering the shrimp sector commercial dependency to China, it is necessary to implement a comprehensive territorial impact analysis methodology that involves a framework of territorial endogeneity, meaning an understanding of how regions integrate into global value chain dynamics as suggested by Dussel Peters (2018).

3.1. Origin and Evolution of the Shrimp GVC in Ecuador

The Ecuadorian shrimp industry originates in the late 60s in El Oro province, in Southern Ecuador, "back then, shrimp were caught in high seas, until for the first time in 1966 in Santa Rosa, shrimp farming began in ponds with the native species L. Vannamei and Litopenaeus stylirostris" (C-Condem 2007:24). Industrial shrimp farming emerges in a context of weak state capabilities, expanding in many cases through the illegal occupation of extensive areas of the mangrove ecosystem. In the 1980s, the industry experienced a 600 % growth, occupying an estimated 439 hectares of the mangrove ecosystem, distributed across Esmeraldas, Manabí, Guayas, and El Oro (C-Condem 2007) (Table 2). By 2015, shrimp farming ponds had reached 213,032 hectares, compared to the 148,230 hectares of remaining mangroves on the Ecuadorian coast (Piedrahíta 2018). However, these numbers are challenged by local organizations that advocate for the preservation of the mangrove ecosystem, who call them conservative and misleading, "from an ecosystem perspective, the impact is not only on the mangrove forest; you need to include the salt ponds, the other species that make up the ecosystem, and water mirrors" (Torres 2025).

Table 2. Ecuador: Main Regional Characteristics of the Shrimp Industry (1976-2000)

	TOTAL		ESMERALDA		MANABÍ		GUAYA		EL ORO	
	Farmers	Has	Farmers	Has	Farmers	Has	Farmers	Has	Farmers	Has
1976	6	439	0	0	1	20	2	300	3	119
1980	156	14,707	1	50	28	1,772	104	10,944	23	1,941
1985	940	93,222	32	2,241	112	4,313	581	71,020	215	14,548
1990	1,780	128,071	136	4,363	347	10,716	877	90,010	420	22,982
1995	1,994	138,710	170	6,846	404	12,089	972	96,587	448	24,188
2000	2,036	152,523	180	9,949	409	12,459	998	105,482	449	24,633

Source: Own elaboration based on Marriot (2003:3).

According to the National Coordinating Corporation for the Defense of the Mangrove Ecosystem (Corporación Coordinadora Nacional para la Defensa del Ecosistema Manglar) (C-Condem), the industry's growth between 1969 and 2006 resulted in a 70 % decline of the ecosystem. Similarly, research developed by Machado (2013) backs up this data: "Ministerial Agreement 498, from 1986, issued by the Ministry of Agriculture and Livestock, declared 362,742 hectares of mangrove forested land as a protective forest. However, in the 2000 Forest Map of the Integrated Natural Resources Survey Center for Remote Sensing (Clirsen), only 108,299 hectares of mangrove were detected" (Machado 2013).

Since its inception, the shrimp industry has tended to expand in hectares or income, with brief interruptions or declines caused by depressions in international demand and, primarily, by plagues and diseases that affect farmed shrimp. By the late 90s, the industry faced a crisis period due to diseases that proliferated in shrimp pools, causing losses in the millions for the industry: "This type of production, by the year 2001, represented 96 % of total shrimp industrial production (C-Condem 2007:24). According to date by the National Chamber of Aquaculture (2024), shrimp production declined by 252 million pounds to 209 million in 1998 due to a disease known as Taura's Syndrome,[1] and in the year 2000, with the expansion of the White Spot Virus, it declined again, falling to 82 million pounds with a 60 % reduction in exports. Production levels achieved before 1998 were finally reached by 2004, marking sustained growth that year.

The importance of shrimp in the country's export matrix encouraged a series of efforts to overcome the industry's sanitary crisis. For this endeavor, the establishment in 1989 of the country's first aquaculture program at the Escuela Superior Politécnica del Litoral (ESPOL) was crucial, along with the creation of the National Center for Aquaculture and Marine Research (CENAIM), which received support from the Japanese government. By the first few years of the 21st century, innovation and research had increased: "Due to high mortality during production, hatcheries that carried out broodstock maturity processes began using pond-raised animals that had survived the viruses, and from these animals they developed new generations that were later transferred to grow-out ponds to produce the new crops" (Piedrahíta 2018). These advances enabled production to recover to pre-crisis levels and multiply them exponentially (Table 3); however, they did not

1 Taura Syndrome is the name of a disease that causes the death of shrimp species and is linked to water contamination from pesticides used by the banana industry to combat black sigatoka, as well as from fungicides used in shrimp ponds (Marriott 2003).

diminish the use of chemicals, pesticides, chlorinated compounds, and antibiotics, which contribute to high levels of pollution in ecosystems.

In 2007, crustacean exports represented 4.1 % of total Ecuadorian exports. Compared to the 22.2 % it represented in 2022, the sector has achieved a growth of 447 %. Chinese demand for shrimp and prawns has played a key role in this growth; as previously highlighted, more than 50 % of exported shrimp is destined for the Chinese market. The expansion of shrimp farming hectares, driven by the growing demand for crustaceans and the lack of environmental commitment of local economic and political elites, has resulted in the accelerated destruction of the mangrove ecosystem and the social fabric of mangrove communities over the past two decades.

3.2. Geographic Scope of the Shrimp GVC

By 2023, the Ecuadorian shrimp industry comprised 893 companies dedicated to shrimp farming in ponds, 30 companies focused on the preparation, preservation, and processing of shrimp and

Figure 5. Ecuador: Geographic Distribution of Shrimp Farming Ponds

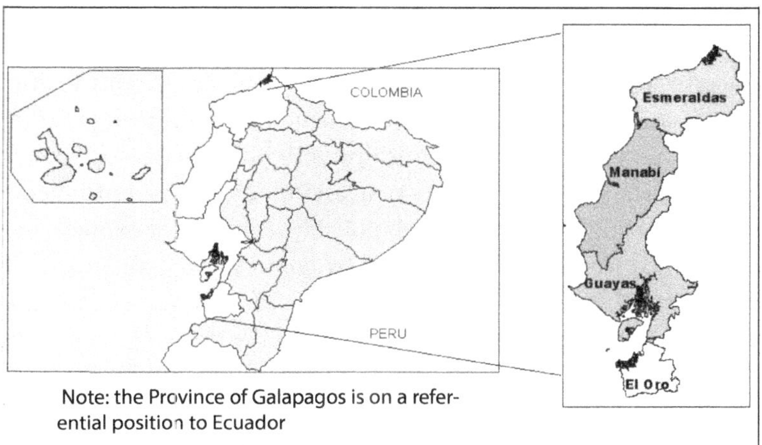

Source: Own elaboration based on C-Condem (2007:5).

prawns, and 180 companies engaged in the wholesale trade of shrimp and prawns (Corporación Financiera Nacional 2024). The ponds are located along the country's coastal region, including the provinces of Guayas, Santa Elena, El Oro, Manabí, and Esmeraldas.

Guayas province is the industry's core, consolidating itself in the 21st century as the main area for shrimp farming and harvesting. El Oro ranks as the second largest farming center, while Manabí serves as a key export hub through the port of Manta. Lastly, Esmeraldas, Los Ríos, and Santa Elena contribute to national production with smaller areas dedicated to farming and hatcheries. The global geographic scope refers to the breakdown of exports to international markets by destination. In the case of Ecuadorian shrimp, the main markets in 2024 were China (42.89 %), the United States (28.59 %), Italy (4.6 %), Spain (4.06 %), and France (2.26 %) (Table 1).

3.2. Production Structure and Governance

The shrimp sector in Ecuador is characterized by a dynamic that combines both hierarchical and relational industrial structures. Large companies are vertically integrated, controlling multiple stages of production and allowing for the optimization of operations. Large producer-exporters integrate their own farming operations, packing plants, processing companies, and export businesses; they have significant influence abroad, strong market control, and privileged relationships with political power. Alongside these large corporations, small and medium-sized producers coexist, relying on long-term relationships with major exporters to access international markets, thereby consolidating a network of suppliers. The enormous asymmetries between large, medium, and small businesses tend to concentrate the greatest benefits in the former, which act as oligopolies, controlling and limiting access for other actors.

According to the National Financial Corporation (CFN), by 2024, there were 79 large companies dedicated to shrimp farming, seven large companies dedicated to the processing and preservation of shrimp and prawn products, and eight large companies committed to wholesale sales (Table 3). Due to their integrated nature, many of these companies converge into a dozen corporations that control national production and the global export of the product. The relevance of large corporations is clear when we consider the employment they generate. In 2024, large companies created 19,077 direct jobs in the process of farm exploitation, product processing and preservation, and wholesale marketing, compared to the 8,668 jobs collectively generated by small and medium-sized companies (Table 3).

Table 3. Companies in the Shrimp GVC and Jobs by Type of Company (2024)

	Shrimp hatchery exploitation		Preservation and processing of shrimp and prawn products		Wholesale sales of shrimp and prawns	
	Firms	Employment	Firms	Employment	Firms	Employment
Large	79	14,094	7	3,261	8	1,722
Medium	163	4,917	3	234	14	185
Micro	439	1,476	19	66	86	262
Small	212	1,385	1	4	30	139
Total	893	21,872	30	3,565	138	2,308

Source. Own elaboration based on National Financial Corporation (2024)

The shrimp industry follows a production chain structured in stages: "The main links in this chain are the hatcheries, grow-out ponds, feed producers, packing plants, and exporters" (Marriott 2003:9). In the initial stage, hatcheries supply post-larvae, a process that requires essential inputs such as water, oxygen, probiotics, and specialized feed. Larvae production for the industry began to develop strongly in the late 1990s, due to the growing scarcity of gravid females captured at sea and later transferred to farming ponds (Marriott 2007). The state promoted the innovation in post-larvae production through the Aquaculture Research Institute of ESPOL in coordination with CENAIM.

Currently, several laboratories are responsible for post-larvae production. It is worth noting that participation in this stage is mainly by large national corporations that also operate on other stages of the production chain. Among these are Acuagran (Granjas Marinas Group), Génesis (Nobis Group), Camaronera Nacional (Pronaca Group), Omarsa (Aquaculture Laboratory), and Shrimp Improvement Systems (SIS) Ecuador. There are also small cooperatives and medium-sized laboratories in Manabí and El Oro that primarily supply microenterprises, as well as CEPIA (Aquaculture Production and Research Center), which is linked to public and private universities in the city of Guayaquil. The absence of a significant foreign presence in this stage reflects the success of the strategy of the shrimp industry in aligning with university-based research, which allowed it to develop innovation capacities adapted to local conditions.

In the next stage, post-larvae are used along with other inputs such as feed, aerators, and disease control supplies to support the growth and harvest of live shrimp ready for processing. The feed industry for shrimp farms in Ecuador has grown in tandem with exports and is dominated by large national corporations and multinational companies with subsidiaries in the country. Regarding the national corporations, Alimentsa, Pronaca, and Expalsa stand out; the main foreign corporations based in Ecuador include the Dutch company Skretting Ecuador from the Nutreco group –the world's leading aquaculture feed producer with operations on five continents– Vitapro, Cargill Ecuador under the Purina brand, and the Danish corporation Biomar. Unlike the post-larvae production stage, this segment is led by foreign corporations and, nationally, by the Pronaca group.

During the harvesting process, employment is primarily low-skilled and pays no more than the minimum living wage of USD 470 per month. There is a high level of informal labor, especially during harvest weeks when more workers are needed. Local populations are usually employed for these tasks and, occasionally, in security-related roles that are often outsourced to private security companies.

Working in shrimp farm security in Ecuador is not an easy task. A 2023 BBC report on the shrimp industry in Ecuador revealed that, "an industry that moves billions of dollars every year in a country with serious security problems is almost inevitably a target of crime (...) We receive threats. They send you messages through other people saying that if you report it or go to the police, they will kill you." The issue of security has led this sector to obtain special permits for carrying firearms and to maintain armed guards on the farms. However, this has also resulted in abuses against local populations who often approach the shrimp farm walls, the few remaining mangrove areas, to collect shellfish and crabs.[2]

Once the shrimp has been harvested, it is necessary to process them for exportation. Using cold storage logistics and packaging materials, the shrimp are prepared for export and distribution. As previously noted, the integrated nature of the large companies that control Ecuador's shrimp export market is evident at every stage of the process. In the packing stage, the leading companies, in order of importance, are: Songa, Promarisco, Expalsa, Santa Priscila, Eurofish, Nueva Pescanova Ecuador, Frimarsa, Balcazar e Hijos, and Proexpo. Packing plants are typically concentrated in intermediate cities from which shrimp is exported, namely, Guayaquil, Durán, and Manta. This work requires low skill levels and involves long, exhausting hours; there is a strong preference for female labor in the packing plants, which often prioritize hiring women.

In the export and distribution stage, processed shrimp are shipped to international markets, where companies sell directly to importers and retailers, who handle the final stage of the value chain: consumer sales, which include branding and marketing processes (FIT Lima, 2023). The main shrimp exporters in

2 In the documentary *Manglar: Ley de Mujer*, directed by Ecuadorian filmmaker Pocho Alvarez, numerous cases of human rights violations are recounted, including the murder of community members during confrontations with security guards. Likewise, Machado reported for the investigative journalism outlet *Plan V*: "Willian José Navarro, 36 years old, told *Plan V* that in May of this year, while he was collecting crabs, guards from a shrimp farm in the Boca del Lagarto estuary shot at him. 'They gave me no warning, they just insulted me and shot me. We were about 10 meters from their fences'" (Machado 2013).

Ecuador, in order of importance, are Omarsa, Songa, Promarisco, Eurofish, Pescanova Ecuador, Empacreci, Expalsa (Nobis Group), Alpesa, Báltica, and Proexpo (National Chamber of Aquaculture, 2024). As in the previous stages, and even more intensely, the control is oligopolistic, implying a strong corporate power[3] that has historically hindered the access of other actors.

3.3. Economic and Institutional Conditions

In the Ecuadorian shrimp industry, evidence suggests economic upgrading in several dimensions, including processes, products, and functions. Process upgrading involves the improvement of procedures and technologies to enhance productive efficiency, such as automated feeding systems and selective breeding programs. Product upgrading increases the value of the final product, such as diversifying the offer with premium shrimp products. Finally, functional upgrading refers to entering higher-margin activities, such as incorporating marketing strategies to eliminate intermediaries and increase efficiency. These upgrading strategies, in turn, are influenced by the institutional, economic, and social contexts that directly affect the shrimp value chain.

Regarding the institutional context of the Ecuadorian shrimp sector, we can identify, on the one hand, labor and fiscal regulations, and on the other, subsidies and support granted to the industry. Labor regulations in Ecuador establish a minimum wage (USD 470 million in 2025) and benefits that include social security and overtime payments. This increases production costs compared to competitors in Vietnam and India (Ecuador Times 2023); however, labor costs are offset by high productivity and the quality of the product, which makes it the preferred choice in the Chinese and U.S. markets (Marriott 2003; Piedrahíta 2018). In a BBC report published in April 2023, it was highlighted that to meet Chinese market demands, "Ecuadorian aquaculturists began to adapt

3 The relevance of this corporate power is also evident in the sector's close ties, and in many cases, overlap, with political elites. A clear example of this is the Nobis Group, which belongs to the family of the current President of the Republic, Daniel Noboa.

their production techniques to the new demand: among other measures, they extended the rearing period from 3 to 4 months to increase the size of the shrimp from an average of 18 grams to about 30 grams." This innovation has allowed Ecuador to surpass India, its main competitor in that market, whose shrimp are on average smaller (Amerise 2023).

Regarding fiscal regulations, shrimp companies pay a corporate tax rate of 25 %, with certain benefits, including cost deductions for research and development. Directly and indirectly, the industry has been historically subsidized and supported by the state and public policy, which has contributed to its development and growth. Throughout the years, governments have invested in improving the sector's competitiveness through infrastructure development and research initiatives. Along these lines, the decision to create the Faculty of Aquaculture at ESPOL and the establishment of CENAIM emerged, which enabled research that led to genetic improvements, increased feed efficiency, and improved farming practices. Similarly, and more recently, it is relevant to highlight the project "Improvement of Competitiveness in the Aquaculture and Fisheries Sector" and the "National Shrimp Farm Electrification Plan." The latter enables the improvement of shrimp farming efficiency and sustainability, as well as reducing dependency on fossil fuels, which leads to lower energy costs in the long term and improved sustainability.

Finally, the sector is regulated by the Ministry of Foreign Trade (MCE), the Ministry of Agriculture, Livestock, Aquaculture and Fisheries (MAGAP), Agrocalidad, and the National Fisheries Institute. Representing the interests of companies in the industry is the National Chamber of Aquaculture (CNA), established in 1993 (Table 4). Since its creation, the CNA has exerted significant political influence and has had strong negotiating power over sector regulations.

Table 4. Ecuador: Institutions that Regulate the Shrimp Sector

Actor	Role	Influence
Ministry of Production, Foreign Trade, Investments, and Fisheries	Regulates aquaculture policies, trade agreements, and the development of the Ecuadorian industry.	High. Directly determines the sector's functioning through policies, regulations, and negotiations with trade partners.
National Chamber of Aquaculture	Represents the industry's interests.	High. Influences policies and negotiates export conditions.
AGROCALIDAD	Sanitary and phytosanitary control agency ensures quality and health standards.	High. Implementation of regulations determines the eligibility of exports.
National Fisheries Institute	Conducts research for the technical upgrading of the industry.	Medium. Provides guidance and seeks innovation but lacks regulatory power.

Source: Own elaboration.

Similarly, it is essential to note the existence of credit lines in both public and private banking for the expansion of shrimp farms, investments in biosecurity, and technological improvements. Due to the oligopolistic nature of the shrimp sector, large companies benefit the most from financing, thereby increasing their export potential while limiting that of small and medium producers. For them, access to funding remains a challenge, as well as the high costs associated with certification and biosecurity requirements for export.

Regarding market conditions, access to key buyers such as China, the United States, and Europe enables the sector to position itself in premium markets. Meaning, production in Ecuador is based on a shrimp species (*Litopenaeus vannamei*) that, due to its taste and nutritional content, has become one of the most popular choices for consumption. It is also fed with high-quality, organic food and utilizes high-level technologies for sanitary control, such as Biofloc for pollution prevention. Similarly, the size of Ecuadorian shrimp has made it the favorite compared to its Asian competitors.

Ecuadorian shrimp exports also have certifications that guarantee their quality, safety, sustainability, and good practices. For example, Ecuadorian shrimp is certified by the ASC (Aquaculture Stewardship Council), holds four BAP (Best Aquaculture Practices) stars –the highest rating– and has HACCP (Hazard Analysis and Critical Control Points) certification, which is required for export to the United States and China. To access the Chinese market, it also has the AQSIQ certification. Due to the reasons mentioned above, Ecuadorian shrimp is sold at premium prices, while Vietnam and India emerge as competitors due to their lower prices (Ocean Treasure 2025). Therefore, dependence on the Chinese market represents a risk in the case of changes in demand or trade policies.

3.4. Analysis of Actors at the Local Level

The Ecuadorian shrimp industry comprises a diverse range of actors with varying levels of influence, operating across the various scales of the Global Value Chain (GVC). At the local level, small producers face difficulties in accessing financing and depend on large companies to export due to certification requirements. In contrast, large shrimp companies have significant control over both production and sector regulations. Local communities and labor unions play a key role by providing labor, although their ability to influence working conditions and environmental sustainability is limited.

At the government level, municipalities are responsible for regulating land use and monitoring the environmental impact of the shrimp industry. At the same time, the Ministry of Production, Foreign Trade, Investment, and Fisheries establishes the policies and trade agreements that govern the sector. The National Chamber of Aquaculture represents the interests of producers and exporters, exerting influence in both commercial and regulatory negotiations (Ríos 2022). Finally, NGOs and environmental groups denounce unsustainable practices and the lack of transparency

Table 5. Ecuador: Analysis of Actors Operating Locally of the Shrimp GVC

Actor	Role	Influence
Small-scale shrimp farmers	Independent farms or cooperatives that produce shrimp for local markets and export.	Low. Depends on government policies and financing. They also rely on large companies for export due to the difficulty in obtaining licenses.
Large shrimp companies	Vertically integrated companies with farms, processing plants, and export networks.	High. Control a significant share of production, influence regulations, and have direct access to international markets.
Local communities and unions	Provide labor. Concerned about employment conditions and sustainability.	Low-Medium. May influence labor policies and sustainability practices but depend on the employers.
Municipal governments	Regulate land use, protect the environment, and develop local infrastructure.	Medium. Have authority over land use, pollution control, and some local production regulations.
NGOs and rights advocates	Seek sustainability and transparency in the implementation of environmental and human rights measures.	Medium-Low. Can pressure governments and markets to adopt sustainability and rights guarantees, but lacks regulatory power.

Source: Own Elaboration.

within the industry, pressuring governments and markets to adopt stricter environmental and labor regulations.

4.5. Territories and the Socio-environmental Issue

Regarding socio-environmental impact, shrimp farming affects mangrove ecosystems and is considered one of the most destructive industries and the main threat to its survival. "Potential impacts to the environment can happen in two stages: during placement, design, and construction of the farming pools, and their operations; the environmental damage is more damaging than the pools placement in fragile ecosystems" (Marriott 2003:35). Despite these warnings, the lack of regulation and oversight, combined with high productivity (reaching up to three harvests per year), low investment (due to the illegal occupation of estuaries, salt flats, and saline lands), and precarious wages, has led to the uncontrolled expansion of shrimp farms, with devastating effects on coastal marine ecosystems.

In an interview for BBC (2023), biologist Bruno Yánez affirms that "although there is a permanent ban, large and small shrimp farmers continue to cut down mangroves to expand their ponds." The impact on mangrove forests, which continue to be cut down despite state prohibitions, jeopardizes food sovereignty and the economies of the people who have historically inhabited these territories. The mangrove communities, as they call themselves, live off the artisanal harvesting of shells and crabs, which they need from this ecosystem to survive. Similarly, the loss of mangroves affects artisanal fishing, as these ecosystems serve as spawning grounds for many marine species, including the red snapper. The low productivity of mangroves is also a consequence of the intensive use of toxic and persistent chemicals, which generate high levels of pollution and directly affect the coastal marine ecosystem. This is particularly evident in areas where shrimp farms discharge untreated water after harvesting (Torres 2025).

Mayra, a woman from a mangrove community, has lived her entire life in Muisne, and remembers with nostalgia when the mangrove fed everyone, "now we just have to scrape by"[4] when the shrimp farmers finishing harvesting; there is no more mangrove, only in the walls of the shrimp farms and the guards will not let us get near." These testimonies echo those documented by Pocho Alvarez and C-Condem (2023): "three decades ago, a shellfish gatherer could extract over a thousand shells from the swamp in just a few hours; now it takes an entire day to gather fewer

4 On Ecuador's coast, the mangrove communities refer to *raspar* as the activity of cleaning the shrimp ponds after the harvest.

than a hundred shells, which sell for nine dollars per hundred" (Plan V 2023).

The remaining mangrove trees serve as natural barriers for shrimp farms. The law grants traditional shellfish and crab gatherers the right to work in these mangroves. However, their rights are continually violated by shrimp farm owners who do not hesitate to use aggressive dogs, electric fences, and armed guards to intimidate them. According to C-Condem, between 2006 and 2023, up to 100 community members were killed in conflicts with armed shrimp farm guards, attacked by aggressive dogs, or electrocuted by fences while collecting shellfish and crabs (Torres, 2025). In a 2013 interview, Luis Navarro, a member of the 19 de Octubre Shellfish Gatherers Association, stated that "at least two more members have been attacked by dogs guarding the shrimp farms: there are many places where people are afraid to collect crabs or shells because the guards shoot at us" (Machado 2023). According to Marianeli Torres, founding member of C-Condem, the situation remains unchanged: in most cases, conflicts are resolved privately through minimal compensation to the impoverished families of the victims (Torres 2025).

Regarding the employment of the local population, the industry relies on low-skilled rural labor. Although there are aquaculture training programs aimed at improving skill levels, these are not accompanied by policies focused on enhancing job quality. Moreover, in shrimp farms, there are reports of labor challenges, including long working hours, job insecurity, and a lack of unionization in the farms and processing industry, which can result in high rates of labor turnover. The precarious nature of employment, combined with the environmental degradation caused by the industry, exacerbated by state neglect and policies favoring the corporate interests of the shrimp sector, helps explain the poverty and exclusion that characterize the regions where export-oriented shrimp farming takes place.

Data from the latest national census (2022) reveal a negative correlation between the shrimp industry boom and the living conditions of local populations, characterized by a high deficit of basic services and high levels of poverty due to unmet basic needs (NBI) (Table 6).

Table 6. Ecuador: Poverty Due to Unsatisfied Basic Needs (NBI) and Lack of Basic Services in Shrimp-Producing Cantons

Province	Canton	% Poverty due to NBI	% Lack of basic services
Guayas	Guayaquil	28,74 %	23,50 %
	Balao	46,71 %	42,09 %
	Durán	65,37 %	63,76 %
	Naranjal	53,51 %	49,48 %
	Playas	48,11 %	43,64 %
El Oro	Machala	33,49 %	29,99 %
	Arenillas	39,70 %	38,56 %
	El Guabo	52,36 %	49,60 %
	Huaquillas	41,34 %	41,29 %
	Santa Rosa	30,32 %	28,05 %
Manabí	Portoviejo	43,25 %	42,59 %
	Chone	68,86 %	68,30 %
	Manta	32,41 %	30,21 %
	Montecristi	78,80 %	78,46 %
Esmeraldas	Esmeraldas	38,44 %	35,26 %
	Eloy Alfaro	87,61 %	85,93 %
	Muisne	92,31 %	91,53 %
	San Lorenzo	73,79 %	71,67 %
	Atacames	70,99 %	68,03 %
	Rioverde	91,98 %	91,28 %
Santa Elena	Santa Elena	50,65 %	48,62 %
	La Libertad	44,57 %	41,18 %
	Salinas	43,49 %	38,84 %

Source: Own elaboration based on INEC (2022).

From an entrepreneurial perspective, environmental degradation can ultimately lead to limited production capacity and impact the sector's sustainability (Witherow 2023), thereby increasing the industry's vulnerability to climate change simultaneously. In this regard, it is essential to note that mangroves act as a natural barrier, protecting coastlines from surges and tidal waves. Their indiscriminate destruction over the past three decades has left coastal areas exposed, increasing risk levels. Additionally, ocean warming presents new challenges related to the spread of bacteria and diseases (Merchan 2024).

Finally, generalized precariousness also leaves these populations vulnerable to the wave of violence affecting the country. Impoverished fishers are being recruited –both voluntarily and, in many cases, involuntarily– into drug trafficking networks. Unemployed youth, with no access to education or training opportunities, are easily drawn in by criminal gangs, entering a world of violence and drug use with no hope or way out. According

Figure 6. Ecuador: Homicide Rate in Cantons with More Than 100,000 Inhabitants (2022 and 2023)

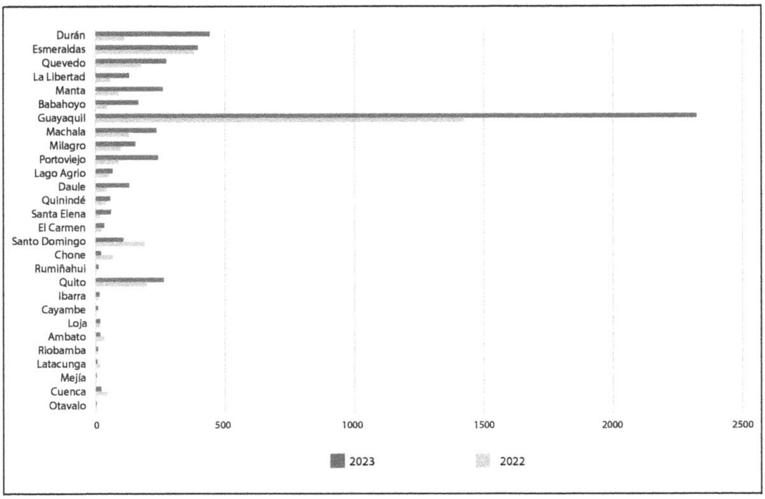

Source: Own elaboration with data from Ecuadorian Observatory for Organized Crime (OECO).

to data from Ecuador's Ministry of Education, "in the past eight years, more than 39,000 students have dropped out of school in Esmeraldas" (Machado 2023).

According to the Ecuadorian Observatory for Organized Crime (OECO), the coastline provinces presented a homicide rate in 2023 that was classified as exceptional. The annual OECO report (2023) shows the gravity of the situation in shrimp farming cantons; such is the case of Durán, Esmeraldas, La Libertad, Guayaquil, Manta, Machala, Portoviejo, Santa Elena and Chone, which show homicide rates well above standard Latin American levels (graph 6 and graph 7). Although criminal violence is not a direct effect of the shrimp industry, widespread poverty and lack of opportunities do have direct effects on this critical situation, which affects these provinces and mainly, sea-access cantons. The historical absence of a social and environmentally sustainable approach in the development of the export shrimp industry and its value chain indirectly contributes to the spread of violence during these dark years in Ecuador's history.

5. Conclusions

This research aimed to analyze the territorial impacts of the export-oriented shrimp value chain in Ecuador. As we have seen in this chapter, demand from China played a significant role in the industry's growth starting in 2006. Today, China is the leading destination for shrimp and prawn exports, accounting for 50.62 % of total exports of these crustaceans. This growth has led to a considerable increase in Ecuador's revenues and the progressive upscaling of the shrimp industry, making the country the world's leading shrimp exporter.

Historically, the growth of Ecuador's shrimp industry has been characterized by dispossession practices with complex social and environmental consequences for local populations, particularly for the ancestral communities residing within the mangrove ecosystem. Shrimp ponds have proliferated at the expense of mangrove destruction, increasing the vulnerability of these territories to flooding and wave surges common along the Pacific coast. Pollution and the expansion of shrimp farms have had severe consequences for food sovereignty and the quality of life of these communities. All of this has occurred amid limited state engagement with these territories and a strong presence of corporate power from the shrimp sector within the state and public policy.

Currently, the export-oriented shrimp value chain to China, in its production phase, is carried out by small and medium-sized national companies linked to large exporters who hold the licenses and meet the requirements to access the Chinese market. This research did not find the presence of Chinese companies in the territories where shrimp and prawns are farmed and harvested. Although the negative impacts of the industry are a direct result of the lack of commitment by local business owners and national political elites, who have historically protected the sector at the expense of mangrove communities and their territories, the recent decade's industry growth and its impacts have been driven by the rising demand for shrimp from China. This highlights the importance of discussing the role of export destination countries in shaping the consequences and territorial dynamics associated with such activities.

China's relevance as a destination market makes it a key actor for demanding better social and environmental practices from its suppliers. The signing of the free trade agreement and its implementation in 2024 could provide an opportunity for Ecuadorian producers to establish incentives for pursuing a socially and environmentally sustainable industry. However, a significant limitation is the Ecuadorian government's decision to exclude environmental and labor chapters from the trade agreement. Regarding China, there are negative precedents in Ecuador's experience, such as the Coca Codo Sinclair hydroelectric project, where journalists and researchers have documented reports of mistreatment, precarious labor conditions, and rights violations.

Despite this, the increase in trade between China and Ecuador creates new opportunities for cooperation, allowing for the establishment of joint programs to restore coastal and marine ecosystems. Such cooperation aligns with a mutual interest in maintaining the shrimp value chain, as continued environmental degradation and pollution would have negative consequences, leading to food insecurity for mangrove communities in Ecuador and simultaneously threatening the stability of a high-demand, high-value product supply in China. The economic, social, and environmental sustainability of the industry must be a priority in negotiations between China and Ecuador.

Lastly, it is essential to highlight that the abandonment of coastal cantons and the worsening of living conditions, driven by environmental contamination and the destruction of local economies, have facilitated the infiltration of criminal groups into these territories and their marginalized societies. Today, ecological degradation is compounded by the breakdown of the social fabric and the extremely high levels of violence affecting coastal cantons with access to the sea. While shrimp exports continue to grow in revenue, the territories from which the so-called "pink gold" is extracted are impoverished and reduced to poverty and destitution. In conclusion, we can state that the significant contribution to the GDP from the exponential growth of shrimp and prawn exports to China is not matched by benefits in the territories where these resources are produced. This inequality-reproducing dynamic must be disrupted through decisive public policy intervention, which is a necessary condition for the sustainability of this global value chain.

References

Agamben, Giorgio. 1998. *Homo Sacer: El Poder Soberano y la Vida Desnuda*. Adriana Hidalgo Editora: Buenos Aires.

Amerise, Atahualpa. 2023. "Cómo Ecuador se convirtió en el mayor exportador mundial de camarones (y qué papel clave jugó China)". BBC *News Mundo*, April 21.

BCE (Banco Central del Ecuador). 2025. *Estadísticas de Comercio Exterior*. (at: https://www.bce.fin.ec/comercio-exterior)

BCE (Banco Central del Ecuador). 2024. "Suscripción del Tratado de Libre Comercio con China: Una Gran Oportunidad para Ecuador". *BCE*: Quito.

Gómez, Bolaños, Javier Mauricio, Mora, Sánchez, Norman Vinicio and Espinoza Carrión, Cecibel del Rocío. 2020. "Disrupción, Resiliencia y Evolución del Sector Camaronero Ecuatoriano entre 2010 y 2019". *593 Digital Publisher CEIT*, pp. 285-299.

CNA (Cámara Nacional de Acuacultura). 2024. "Estadísticas CNA. Exportaciones Mensuales". CNA: Guayaquil.

Defensa del Ecosistema Manglar del Ecuador. 2007. *Certificando la Destrucción. Análisis Integral de la Certificación Orgánica a la Acuacultura Industrial de Camarón en Ecuador.* Fundación ICO: Ecuador.

CECONDEM. 2023. "Manglar ley de mujer" [video]. *CECONDEM* (at: https://www.youtube.com/watch?v=ylOdC9k3MEQ)

Corporación Financiera Nacional. 2024. "Ficha Sectorial del Camarón". *Corporación Financiera Nacional.* (at: https://www.cfn.fin.ec/wp-content/uploads/2024/07/Ficha-Sectorial-Camar%C2%A2n.pdf)

Dussel Peters, Enrique. 2018. "Cadenas Globales de Valor. Metodología, Contenidos e Implicaciones para el Caso de la Atracción de Inversión Extranjera Directa desde una Perspectiva Regional". In, Dussel Peters, Enrique (coord.). *Cadenas globales de valor: Metodología, teoría y debates.* UNAM/Cechimex: México, pp. 45-66.

Dussel Peters, Enrique (edit.). 2018. *Cadenas Globales de Valor: Metodología, Teoría y Debates.* UNAM/Cechimex: México.

Dussel Peters, Enrique (edit.). 2019. *China Financing in Latin American and the Caribbean.* Red ALC-China, UDUAL and UNAM/Cechimex: México.

Ecuador Times. 2023. "Producing Ecuadorian Shrimp Is 24% More Expensive Than in 2021". *Ecuador Times*, February 21.

FIT Lima (Flanders Investment and Trade). 2023. "Aquaculture Sector in Ecuador". *FIT*: Lima.

Bellamy Foster, John and Clark, Brett. 2020. *The Robbery of Nature: Capitalism and the Ecological Rift*. Monthly Review Press: New York.

Gallagher, Kevin and Porzecanski, Roberto. 2010. *The Dragon in the Room: China and the Future of Latin American Industrialization.* Stanford University Press: California.

Gereffi, Gary and Fernandez, Stark, Karina. 2016. *Global Value Chain Analysis: A Primer.* Duke Center on Globalization, Governance & Competitiveness: North Carolina

Hearn, Adrian and León Manríquez, José Luis. 2011. *China Engages Latin America: Tracing the Trajectory*. Lynne Rienner Publishers: Boulder.

Jenkins, Rhys. 2009. "El Impacto de China en América Latina". *Revista CIDOB d'Afers Internacionals*, pp. 251-272.

Jenkins, Rhys. 2010. "China's Global Expansion and Latin America". *Journal of Latin American Studies* 42(4), pp. 809-837.

Jenkins, Rhys. 2015. "Is Chinese Competition Causing Deindustrialization in Brazil?". *Latin American Perspectives* 42(6), pp. 42-63.

Jenkins, Rhys, Dussel Peters, Enrique y Mesquita Moreira, Mauricio. 2008. "The Impact of China on Latin America and the Caribbean". *World Development* 36(2), pp. 235-253.

Machado, Decio. 2013. "La Historia Oculta del Camarón". *Plan V*, September 25.

Machado, Jonathan. 2023. "Esmeraldas: Más niños y jóvenes abandonan la escuela o pierden el año". *Primicias*, July 27.

Marriott García, Francisco. 2003. "Análisis del Sector Camaronero". *Banco Central del Ecuador*: Quito.

Merchán, Javier. 2024. "2025: Retos De La Industria Camaronera En Ecuador". *FIDEVAL Fondos y Fideicomisos,* November 12.

Ministerio de Producción Comercio Exterior Inversiones y Pesca. 2022. "Tratado de Libre Comercio Ecuador-China". *Ministerio de Producción Comercio Exterior Inversiones y Pesca*: Quito.

OEC (Observatory of Economic Complexity). 2023. "Ecuador Crude Petroleum Exports". OEC.

Ocean Treasure. 2025. "Challenges and Outlook for Ecuador's Shrimp Industry: A Comprehensive Analysis". *Ocean Treasure*, February 7.

OMSA (Organización Mundial de Sanidad Animal). 2023. "Infección por el virus del síndrome de Taura". OMSA.

Piedrahita, Yahira. 2018. "Current Situation of the Shrimp Industry in Ecuador". CNA.

Plan V. 2023. "El documental que cuenta cómo fue el despojo de los pueblos del manglar". *Plan V*, August 2.

Ray, Rebecca and Myers, Margaret. 2024. "Feeling the Stones: Chinese Development Finance to Latin America and The Caribbean, 2023". *Inter-American Dialogue by Boston University Global Development Policy Center.*

Reyes Herrera, Milton and Chun Lee, Po. 2017. *La Relación China–Ecuador en el Siglo XXI: Elementos Relevantes para la Discusión.* Instituto de Altos Estudios Nacionales: Quito.

Ríos, Haylis. 2022. *Importancia del Sector Acuícola en el Desarrollo Económico en el Ecuador Durante la Última Década.* Universidad Técnica de Machala: Ecuador.

Sacher, William. 2017. *Ofensiva Megaminera China en los Andes: Acumulación por Desposesión en el Ecuador de la Revolución Ciudadana.* Editorial Abya Yala: Quito.

Salinas de Dosch, Ana Lucía. 2012. "China 's Emerging Role in Ecuador". *México y la Cuenca del Pacífico* 15(43), pp. 43-63.

Seafood Watch Staff. 2021. "Whiteleg Shrimp: Ecuador – Semi-Intensive Ponds". *Monterey Bay Aquarium Seafood Watch*, March 1.

Trading Economics. 2025. *Ecuador Exports* (at: https://tradingeconomics.com/ecuador/exports)

United Nations. s.f. *UN Comtrade Database.* (at: https://comtrade.un.org)

Vadell, Javier Alberto, Lo Brutto, Giuseppe, Leite, Alexandre Cesar and Crivelli, Eduardo. 2020. "El Rol de la Cooperación de China en la Transformación Estructural del Sur Global". *Geosul* 35(77), pp. 451-475.

Viola, Reyes, Carolina. 2016. "Territorios y Cambio Estructural en Hábitats Periurbanos: Coca Codo Sinclair, Inversión China y el Cambio de la Matriz Energética en el Ecuador". *Revista Ciencias Sociales* 38, pp. 67-84.

Viola, Reyes, Carolina and Mora Vera, Daniela. 2025. "Economía Política de la Cooperación Sur-Sur de China en Latinoamérica". *Revista Estado y Comunes.*

Viola, Reyes, Carolina. 2021. "Il Serpente e il Drago: Riflessioni sulla Territorializzazione degli Investimenti Cinesi nell'Amazzonia Ecuadoriana". In, Graziano Mazzocchini and Giuseppe Cocco (edit.). *Dopo la marea Crisi del progressismo e nuovi processi costituenti in America Latina.* Rivista Machina. pp.32-41.

Witherow, Sebastian. 2023. "Shrimp Farming in Ecuador: A Sustainability Assessment". *Esri StoryMaps*, May 14.

WRM (World Rainforest Movement). 2021. "Ecuador: The Certification of Industrial Shrimp Aquaculture Intensifies Rights Violations and the Destruction of Mangroves". *WRM*, March 9.

ABOUT THE AUTHORS

Pedro Henrique Batista Barbosa is a Brazilian career diplomat. He holds a bachelor's degree in Law from PUC-Rio, a master's degree in Diplomacy from the Diplomatic Academy Rio Branco Institute, and a doctorate in International Politics from Renmin University of China. In recent years, he has been a research fellow at the Global Development Policy Center (GDPC) of Boston University, the Center for Chinese-Mexican Studies (CECHIMEX) at the National Autonomous University of Mexico (UNAM), and the Inter-American Dialogue. He has published extensively on Brazil–China relations, particularly in the energy sector (electricity and oil & gas). In 2019, he edited the volume *Challenges and Opportunities in the Brazil–Asia Relationship from the Perspective of Young Diplomats* (FUNAG), and in 2024 he published the book *China, Brazil and Petroleum: The Role of China in Brazil's Transformation into an Oil Power* (Palgrave Macmillan).

Andrés Bórquez is an Assistant Professor at the Institute of International Studies, University of Chile. He holds a Ph.D. in International Politics from Fudan University, China. His research focuses on China–Latin America relations and the development partnership between Chile and ASEAN. He is also the Coordinator of the Master's in Asia Studies at the University of

Chile and Editor of *Latin American Asian Studies*. Additionally, he is a principal researcher at the Millennium Nucleus on the Impacts of China in Latin American Countries. https://orcid.org/0000-0002-3904-409X

Marco Curi is a Junior Researcher at the Center for China and Asia-Pacific Studies at Universidad del Pacífico. He contributes to the "Capitalizing on the New Climate Economy in the Americas" project. His research focuses on China's role in advancing a just energy transition in Peru and its impact on sustainable development. He holds a degree in Economics and International Business from Universidad Peruana de Ciencias Aplicadas, where he leads the Foreign Trade Agency within the Economic Observatory. A former scholar of the Ministry of Foreign Trade and Tourism of Peru and The Fund for American Studies, he focuses on China–Latin America trade relations and the challenges of achieving a just energy transition. Marco also lectures on global trade dynamics and economic policy.

Enrique Dussel Peters holds a Ph.D. in Economics from the University of Notre Dame (1996). He has been a professor at the Graduate School of Economics at the National Autonomous University of Mexico (UNAM) since 1993. He coordinates the Center for Chinese-Mexican Studies (CECHIMEX) at UNAM's School of Economics and the Academic Network of Latin America and the Caribbean on China (Red ALC-China). A Level III member of the National System of Researchers, he has authored numerous books and chapters in Spanish, German, English, Chinese, and Portuguese on political economy, industrial organization, development, global value chains, and Latin America–China relations. http://dusselpeters.com.

Dorotea López is a Professor and Director at the Institute of International Studies. She holds a degree in Economics from the Instituto Tecnológico Autónomo de México (ITAM), a Master of Philosophy in Economics from the University of Cambridge,

United Kingdom, and a Ph.D. in Social Sciences from the University of Chile. She is a principal researcher at the Millennium Nucleus on the Impacts of China in Latin American Countries. Her research interests include trade policy and services. https://orcid.org/0000-0003-4819-7351.

Eduardo Daniel Oviedo is a Principal Researcher at CONICET and a Professor at the National University of Rosario (UNR), Argentina. He completed postdoctoral studies at UNR, holds a Ph.D. in Political Science from the Catholic University of Córdoba, and earned a master's degree in Law from Peking University. His most recent book is *International Relations in the Time of China's Rise and Argentina's Decline*. He currently serves on the Executive Council of the International Confucian Association.

Lesbia Pérez-Santillán is a Postdoctoral Researcher at the National Council of Humanities, Sciences, and Technologies (Conahcyt) in the Department of Economics at the Metropolitan Autonomous University (UAM), Iztapalapa. She is a Level 1 member of the National System of Researchers (SNI) and holds a Ph.D. in Economics from the Graduate School of Economics at the National Autonomous University of Mexico (UNAM). She is also a member of the Academic Network of Latin America and the Caribbean on China (Red ALC-China) and collaborates with the China–Mexico Studies Center at UNAM's School of Economics. Her research focuses on international trade, global value chains, input–output analysis, and Latin America–China economic relations.

Carlos Eduardo Piña is a political scientist specializing in oil trade and politics. He earned his degree from the Central University of Venezuela (UCV) and is completing a master's degree in International Relations at the National Autonomous University of Mexico (UNAM). He is a member of the Academic Network of Latin America and the Caribbean on China (Red ALC-China).

Juan E. Serrano-Moreno is an Assistant Professor at the Institute of International Studies, University of Chile. He holds a Ph.D. in Political Science from the University Paris 1 Panthéon-Sorbonne and has taught at universities in France, Spain, and Chile. His research focuses on China–Latin America relations and environmental governance. He is also an attorney with the Madrid Bar Association and the Coordinator of the Master's in International Strategy and Trade Policy at the University of Chile. ORCID: 0000-0002-8466-1556

Giuliana Vera-Díaz holds a Bachelor's degree in International Relations with a concentration in Cooperation for Development at the Pontificia Universidad Católica del Ecuador (PUCE) and is a researcher at the Socio-Environmental Observatory of Chinese Investment in Ecuador and Latin America (OSICHEL). She is also an academic and research assistant at the Asian Program from the Facultad Latinoamericana de Ciencias Sociales (FLACSO), Ecuador. She has been a trainee at the Center for EU-Asia Connectivity of the European Union, in foreign policy with the Global Interest and Competition in the Asia Indo-Pacific Region research project.

Carolina Viola-Reyes holds a Ph.D in political science from the Latin American Faculty of Social Sciences (FLACSO, Ecuador). She is also a research faculty member at the Pontificia Universidad Católica del Ecuador (PUCE) and the Coordinator of the Research Group: Socio-Environmental Observatory of Chinese Investment in Ecuador and Latin America (OSICHEL). Author of various articles on democracy, extractivism, and the new global geopolitical order, such as "Il serpente e il drago: Riflessioni sulla territorializzazione degli investimenti cinesi nell'Amazzonia Ecuadoriana" (journal Machina), the chapter "Energy Integration in South America and Global Geopolitics in the book *Energy Integration in South America and Global Geopolitics* and, recently, for the journal Estado y Comunes, Political Economy of the Chinese cooperation in Latin America.

Kehan Wang is a Postdoctoral Researcher at the Center for China and Asia-Pacific Studies at Universidad del Pacífico in Lima, Peru. His research examines natural resource governance in Latin America, with a focus on conflict management and corporate–community dynamics. He holds a Ph.D. in Political Science from Boston University, where he worked closely with the Global Development Policy Center as a Global China Fellow. His work addresses Environmental, Social, and Governance (ESG) regulations in South America's renewable energy value chains, as well as the compliance of Chinese companies operating in the region.

Universidad Nacional Autónoma de México
Facultad de Economía
Centro de Estudios China-México
Unión de Universidades de América Latina y el Caribe
Red Académica de América Latina y el Caribe sobre China

**LATIN AMERICAN EXPORTS TO CHINA.
LOCAL EXPERIENCES AND CHALLENGES**

Esta edición se terminó de editar en mayo de 2025
Su composición se realizó con las familias tipográficas:
Minion Pro 7:10; 8:10; 11:14
Montserrat 7:14; 10:14; 11:14; 12:14; 14:18 18:20; 20:25; 24:32

El cuidado de la edición estuvo a cargo de:
Silvia Jiménez Barba